Actor's Playbook

Theatre Arts

The Dynamics
of Acting

Fourth Edition

National Textbook Company
a division of *NTC Publishing Group* • Lincolnwood, Illinois USA

Development: Word Management, Inc

Design and Production: Stet Graphics, Inc

Published by National Textbook Company, a division of NTC Publishing Group

© 1997 NTC Publishing Group, 4255 West Touhy Avenue

Lincolnwood (Chicago), Illinois 60646-1975 U.S.A.

6 7 8 9 ML 0 9 8 7 6 5 4 3 2 1

Table of Contents

Cinderella, Cinderella
A Participation Play
by
Stephen and Katherine Hotchner

Characters

Cinderella
Cecily
Denise
Stepmother
Fairy Godmother
King
Duke Ferdinand
Prince

Production Notes

General Properties:

Rocking chair, two chairs. Fairy Godmother's wand, placed under a seat in the auditorium before performance.

Personal:

Cinderella: Bucket filled with sponges, dustpan, broom and rags; Cecily's gloves.

Stepmother: Cherry pits, key.

Godmother: Huge handbag containing yarn, thread, crowns, hairbrush, necklace, slippers for Cinderella, and other items as desired; large gift-wrapped package supposedly containing Cinderella's dress for the ball.

Costumes:

Cecily: Denise and Stepmother are dressed for the ball in evening gowns. Stepmother also has cloak and gloves.

Cinderella: is dressed in rags in the scenes at home. Her dress for the ball is a beautiful floor-length gown with ruffled sleeves, and studded with diamonds. Her wedding gown may be the same, with the addition of a train.

Fairy: Godmother is dressed like a cleaning lady, in shirt and long overalls. Her sleeves are rolled up.

Time: Long ago.   Place: Far away.

AT RISE OF CURTAIN, a single rocking chair and two chairs which will double in function as thrones and as chairs. Enter CINDERELLA L with a bucket filled with sponges, dustpan, broom and rags.

• • • • • • • • • • • • • • • • • • • •

CINDERELLA: *(to audience).* Hello. Who are you? You look so nice. You remind me of the friends I used to have before my stepmother drove them all away. Now I don't get to play much. I work all the time. And I get so tired. Look at this house. The floors need scrubbing, the windows need polishing and the fireplace needs sweeping. I'll never get it all done. Oh, if only . . . But no, no, it's no use. I wanted so to go to that ball. I would dance and dance and . . . What's the use of dreaming. If only . . . do you think . . . you could help me. *(Moves into audience, to one child.)* Would you help me scrub the floor? *(Repeats this to another child and brings them both on stage.)* Here are some sponges. You can start right away. And now the windows. *(Again she chooses two children with:)* Would you like to polish a window? And you? *(Leads them up on stage.)* Right there. And there are your rags. And . . . I can't believe it, the place looks cleaner already. Oh, I forgot the fireplace. *(Selects two more children.)* Here, I'll give you a broom and you a dustpan. And I'll help all of you scrub. The rest of you warn us if you hear my stepsisters coming. They have high, shrill voices. *(After a short pause, Cecily's voice is heard. She must give children some time to clean first.)*

CECILY: *(from offstage R).* Bet you wish you could look as pretty as me.

CINDERELLA: Are they coming? Oh, they are. Quick, everyone, back to your seats. They mustn't find you here.

DENISE: *(also offstage R).* Don't you wish you had my looks. The prince won't even look at you when we get to the ball, bandy-legs.

CINDERELLA: Hurry, hurry. I'll take the rags and the sponges and the broom and the dustpan. Then I'll run upstairs and finish my dress and——(*starts to exit L, then turns.*) Thank you. (*Runs out L with cleaning paraphernalia, leaving the broom behind.*)

(*CECILY enters R dressed in evening gown, followed by DENISE similarly dressed.*)

CECILY: Fatty.

DENISE: I am not fat. Mama, Mama. Cecily called me fatty. (*STEPMOTHER enters dressed for the ball in gown, gloves and cloak.*)

STEPMOTHER: I'm going to say this just once. Tonight you must be beautiful. The Prince is going to choose one of you for his wife at the ball. If you argue, your cheeks will turn puffy and then you'll be as ugly as Cinderella.

CECILY: As ugly as Cinderella. Mama, how can you say that?

DENISE: You're right, Mama, as always. You mustn't argue with me, Cecily.

CECILY: Me argue with you? You started it, you little louse.

DENISE: Why, you . . . you . .

STEPMOTHER: Now, girls. Remember. Dignity, grace, poise.

CECILY: (*curtsying clumsily*). We're sorry, Mama.

DENISE: (*curtsying clumsily*). Beg your pardon, I'm sure.

STEPMOTHER: That's my little darlings. Cecily, we have to go. Where are your gloves?

CECILY: Cinderella was supposed to bring them. (*Sharp change of voice, a fishwife.*) Cinderella!

DENISE: Cin-de-rella! (*CINDERELLA runs in, out of breath. She is dressed in rags still. She stops dead when she sees the sisters glaring at her. She holds out the gloves. CECILY snatches them from her.*)

CINDERELLA: I . . . I . . . didn't mean to be late. I was making a dress.

DENISE: A dress? You, in a dress? You couldn't wear a dress. It would be covered with soot in two seconds.

CECILY: One second.

CINDERELLA: But, Mama . . .

STEPMOTHER: Don't call me your mother. Your real mother died long ago. I am "ma'am" to you.

CINDERELLA: But . . . Ma'am, you said that when I finished my work I could go to the ball if I could find a dress and I've found one and . . .

CECILY: Mama, she's not going to the ball, is she? She's a servant. The Prince will take one look at her and hold his nose.

DENISE: She smells like a servant.

STEPMOTHER: We mustn't be unfair. I did say if Cinderella finished all her work she could go to the ball.

DENISE: Over my dead body.

CINDERELLA: Oh, thank you, Ma—— I mean, Ma'am. I'll run up and finish my dress. (*Starts to leave. STEPMOTHER throws cherry pits into fireplace.*)

STEPMOTHER: Oh, Cinderella. (*CINDERELLA stops, slowly turns.*) Look at the fireplace, will you? Inside the fireplace.

CINDERELLA:.(*walking slowly UR, stares inside fireplace*). Where did all those cherry pits come from? Tons of them. Buried deep in the ashes. It was clean. It was clean.

STEPMOTHER: What a shame, girls. It looks like Cinderella forgot to clean out the fireplace.

CINDERELLA: I didn't. I swear I didn't.

CECILY: Are you calling Mama a liar?

CINDERELLA: But . . .

STEPMOTHER: I'm sorry. It looks like you won't be able to go to the ball. Cecily, take my hand. Denise. I hear the coach. And we mustn't keep the coachman waiting. Good-bye, Cinderella.

CECILY and DENISE: Good-bye, Cinderella. (*They break into malicious laughter.*)

DENISE: Have fun. (*They exit.*)

CINDERELLA: (*waving*) You, too. (*Turns and walks to the rocking chair. She crooks the broom between her elbows.*) Have lots of fun at the ball. You meanies. I'm not going to cry. I'm not going to . . . I won't clean up the fireplace. I won't. I'll sleep and dream. Dream of the ball and my prince and a dress and —— (*Yawns.*) — a nicer place to be than — (*Yawns.*) — here. (*Closes her eyes*)

(*The FAIRY GODMOTHER enters from the audience dressed as a cleaning lady, with long overalls and sleeves rolled up. She carries a huge handbag which is so bulky it resembles an overnight bag and a large package wrapped like a birthday present. The moment she gets on stage she turns to the children, putting her finger to her lips.)*

GODMOTHER: She's asleep. I think introductions are in order. I'm Cinderella's fairy godmother which is just the same thing as your favorite aunt or uncle, and I'm mad. Did you see the nasty trick that stepmother played on my little girl? Cherry pits in the fireplace. Just when you'd all cleaned up so beautifully, too. They play tricks like that on her all the time. If only her real father and mother were alive . . . but those days are gone. I'll start the magic. And in just a second—*(Starts to fumble in her bag for the wand.)* Now that wand was around here somewhere, somewhere. *(Turns bag upside down and dumps it out on floor. All sorts of objects tumble out yarn, thread, crowns for kings and queens.)* Oh, dear. I can't have left my wand at home.I couldn't have done that.Children, would you look for my wand? I could have left it under one of your seats. Yes, I could have done that. I was very nervous before you came. Never talked to so many children before. Don't know if you're going to like me, that sort of thing. Please look. Does anybody see it? Anybody? *(Child replies or waves wand in air.)* Oh, thank goodness. You stay right there. I'll come down and get it. *(GODMOTHER goes down into audience and retrieves wand from child. She begins to put back contents of bag.)* I'm in a terrible hurry. Do you see this package? This is Cinderella's dress for the ball. I must get her to that ball before the Prince chooses a wife. *(Goes into audience.)* Would you help me put on her dress? And you? *(GODMOTHER leads children on stage.)* Come on. Let's wake up Cinderella. Oh, we must hurry, we must hurry. *(GODMOTHER whispers into CINDERELLA'S ear.)* Cinderella.

CINDERELLA: *(waking).* My goodness, who are you?

GODMOTHER: Your fairy godmother, Cinderella, and I arrived late because I couldn't find the right address. You are going to the ball. Oh, please hurry. These children will help you get dressed. Go off stage with them and come back as soon as you can.

CINDERELLA: *(to the two children and the audience).* Well, should I believe her? Can I really go to the ball? *(Children respond.)* I can. Then let's hurry. Come. This way. *(CINDERELLA takes the package and goes offstage with the children.)*

GODMOTHER: No time to lose. No time to lose. By midnight it'll all be over. *(Goes into audience and selects more helpers.)* There's so much more to do. Would you and you put on the slippers? Would you brush Cinderella's hair when she comes out in that beautiful dress. And, and would you put on her necklace. Thank you. *(Leads four children on stage.)* A fairy godmother who can't arrive on time to do her job. Now.

Here is your brush — (*Gives brush to child.*) — and here is your necklace and here are the slippers. (*Hands items to children.*) Are you ready, Cinderella? (*If she is not, GODMOTHER can have children come on stage and clean out cherry pits.*) Ready.

(*CINDERELLA steps out in a beautiful floor-length gown, ruffles on the sleeves, studded with diamonds. She whirls about in the gown.*)

CINDERELLA: This is wonderful. I feel so pretty.

GODMOTHER: Now, sit down, Cinderella. (*CINDERELLA sits in the rocking chair.*) This child is going to brush your hair. And this child will put on your diamond necklace. And these two can help put on your slippers. Oh, do hurry. (*Comes to edge of stage.*) How to get her to the ball. When I wave my wand I want all of you to close your eyes. The lights will go out. There'll be music. Perhaps even thunder and lightning — that always helps. And I want you to wish Cinderella to the ball in a golden coach with four black horses and a coachman with a green hat and a yellow feather. Have you finished combing and brushing her hair? We must hurry. Are the slippers on? And the necklace? The sisters have probably already arrived. Come, children, magic helpers, go back to your seats and help us all wish Cinderella to the ball. (*GODMOTHER takes children back to their seats.*) Now I'll stay with you. Wishing is very hard and I want to help you create the scene. Lights! (*Lights go out.*) Wishing is better in the dark. (*CINDERELLA exits.*) Thunder and lightning. (*Thunder and lightning.*) Music. (*Traveling music begins.*) Clippity clop, clippity clop, clippity clop. (*She slaps her knees, leading the children to create the ride.*)

CHILDREN: Clippity clop, clippity clop, clippity clop.

GODMOTHER: Keep it up. Keep on racing, horses. Coachman, raise your whip. They must run faster than the wind. Don't bounce too hard, coach. We don't want to tumble Cinderella into a ditch. Ride, horses, ride — wish, children, wish. Wish for a ball and a King and a Prince and a Duke and the one true love that the Prince has been waiting for. Cinderella! Lights!

(*Lights on. A forlorn-looking KING sits on one of the thrones. The other throne, the Queen's, is empty. There are no guests.*)

GODMOTHER: Where is the Queen? Where are the guests, the lovely ladies? Their escorts? Oh, no. I forgot to wish for them.

KING: Ferdinand? Duke Ferdinand? You booby. You nincompoop. (*Enter the DUKE FERDINAND pursued by STEPMOTHER and her two daughters.*)

DUKE: Yes, your booby — I mean, your majesty. Oh, good heavens, the

Queen, the guests, the ladies, the ball . . .

STEPMOTHER: Here are all the ladies you will need, your majesty.

CECILY: *(curtsying terribly).* Pleased, I'm sure.

DENISE: *(curtsying and tripping over her toes).* Delighted.

KING: Who are these impostors! I want beautiful damsels by the dozens. Otherwise the Prince won't even come in from the garden. Duke, if you don't get me some beautiful ladies in two minutes I'll . . . My Queen, where is my Queen? Oh, I can't understand any of this. You can't have a ball without guests. And my Queen. She was such a nice Queen.

GODMOTHER: It's now or never, kids. *(Calling out.)* Your majesty!

KING: Who is that? Duke, find out who that is.

DUKE: His majesty Cybil the Third requests your name.

GODMOTHER: *(coming up on stage)* Never mind my name. You wouldn't believe me if I told you. First, your majesty, let me compliment you on your good taste. Your Prince would never accept those women as his love.

STEPMOTHER: Well, I never.

CECILY: Charmed, I'm sure.

DENISE: Delighted.

STEPMOTHER: Oh, be quiet, you two, and stop curtsying.

GODMOTHER: Your majesty, to have a ball you need guests, especially beautiful ladies with their escorts . . . correct?

KING: Correct. I like this woman, Duke.

GODMOTHER: Now, if you will look out at that audience you will see some of the most beautiful ladies in the land.

KING: *(letting the GODMOTHER "lead" him to the edge of the stage; looking out into audience and beaming with pleasure)* Why, yes, yes! But . . . but . . all those . . . *(Runs back to GODMOTHER.)*

GODMOTHER: We better be very quiet. He's very shy. If you look even harder you may even find your Queen.

KING: *(goes toward children again, finding his Queen and breaking into bellows of laughter).* My Queen. I found my Queen. But how am I possibly to persuade these children to come up here and . . . well, it's not proper. Do you think it's proper, Duke?

DUKE: Never!

STEPMOTHER: Scandalous.

CECILY: Disgraceful.

DENISE: I won't have it!

KING: *(sighing)* It sounded like a good idea but . . . but you heard.

GODMOTHER: Your majesty, come closer.

KING: Oh, all right. *(Goes back to GODMOTHER.)*

GODMOTHER: Your majesty, you do need a ball. And to have a ball you must have lovely ladies. And to have a ball you must have a Queen. They'll give you a ball. Won't you?

KING: You will? Oh, so many queens!

GODMOTHER: Sh-h-h! Don't frighten them. They've never met a king before.

KING: Oh, I do understand. I am rather awesome. But . . . how do I get them up here?

GODMOTHER: Just ask.

KING: Just . . . ask?

GODMOTHER: With complete sincerity and the deepest respect.

KING: My son insists on marrying for love. And so I — that is, the Duke and I — had this idea. If we gave a ball where the loveliest ladies in the land gathered for an introduction, my son, the Prince, would find his love. Please. I would be most honored if some of you ladies would come to my ball. *(To GODMOTHER.)* Is that enough?

GODMOTHER: Would you come to a ball without an escort?

KING: Of course not. And, gentlemen, if you would escort a lady of your choosing to the ball, I'd be so pleased I might just do a jig.

GODMOTHER: Don't make promises you can't keep.

KING: But I would do a jog.

GODMOTHER: That's all right, then.

KING: *(moving into audience)* Would you be a lovely lady? And you? And you? And you? *(Picks four or five lovely ladies.)* Go to the ball. *(The four lovely ladies go on stage where the DUKE and GODMOTHER position them.)* And would you be an escort? And you? And you? And you? *(Picks four gentlemen, moves back on stage with them.)* Then we have a ball. *(Starts dancing a jog.)* Tra la la, la la, Tra la la la la. I'm very happy.

GODMOTHER: Your majesty?

KING: Yes?

GODMOTHER: Your Queen awaits you.

KING: Can I have more than one queen?

GODMOTHER: The Queen can have attendants.

KING: *(toward audience).* Would you be my Queen? I would be so honored. I . . . *(Hands go up.)* Yes, my queen. Take my arm. And you two can be her attendants. Come, my Queen. Let us join the guests at the ball. *(They start walking, with great dignity onto stage.)* I missed you, Queenie. One moment you were on your throne. The next moment . . . gone. *(They are now on stage. The KING helps the Queen ascend her throne.)* There. The seat is comfortable, I trust. And, attendants, if you will stand on either side of the Queen. But the crown . . .

GODMOTHER: *(taking crown from bag)* Here, your grace.

KING: *(placing crown on his Queen).* Lovely, lovely. And now, bring on the Prince.

GODMOTHER: Ball music, please.

(Ball music begins. A PRINCE enters, young and sulking, hands in pockets. He refuses to look at any of the ladies.)

KING: Son. You've forgotten your manners.

PRINCE: I don't want a ball.

KING: Do it for your old dad.

PRINCE: Oh, all right. *(Starts toward ladies. STEPMOTHER stampedes him.)*

STEPMOTHER: Look, your grace. I have two lovely daughters. They have class. Stick up your chins, quickly! *(One of the daughters pushes in front of the other one to gain the Prince's attention.)* And I don't suppose you've ever seen any ladies more beautiful.

PRINCE: Why did I come in from the garden? Father, you promised me a princess.

CECILY: Well, here I am. ⎫
DENISE: Pleased to meet you. ⎭ *(Simultaneously.)*

STEPMOTHER. My daughters.

KING: Silence. *(STEPMOTHER advances on the King.)* Duke, Duke, help, help.

DUKE: Yes, your majesty. *(To the ladies chosen from the audience.)* Ladies, lovely ladies, stand over here. Thanks. Ah, you see, the Prince will be able to really see you from a distance.

STEPMOTHER: Fine idea. Girls, pose over there.

CECILY and DENISE: Yes, Mama.

KING: That's better. *(Gestures toward the lovely ladies and their escorts.)* Now, son. Find your love. *(The PRINCE approaches the first couple.)*

PRINCE: *(stepping up to girl and kissing her hand.)* You're very beautiful. *(Steps up to second girl and kisses her hand.)* And you're very nice. *(Steps up to third girl and kisses her hand.)* And you're lovely, too. *(Sighs.)* But I'm not in love with any of you. Please don't be insulted. It's not that I don't want to be. But the girl I'm looking for . . . the girl I'm looking for . . . oh, well. *(Picks one girl to dance.)* Would you like to dance? You would? Thank you.

KING: Come, everyone. Dance. *(Dance music begins. The KING, DUKE, GODMOTHER and PRINCE each take two or three children and lead them in a ring dance. GODMOTHER allows dance to go on. Then . . .)*

GODMOTHER: Now, Cinderella.

(CINDERELLA runs on R, stops, looks at the PRINCE bashfully, and bows her head.)

PRINCE: *(to his partner).* Thank you for the dance. *(He steps up to CINDERELLA and takes her hand.)* May I have this dance?

CINDERELLA: I'd love to.

GODMOTHER: Dance music. *(Romantic dance music begins. CINDERELLA and the PRINCE begin to waltz around the ballroom. They gaze enraptured into each other's eyes. Then, GODMOTHER suddenly jumps.)* Oh, no! This is terrible. *(Steps up to audience while dance continues.)* I forgot to tell Cinderella what happens at midnight. Her dress will turn into rags. And a clock will sound twelve times like this. Dong. Dong. Now you must be the clock. When I give you the signal you must go Dong, Dong twelve times. Then you and I must wish her back to her house before that wicked stepmother and her daughters arrive home. Ready. Sound the midnight chimes. Now.

CHILDREN: Dong, dong, dong, dong, dong, dong, dong, dong, dong, dong, dong, dong.

CINDERELLA: What's happening to me? I feel funny . . I . . Godmother, help me.

GODMOTHER: Run, Cinderella, run home. Your time has run out.

PRINCE: Don't go. Please don't go.

CINDERELLA: I must. *(She runs down the aisles of the theater, then doubles back again, losing one slipper as she goes. She leaps back onto the stage and runs out UR. The PRINCE chases her, stops in the middle of one aisle and picks up the slipper.)*

PRINCE: I've lost her.

KING: Sound the guards. Give chase. Give chase.

DUKE: Sound the guards.

PRINCE: But I've got one slipper.

GODMOTHER: *(going to couples and leading them back to their seats)* Quickly, children. You must go back to your seats. We must wish Cinderella home. You, too, Queen and attendants.

KING: She can't be gone. Duke, I'll have your head if you don't find her. *(DUKE runs out UR, where Cinderella was last seen.)*

STEPMOTHER: But, your majesty, my daughters will . . .

KING: Out of my sight. Duke! *(The STEPMOTHER and daughters exit angrily. GODMOTHER comes back on stage and helps Queen and attendants back to seats. The DUKE re-enters)*

DUKE: Yes.

KING: My son has found a slipper that belongs to that girl. Take him and search the kingdom, and find the girl whose foot fits that slipper. Go.

DUKE: Yes, your majesty. *(The DUKE and the PRINCE exit L.)*

GODMOTHER. Lights. *(Lights dim.)* Wish hard, hard. The King's guards are gaining. This is a wild ride. Clippity clop, clippity, clop. Sound the horses' hooves.

CHILDREN: Clippity clop, clippity clop.

GODMOTHER: Ride, horses, ride. Coachman, raise your whip. They're gaining. Quickly. Ride faster than the wind. Clippity clop. clippity clop. Now you're home, Cinderella.

(CINDERELLA runs in L, frantically, with a slipper in her hand. She is once again back in rags.)

CINDERELLA: Where shall I hide the slipper? I must hide the slipper before they get home.

GODMOTHER: What do you think, children? Where should she hide it? Under the mantlepiece.

CINDERELLA: Yes, but . .

GODMOTHER: Under the chair. *(Any suggestions tried out simultaneously by the frantic Cinderella.)*

CINDERELLA: They'll find it. Oh, what am I going to do? Here they come.

STEPMOTHER: *(offstage)* I've never been so mortified in all my life.

CINDERELLA: Oh, children, what should I do with the slipper? I know I'll need it when the Prince comes. And he will come.

STEPMOTHER: *(offstage)* Why, that stupid prince might have even preferred Cinderella.

CINDERELLA: Here. I'm going to give the slipper to you. *(She gives the slipper to the GODMOTHER. GODMOTHER quietly hands the slipper to a child.)* Hold onto that slipper until the right moment comes. Hold onto it. *(CINDERELLA runs to the rocking chair, takes the broom in her hands and pretends to be asleep. The GODMOTHER runs into the audience and takes her place just as the STEPMOTHER sweeps in with the two daughters following her.)*

CECILY: Look at her. Dirty thing. *(Kicks CINDERELLA awake.)* Wake up, you ash heap.

DENISE: Wake up, cinder pot.

CINDERELLA: Oh, hello. Did you have a good time at the ball?

CECILY: Did we have a good time at the ball? Little stupid.

DENISE: The Prince had the nerve to reject us.

CINDERELLA: He must have had very bad taste.

CECILY: She has a little sense, mother.

STEPMOTHER: Did you pick the cherry pits out of the ashes, Cinderella?

CINDERELLA: Yes, Ma'am.

STEPMOTHER: Yes, Ma'am. Isn't she sweet? Isn't she dutiful, girls?

CECILY: I hate her.

STEPMOTHER. Now, Cecily. Give Cinderella your breakfast order and wake up times and then come to bed.

CECILY: Cinderella, I want to wake up at eleven o'clock, no later, no earlier. And for breakfast I desire eleven pancaakes, four sausages, three eggs and a large glass of orange juice.

DENISE: And I desire the same. Oh, Mama, why don't you give Cinderella away? It's all her fault.

STEPMOTHER: Now, now, girls. Come to bed. By the way, Cinderella, I will arise at eleven-thirty and I expect my usual toast and tea. Good night.

CECILY and DENISE: Good night.

CINDERELLA: Good night. *(Sighs, then waits until they exit R.)* Oh, Prince. Please come. Please, please come.

(CINDERELLA falls asleep. The GODMOTHER comes up to the stage, on tiptoe.)

GODMOTHER: Lights out, please. *(Lights darken.)* I'm exhausted. I thought we'd never get Cinderella home safely. Wishing is terribly hard work. Close your eyes. The night will pass. *(Night music begins.)* And when the morning comes we'll have our work cut out for us. Even if the Prince should come I don't trust that stepmother.

(Music plays for an interlude of a few seconds. Then there is loud terrific knocking offstage, or at the back of the theater if possible. Knocking continues awhle, then CINDERELLA wakes up with a start just as the STEPMOTHER enters R. GODMOTHER scurries back into audience.)

STEPMOTHER: Anwer the door. Don't just stand there. *(The DUKE and the PRINCE have entered R and pantomime looking through a peephole in the door.)*

DUKE: Open up in the name of Prince Harry.

STEPMOTHER: What? Who?

DUKE: Open up in the name of Prince Harry.

STEPMOTHER: The Prince. Oh my, the prince. Get away from that door immediately, you ninny.

CINDERELLA: Whoever has the slipper, please hold onto it tight.

STEPMOTHER: What did you say? Oh, never mind. *(Looks through peephole.)* Yes?

DUKE: By royal proclamation of his majesty, Cybil the Third, I hereby order you to . . .

PRINCE: Please open the door. I must try this slipper on the lovely lady who wore it last night. I want to make her my wife.

DUKE: Well put, your grace.

STEPMOTHER: Just a minute.

DUKE: We're freezing. Hurry up.

STEPMOTHER: Certainly. Denise. Cecily. Come down here this instant. *(CECILY and DENISE enter, dragging their feet, half awake, yawning.)*

CECILY: So early.

DENISE: Very, very early.

STEPMOTHER. Wake up, you two, wake up. The Prince is outside ready to try on a slipper. And if the slipper fits . . . a kingdom is ours.

DUKE: Freezing. You are keeping his grace out in the cold.

CECILY: But if he wants to try the slipper on everyone in the house, then Cinderella could try it on, too. And if Cinderella . . .

DENISE: But the slipper couldn't fit her. Could it?

DUKE: Toes turning to ice. Royal toes of Prince Harry will now have to be thawed out in front of a roaring fire.

PRINCE: My heart is ice, that's certain.

STEPMOTHER. Just another teeny minute. Look at Cinderella, hard. *(All three stare at CINDERELLA. She backs away.)* Now imagine her in that beautiful gown the mysterious girl wore last night, the diamond-studded necklace . . .

DUKE: Royal Prince Harry's toes getting numb . . .

PRINCE: Oh, I'm all right. It's hopeless anyway.

STEPMOTHER: And sequins and ruffles and a clean face. Well?

CECILY: Lock her up.

DENISE: Throw the key away.

STEPMOTHER: Get her. *(DENISE and CECILY grab CINDERELLA.)* Take her up to the top room. Then bring me back the key.

DENISE: Yes, Mama. Come, Princess.

CECILY: Come to your kingdom.

CINDERELLA: *(as they lead her out struggling)* It can't end this way. It can't. *(They exit L.)*

DUKE: Royal Prince is now a royal piece of ice. If you don't open this door this instant, we shall go to another house.

STEPMOTHER: One more teeny weeny minute.

DUKE: Your teeny weeny minutes are freezing our toes off!

STEPMOTHER: *(turning to door)* Coming, your grace. *(Pantomimes opening the door. DUKE enters in a huff. The PRINCE follows dejectedly behind him.)*

DUKE: In the name of his majesty, Cybil the Third, I warn you that you have nearly caused the Prince a severe case of frostbite.

PRINCE: Get it over with, Ferdinand. I don't mind the cold at all. It matches the despair I feel in my heart.

DUKE: You have daughters?

STEPMOTHER: Two. Each as lovely as a princess.

DUKE: Is there anyone else in this household besides them? I have been ordered to try this slipper on every eligible damsel in this land.

STEPMOTHER: Cecily, Denise. *(CECILY and DENISE enter L. They sit on thrones used in ball scene and hold out their feet.)*

CECILY: Me first.

DENISE: No, me. I've got the prettier toes.

DUKE: *(trying the slipper on DENISE)* Here goes. Well . . . it's beginning to fit.

DENISE: Of course it fits. Prince Harry is my one true love. I remember dancing with him all night.

DUKE: It doesn't fit and that's all there is to it.

DENISE: It does so. I always fit my shoes snugly.

DUKE: Maybe her foot. *(He moves to CECILY with the slipper and tries it on her.)*

GODMOTHER *(from her place in the audience)* Children. Tell the Prince what happened. Tell him.

PRINCE: *(turning)* What did you say? I'm sorry. I can't understand you. Something about a cinderheap.

STEPMOTHER: Don't pay attention to them, Prince. They're the kind of children who don't clean their rooms.

PRINCE: *(still turned toward audience)* I still have trouble understanding you. Perhaps it was the cold. I think my ears are numb. There is a cinderblock in the house. A she. Wait a minute. Perhaps if one of you spoke to me alone. I'll pick out someone. There's a Cin . . . a cin . . de . . rel . . . la. What's a Cinderella?

STEPMOTHER: Just a name Denise gives to her favorite doll.

PRINCE: Is that right? Is Cinderella a name Denise gives to her favorite doll?

CHILDREN: No.

STEPMOTHER: Really, your majesty, if you will just see how beautifully that slipper is fitting on . . .

CECILY: (*giving a cry of agony as the Duke attempts to shove the slipper all the way up her foot*) Oh, the pain, the pain.

STEPMOTHER: Try harder.

CECILY: Oh Mommy, the slipper just doesn't fit. My toes are all sore.

STEPMOTHER: You could suffer for my sake.

DUKE: No use going on. The mission is a failure.

PRINCE: There's a Cinderella in this house. And she's not a doll and she's not a name for a pet. She's . . .

DUKE: Time to leave, your grace.

STEPMOTHER: I don't care if your toes bleed.

PRINCE: Silence! I want silence in this house. These children have something very important to tell me. Now I shall go among you and you will talk to me one at a time. (*Prince goes into audience and listens. To one child at a time.*) I see. So Cinderella is a girl who lives in this house and they've locked her up. Where is the key? Who has the key?

CHILDREN: The stepmother.

PRINCE: (*marching back to STEPMOTHER*) I want Cinderella down here immediately.

STEPMOTHER: I don't know what you're talking about. There is no Cinderella in this house.

PRINCE: The children say there is.

STEPMOTHER: (*turning her back to the audience*) Are you going to take my word or believe them?

PRINCE: Now I warn you. If you don't make those ill-mannered daughters of yours get Cinderella down here immediately I'll have my soldiers tear your house down brick by brick until we find her.

STEPMOTHER: (*after a stony silence*) Oh, very well. (*Takes out the key and hands it to CECILY and DENISE, both of whom are limping.*) Get the little cinderheap and bring her here.

PRINCE: Thank you, children. You've been very helpful.

STEPMOTHER: (*as CECILY and DENISE exit*). Oh, your grace. The edict says that every eligible damsel can try the slipper on, is that correct?

PRINCE: Correct.

STEPMOTHER: I'm an eligible damsel and I wish to try on the slipper. *(She goes and sits in the rocking chair and holds out her foot.)*

DUKE: This is ridiculous. You know very well that . . . that . . .

PRINCE: Try it on. It won't do her any good.

GODMOTHER: It's a trick, magic helpers. Child with the slipper, get ready. *(DUKE is trying the slipper on. Suddenly the STEPMOTHER gets up and pretends to hop about in pain.)*

STEPMOTHER: Ow! This slipper is killing me. *(She goes DR.)* I have to get it off.

PRINCE: You shouldn't have tried it on in the first place.

STEPMOTHER: *(pantomiming opening door).* I have to get it off. Oh, the pain. *(She throws the slipper off R with all of her strength. The PRINCE and the DUKE rush to the door.)*

DUKE: The slipper. It's rolling . . .

PRINCE: And rolling . . .

DUKE: It fell into . . .

PRINCE and DUKE: The well.

STEPMOTHER: I'm sorry. It hurt my toes so much I had to get it off. What a shame. Some say that well has no bottom. *(Enter CINDERELLA L with a dejected pair of daughters behind her. DUKE has sprawled into the rocking chair and the PRINCE has sat down on the edge of the stage, his head in his hands.)*

STEPMOTHER: Why, Cinderella. Just in time. What a pity there's no slipper for you to try on.

CINDERELLA: *(to the children)* She thinks she's clever, doesn't she? Your grace . . . stand up. *(The PRINCE stands up, unable to take his eyes off CINDERELLA.)* Walk to the edge of that stage and say these words: Magic slipper, magic child, Give me back my love.

PRINCE: But . . .

CINDERELLA: Believe, your grace, believe.

PRINCE: *(holding out his hands to audience)* Magic slipper, magic child, Give me back my love.

GODMOTHER: Now, child with the slipper. Go and give the gift of a kingdom to Cinderella. *(A child comes out of the audience and makes his or* *her way to the stage. handing the slipper up to the PRINCE, who takes it as though it were a precious gem.)*

STEPMOTHER: I'm not going to stay around here to see this. *(She exits R.)*

CECILY: Mother, you're not as clever as you think you are. In fact, you're stupid. *(Exits R, limping.)*

DENISE: Oh, my toes still hurt. *(Exits R, limping.)*

PRINCE: Sit down, Cinderella. Even in those rags I recognize you.

CINDERELLA: *(sitting down on throne L).* Yes, your grace.

DUKE: A cinder girl for a princess!

PRINCE: Quiet, Duke. The slipper fits. So, it was you.

CINDERELLA. Yes, my prince.

PRINCE: Who am I to thank for all this?

CINDERELLA: The children, your grace. And an absentminded fairy godmother. They were quite a team.

PRINCE: In payment for services rendered to the future king of this land, I invite you all to our wedding. Pets are welcome, of course.

DUKE: Pets at a wedding?

PRINCE: Quiet, Ferdinand. Come, my princess. *(The PRINCE takes Cinderella's arm.)*

GODMOTHER: Wedding music, please. *(Wedding music begins. The PRINCE and CINDERELLA go off stage.)*

(The GODMOTHER chooses eight children to hold CINDERELLA'S wedding train when she enters. She chooses these children from the seats closest to her. The KING re-enters and with the DUKE forms two rows of children into an arch, through which Cinderella and the Prince will pass. They show the children how to raise their hands like trees to form the arch. They tell the rest of the audience to form the magic arch by standing up in their seats when CINDERELLA enters. CINDERELLA and the PRINCE re-enter.)

GODMOTHER: Hold the wedding train, children. Two by two, hand in hand. Come, children, follow Cinderella, hold the veil. *(The wedding music turns to a processional as the children, helped by the GODMOTHER, hold the wedding train and follow CINDERELLA and the PRINCE as they circle through the audience and finally back on stage.)*

GODMOTHER: *(after the PRINCE and CINDERELLA are back on stage)* You can go back to your seats now, children. *(As they do so.)* Everyone close your eyes and take a few seconds to wish Cinderella and yourselves a long and happy life. (*A moment of silence, then:*)

KING: In the name of Cybil the Third, myself, I declare my son the Prince married to Cinderella. Everyone. Hip, hip, hurrah. Hip, hip, hurrah. Hip, hip, hurrah. (*As CINDERELLA and the PRINCE leave.*) Farewell.

DUKE: Farewell.

GODMOTHER. Farewell. (*Lights darken. All leave. Then when lights come back on, all the actors return and say good-bye to the children.*)

End of Play

2

Hansel and Gretel

An Adaptation
by
William Glennon

Characters

Hansel
Gretel
The Bird
The Gnome
The Witch
Father
Mother

Production Notes

Time: Long ago.

Place: In and near a deep forest

Act Three: The Witch's Hut

At Rise: GRETEL is sweeping in front of the house. HANSEL in the cage, the BIRD and GNOME on guard, marching back and forth slowly now. A moment's silence.

● ● ● ● ● ● ● ● ● ● ● ● ● ● ● ● ●

HANSEL: You must be tired.

GRETEL: Yes, I am.

BIRD and GNOME: Yes, I am!

HANSEL: No wonder. Sweeping, cleaning . . . working for the Witch. You've swept in front of her house every day for two weeks now. Surely there can't be much dirt left.

GRETEL: There isn't. But she insists. Sweep! Clean! Scrub! I like things neat and tidy!

BIRD and GNOME: She likes things neat and tidy!

HANSEL: *(cups his hands and peeks inside)* Oh, my! Guess what I have here!

BIRD and GNOME: She likes things neat and . . . what?

GNOME: What do you have there?

BIRD: Yes, what?

HANSEL: A secret.

GRETEL: Hansel . . . you're sweet. I know—you're trying to cheer me up.

HANSEL: A special, special secret. Only for friends, though.

GNOME: Well, we're friends. You're a prisoner, and I'm a friendly guard. What is it?

HANSEL: Never mind. Come look, Gretel.

BIRD: She's supposed to sweep . . .

GNOME: And clean . . .

BIRD: And scrub . . .

GNOME: So keep your secrets to yourself. Besides, it's almost time for you to eat again.

HANSEL: I can't. I've eaten every hour, on the hour, for two weeks now. I'm full.

GNOME: You may be full, but you're not ready yet, that's what she said.

BIRD: And the fence needs mending.

GNOME: Yes, the fence needs mending.

GRETEL: But . . . but there is no fence. How can the fence need mending when there is no fence?

GNOME: Don't you know?

GRETEL: No.

BIRD: You really don't know?

GRETEL: No.

BIRD: Well . . .

GNOME: Well. There *used* to be a fence. A fence made of . . . gingerbread men.

BIRD: Children, really.

HANSEL: Children?! Really?

BIRD: Yes! She's been bringing children here for ages and ages, though not so many recently.

GNOME: That's why she's hungry. She only likes gingerbread—her own special kind.

BIRD: Yes—you see, she changed the children into gingerbread, and put them up around the house, like a fence. But then, she got hungry . . .

GNOME: And the fence is gone. See?

GRETEL: Then it's true! When she says, "The fence needs mending," it means she's going to take some little boy or girl and . . . Why you two ought to be ashamed of yourselves! The very idea! Helping her find children! How could you?

BIRD and GNOME: She speaks and we obey!

(The WITCH, cackling, comes out with a book.)

WITCH: I found it! I found it! You'll all be happy to hear I have found it. Three cheers for me.

GRETEL: Found what?

WITCH: My book! My recipe book! I thought I'd lost it, but I found it! Now, let's see. Here it is! Gingerbread the old-fashioned witch's way. Hold out your arm, Hansel, and I'll see if you're ready. *(HANSEL holds out a bone and the WITCH feels it.)* Great day! You're still as thin as a bone! Extra dumplings for you! Extra everything! We'll step up feedings to every half hour. Tonight's the night! I can wait no longer!! *(She goes in the cottage.)*

GRETEL: She's horrible! She's mean and nasty and horrible! *(The WITCH sticks her head out the window.)*

WITCH: Sticks and stones may break my bones, but names will never hurt me. *(She vanishes.)*

HANSEL: Uh, oh. I wish you could see what I have here.

BIRD: We know. A secret. And it's only for friends.

HANSEL: And you're my friends.

GNOME: Well . . .

BIRD: I'd like to be.

HANSEL: You already are.

BIRD and GNOME: We are?

HANSEL: Certainly.

GNOME: How do you know?

HANSEL: Well, last week you saw me keep this bone.

GNOME: Yes, we saw.

HANSEL: And then, when the Witch asked me to hold out my arm and I held out this bone, you didn't say a word.

GNOME: And the Witch thought the bone was your arm. *(Laughs)*

BIRD: She still does. She thinks you're as skinny as a bone.

HANSEL: That proves you must be my friends. Well?

BIRD and GNOME: Well, we're very fond of you!

HANSEL: Good! And we're very fond of you, too. Aren't we, Gretel?

GRETEL: Yes, but what can we do?

HANSEL: We're four against one!

BIRD: Not one person . . .

GNOME: A Witch, and she's keener than one—stronger, too. She's more like two or eight.

HANSEL: I'll think of something.

GNOME: There's only one sure way to get rid of her.

HANSEL: What's that?

GNOME: Get her in the oven. *Her own oven.*

GRETEL: I couldn't do that. Not to anyone. Not even a witch.

GNOME: But she won't feel a thing. She can't. She hasn't any feelings.

She'll just disappear. Poof!

GRETEL: You're sure? How do you know?

GNOME: Every Gnome knows.

BIRD: I've heard all the creatures and spirits of the forest say, *(The GNOME "mouths" along with BIRD'S quote.)* "The worst thing she does will someday be her downfall." So, you see, I know it, too, and I'm a bird.

GNOME: Well, Gnomes know, and a few select birds. Anyhow, it's true as true can be. In her own oven!

HANSEL: She'll just vanish? Forever?

GNOME and BIRD: You got it. *(Slight pause.)*

HANSEL: You're right. I've got it. *(He motions to them and they gather to hear his whispers.)* Go ahead, *now!* We've got to get her out here and get the key.

GRETEL, GNOME and BIRD: *(Begin to shout and carry on).* "Hansel won't tell," "What's your secret?", "Tell me or I'll tell the Witch!", "What's your secret?" *(Loud and long)*

(The WITCH appears in doorway.)

WITCH: What's going on out here?

GNOME: Hansel has a secret and he won't tell!

WITCH: So what?

HANSEL: It's too special to tell just anyone.

WITCH: Say, that cage door isn't unlocked is it? *(She goes to check, pushing the others aside.)* Good. I wouldn't put a trick or two past you, boy.

HANSEL. No tricks. Just a secret. *(Cups hands, peers in.)* Amusing! Rich!

WITCH: What is? *(As the folowing goes on, GRETEL and the GNOME and BIRD get the key to the cage away from the WITCH without her realizing it.)*

HANSEL: Large and small, all at once!

WITCH: What are you talking about?

HANSEL: My secret.

WITCH: I could care less. What is it?

HANSEL: Want to peek?

WITCH: I might, but I doubt it.

HANSEL: Here.

WITCH: I can't see anything.

HANSEL: It's wet.

WITCH: It is? Well, I still can't see it.

HANSEL: And it's long and sometimes rough and sometimes smooth.

WITCH: You're joking.

HANSEL: And it's deep, and shallow too.

WITCH: Hold it closer, boy—a little closer.

HANSEL: There!

WITCH: Where?

HANSEL: It's a river!

WITCH: A river?

HANSEL: Yes, a river. It's large where it ends at the ocean, and small where it starts in the hills, and it's wet and rough and sometimes smooth, and deep here and shallow there . . . a river!

WITCH: You haven't got any river there.

HANSEL: A make-believe river, not a real one. It's a game. See? Now you know my secret.

WITCH: A game? I hate games! Especially when I'm hungry. Stick out your arm. *(Again the bone.)* Great night! You're thinner than ever! Well, I've got six pots of dumplings cooking in butter, a little snack to tide you over till dinner. *(She starts in.)* It's large and small and wet and rough and deep and silly! Some stupid secret! *(She exits.)*

HANSEL: *(after a little pause)* Did you get it?

GRETEL: *(holding up the key)* Yes!

HANSEL: Good!

GNOME: *(quietly)* Three cheers for us.

All: *(quietly)* Hooray! Hooray! Hooray! *(The WITCH sticks her head out the window.)*

WITCH: Cut down on the noise, I'm cooking.

ALL: *(very loud)* Yes, Ma'am!

WITCH: That's better. *(She vanishes.)*

GRETEL: Well, now that we have the key, I'll open the cage and we can run away.

HANSEL: No!

BIRD and GNOME: No?

GRETEL: No?

HANSEL: No. We've got to overthrow the Witch. And we can't do that if we run away.

GNOME: We'll have to take care. She's got all sorts of tricks and spells up her sleeve.

BIRD: Both sleeves.

HANSEL: Well then, supposing . . . Wait! Listen!

GRETEL: What is it?

HANSEL: I thought I heard Father! *(They listen.)* I guess not. *(He whispers again.)*

GRETEL: I'll . . . I'll try, Hansel! I'll do my best.

HANSEL: Good. First, give me the key.

GRETEL: Here.

HANSEL: Now, Gretel, now . . .

GRETEL: All right. *(GRETEL goes to the cottage and calls in.)* Yooo-hoooo! Yooo-hoooo? *(The WITCH appears at the window.)*

WITCH: Yooo-hooo? What are you yoo-hooing for?

GRETEL: I yooo-hoo for you.

WITCH: Sweep! Scrub! Clean! I like things nice and tidy. And stop yooo-hooing.

GRETEL: You must come out.

WITCH: Why?

GRETEL: There's . . . there's something wrong with my brother.

WITCH: There certainly is! I've fed him enough to fill a giant, and he's still as thin as a bone.

GRETEL: No . . . no, he's turning green, I think.

WITCH: Green? *(She starts out.)* Wait! Is this another game? I hate games! I hate secrets, too.

GRETEL: No, this is no game. No secret.

WITCH: It better not be. (*Out she comes.*) Now, let's see. (*HANSEL has turned, covering and hiding his face and hands.*) I said, "Let's see!"

HANSEL: (*springing into action*) All right!! (*He has opened the cage and leaps out. The BIRD and GNOME join in the fray. They try to get the WITCH into the cage. She is, however, as the GNOME said, more like two or eight.*)

WITCH: What's this? Treachery! Oh, I despise treachery!

HANSEL: Quickly! Here! Into the cage with her!

WITCH: Ha! Into the cage with me? Never! (*The struggle continues, amid general ad libbing.*) I speak!

BIRD and GNOME: You speak and we *disobey*.

WITCH: Whaaaaat! (*More battle.*)

GNOME: At last we've said, "No" to the Witch!

WITCH: (*hitting her stride*). Nothing like a little exercise to work up a good appetite! (*Finally she gets GRETEL in one hand and HANSEL in the other and drags them to the cottage. The BIRD and GNOME try to prevent this, unsuccessfully.*) You two! (*The BIRD and GNOME stop, frightened.*) Little Bird and Little Gnome. You seem to seek another home! Not another sound or peep! Seek your other home in sleep! (*They suddenly fall down and apparently go into a deep sleep. The WITCH laughs.*) No one dares defy me! No one! Especially you two little dears! Into the house with you! Quickly! (*Under vocal protests she pushes HANSEL and GRETEL into the cottage and closes the door.*)

HANSEL: (*from cottage*) You can't keep us in here! You can't lock the door from the outside!

WITCH: Drat that boy!

HANSEL: (*opening the door*) We'll escape!

WITCH: One more step and I'll destroy the Bird and the Gnome.

GRETEL: Don't! They're our friends!

WITCH: They won't be long! Unless you do as I say, I'll cast a spell, and destroy them both.

HANSEL: You win. For now.

WITCH: That's better! Inside! Quickly! (*HANSEL closes the door.*) Time's a-wasting! (*She goes to the oven.*) I hate to rush dinner, but what's a body to do? (*Makes the oven ready.*) Hmmm. An hour at three-fifty should do the trick.

HANSEL: (*in the window*) You'll never get away with this!

WITCH: With what, dear boy?

HANSEL: We know all about the fence you ate. We know why you keep saying, "The fence needs mending." That's not what you mean . . .

WITCH: Well, things have changed. Yes, I was misguided. I see that now. It's my ways that need mending. Oh, indeed they do. I have been wicked, but wicked I shall be no more.

HANSEL: When you say, "The fence needs mending," you intend to take some poor child and pop him in your oven and then have dinner.

WITCH: No more! No more! Gretel?

GRETEL: (*in the window*) Yes?

WITCH: Bring me that pan with the cake batter in it. I'll cook it out here in this oven.

HANSEL: Why? Why not use the stove here in the kitchen?

WITCH: I need the air. Please, dear Gretel. Oh, how wicked I have been! I don't suppose there's any hope for me, and I do so want to take my proper place in society. Come, come. Bring the cake batter. I'll fix a nice dinner for both of you. Then we'll all be friends. No more spells, no more evil deeds, no more secrets. Cross my heart.

HANSEL: What heart?

GRETEL: You cast a spell on the Gnome and Bird. That's really heartless.

WITCH: They're only sleeping. A nice rest. They'll wake up in a little while, in time for dinner. The cake batter, dear. Hee, hee, hee. And I'll let you lick the spoon. (*HANSEL whispers to GRETEL who nods.*) Don't you trust me?

HANSEL: Three guesses.

WITCH: What's the matter with children these days? No trust. (*GRETEL comes out with the batter pan.*)

GRETEL: Well, maybe we do trust you. Here.

WITCH: That's my little plump sweetie! Now, Gretel, dear, see if the oven's hot enough, will you?

GRETEL: Hot enough for what?

WITCH: For my cake. What else? As soon as it's baked, we'll all have a party. The little Gnome and Bird will awaken to a lovely party. Now, if that doesn't sound like fun then I don't know what does. Is the oven hot enough, Gretel, dear? Oh, for pity's sake, you haven't checked!

GRETEL: I . . . I don't know how.

WITCH: Well, I never! A clever little girl like you and you don't know how to see if an oven's hot enough? The idea! Why you just open the door and stick your head inside and see if the air is nice and warm, that's all. Now, go on with you!

GRETEL: Well, all right . . . *(She starts to the oven. HANSEL comes out the door immediately, but the WITCH has anticipated this. With amazing agility, she grabs him, sprinkles some powder on him and pushes him aside. GRETEL is not aware of this as she inspects the oven. At the same time the BIRD and GNOME stir. The WITCH returns to GRETEL.)*

WITCH: Well, dear, I'm waiting.

GRETEL: Such a large oven!

WITCH: Well, this particular cake is known to rise to tremendous heights. Stick your head in dear and see. See if it's warm enough. *(The WITCH puts the cake down, preparing to give GRETEL the "fatal push." The GNOME is now sitting up looking about, sleepily.)*

GRETEL: Stick my head in?

WITCH: Yes!

GRETEL: I don't know how.

WITCH: Don't know how? There's nothing to know! Just stick your head in! Quickly . . . or we'll lose all the heat.

GRETEL: How?

WITCH: How? How do you think? In! Your head, silly girl! In!

GRETEL: It's so very difficult.

WITCH: Great night in the evening. *(By this time the BIRD is awake. The BIRD and GNOME go and shake HANSEL.)*

GRETEL: I'm sorry to be so taxing.

WITCH: Taxing. That's not the word! You're positively . . charming! Yes, charming! A little dense, but charming, nonetheless. For pity's sake, this is your head, and this is the oven! Combine the two, dear—combine the two! As easy as cake!

GRETEL: Feet first?

WITCH: No! Head first!

GRETEL: How?

WITCH: (aside) What a nincompoop of a girl! This way. See? The head first.

GRETEL: Oh, yes.

WITCH: Like this. It's so easy. Easy as pudding. (The WITCH sticks her head in the oven to demonstrate. Immediately, HANSEL, the GNOME and the BIRD are alert and on their feet. Slowly, they advance and join GRETEL.) You see how?

GRETEL: Yes! You wicked creature! (All together they quickly run and push the WITCH into the oven. She screams like a thing possessed until the door of the oven is closed. They stand and look at one another for a moment. HANSEL goes and opens the oven.)

HANSEL: She's gone.

BIRD: She really vanished?

GNOME: Told you so! Poof!

HANSEL and GRETEL: We've overthrown the Witch! (A great cheer from them all, and they prance about happily. FATHER enters.)

HANSEL: I knew I heard you!

FATHER: Hansel! Gretel! Here you are! I've looked everywhere. (A tremendous ad lib from all, as HANSEL and GRETEL greet FATHER.)

GRETEL: Father! You'll never believe it! But after you left us in the forest we met a little Gnome, and a little Bird and they brought us here . .

HANSEL: It's so good to see you, Father. I knew you wouldn't leave us, I just knew it! You've been searching for us, haven't you? I told Gretel! I told her we could trust you. I knew we could.

FATHER: Now, now. One at a time. Let me look at you. You're all right?

HANSEL and GRETEL: Oh, yes, we're fine. At least now we are.

FATHER: I'm so glad. I've been searching and searching . . . (Seeing the others.) Who are they?

GNOME: I'm known as the gnome.

BIRD: And I'm the white bird.

BIRD and GNOME: Please say that you like us, please say a kind word.

FATHER: A kind word?

GNOME: He said it! He said "a kind word"!

GRETEL: These two friends helped us get rid of the wicked witch.

FATHER: The wicked witch?

HANSEL: Yes. We pushed her in the oven and she disappeared. Just before she tried to push Gretel in.

FATHER: You are indeed friends.

HANSEL: What about Mother? Is she all right?

FATHER: Well, she hasn't really been herself since you've been gone.

GNOME: She *wasn't* herself. She was under a spell.

FATHER: The wicked witch?

GNOME: Right.

FATHER: So that's why she wanted to . . .

HANSEL and GRETEL: Leave us in the woods!

GNOME: But now that the witch has vanished, your mother's spell will vanish too.

FATHER: Well, come along, we'd better head home and tell her. If we can find her. She goes into the woods by herself all the time.

HANSEL: We'll find her.

BIRD and GNOME: Bye, Hansel. Bye bye, Gretel.

HANSEL: You're coming with us.

GRETEL: Of course you are. We're friends.

FATHER: More like family really. Please come home with us.

BIRD and GNOME: Home. A real home!

BIRD: Maybe I'll learn how to fly again—now that the witch is gone.

GNOME: And I'll tell you lots of amazing things—things just gnomes know.

FATHER: It's a deal!

MOTHER: (*off*). Hansel? Gretel? Can you hear me?

FATHER: Listen!

HANSEL: It's Mother. We're here, Mother. (*He goes to get her.*)

GNOME: See, she's no longer under the spell. (*All call to Mother, and HANSEL leads her in, and there is jubilation.*)

MOTHER: Thank goodness you're all right. I've been searching all over. I've had such bad dreams. What happened?

FATHER: We'll tell you on the way home. *(After the hugs.)*

MOTHER: Tell me now.

FATHER: Let's see. Well, once upon a time there were two children named Hansel and Gretel.

HANSEL: And they lived on the edge of a great forest with their mother and father.

GNOME: Until they met a Gnome.

BIRD: And a dear sweet little wonderful white bird who . . .

GNOME: Stick to the facts.

BIRD: Who took them to a house made of candy and cake. And that's a fact.

MOTHER: This house! Who lives here?

HANSEL: No one, now. That's a big part of the story.

MOTHER: I hope it ends happily.

FATHER: Oh, it does. It does. Good dreams from now on.

MOTHER: Well, I won't budge 'til you tell me.

ALL: *(taking in lots of air).* Well . . . *(All begin to tell the story with gusto and gesture. MOTHER tries to follow for a little bit, then, smiling, holds her ears against the din and unseen by the "Narrators" tiptoes off in a homeward direction. FATHER then sees she's gone and holds up his hand. Silence.)*

FATHER: Where'd she go? *(A quick look around.)*

ALL: Home! *(They run, following her out.)* Wait for us! *(They start "narrating" again.)*

End of Play

3

Dragon of the Winds

by

Carson Wright

Characters

For 11 Males and 8 Females
(doubling possible to reduce the cast to 15)
Unosuki: a teller of tales
Nokohi: a village housewife
Goi: a boy
Tajo: another boy
Morito: an old farmer
Ikeno: a young farmer
Hanazo: a kite maker
Uji: sign painter
Kesa: a young woman
Masagi: a young woman
Takikuni: an old woman
Sujiki: a geisha
Takahiko: a samauri
Yokinaga: an advisor to the Emperor
Shuishu: Hanazo's mother

Production Notes

Playing time: 37 minutes

Time: Once upon a . . .

Place: A lake shore near the Japanese village of Sarusawa.

Properties:

Basket of laundry - Nokohi

Fishing line - Goi and Tajo

Rakes - Morito and Ikeno

Kite sized package - Hanazo

Measuring tape - Masagi

Sign with Japanese letters - Uji

Basket of laundry - Takikuni

Coin - Hanazo

6 x 2 inch poem papers - Kesa and Nokohi

Paint brush and bucket - Morito

Hedge shears - Ikeno

Box containing Japanese tea service - Geisha's servant (*the box should be large enough to double as a table for the tea ceremony*).

Flute - Geisha's servant

Oriental stringed instrument - Geisha's servant (*any one of several instruments will do*).

Baggage - Geisha's servants

Sword - Takahiko

Swords - Ninja

Lanterns - Geisha's servants

Cane - Shuishu

12-foot wind sock "Dragon" kite - Tajo (the "dragon" was made by sewing a tube from two lightweight pieces of material, one green (*upper*) and one yellow (*lower*). Red "legs" dangled at appropriate places. The head was papier-mâché with wide-open mouth which allowed air to fill the dragon as Tajo runs across the stage holding it aloft on a stick.

The set:

1. The Pier (*a 4 x 8 platform*)

2. 4 ft. wide, 2-step unit

3. 8 ft. Pylons

4. Bushes (*profiles*)

5. The Willow Tree *(profile)*

6. The Log *(or rock, or stump)*

7. Curtain

8. Cyclorama

A lake shore: For the best outdoor effect this set should be backed by a cyclorama or a painted drop. All bushes and trees *(painted or realistic)* should be bright with flowers.

Up Right Center - a pier *(with torri if possible)*. A 4 x 8 platform with a 4 ft. wide step unit will do for the pier. However, a more Japanese look can be achieved by placing two 8 ft. pylons on opposite sides of the pier about 2 ft. from the upstage end and hanging a cross piece that forms a torri (Japanese shrine gate).

Up Left Center - a weeping willow tree *(suggest a colorful profile)*.

Stage Right extending to pier - low bushes, cattails, etc., showing lake's shore line. *(Suggest profiles)*.

Stage Left - bushes *(suggest colorful profiles)*. These may also be scattered around extreme upstage.

Sound:

All songs mentioned can be found on "Popular Koto Melodies of Japan" *(Everest #3347)* Everest Records, 10920 Wilshire Blvd., Suite 410, Los Angeles, CA 90024.

Other sound effects: splashes, thunder.

Lights:

General bright daylight for most of play. Dimming beginning on page 51 at Yokinaga's exit. Early evening at Shuishu's entrance, "lantern" spot in bright moonlight for Geisha's dance. Sunrise beginning page 54 during Unosuki's speech. Full daylight by Uji's speech page 54. Dimming for storm page 55, and lightning flashes page 55. Back to full daylight page 56 to the end of play.

Costumes:

General note: Japanese costumes are not expensive or hard to make. Kimonos are very simple. The plain ones have a square sleeve; the fancy ones have a long hanging sleeve; otherwise they are the same. A happi is a waist-length kimono shirt. The male peasants go barefoot. The women and the other men wear tabi (socks with split toe) and zoris (flip-flop andals). All costume changes called for are optional.

UNOSUKI: Happi tied with rope belt, baggy pants, wrapped leggings, coolie hat, walking staff. Earth colors. No changes.

NOKOHI: Simple gray kimono, cord obi, change to colorful kimono for last entrance.

GOI: Beige happi tied with rope belt, loose brown pants cut just below knees.

TAJO: Same as Goi. Different colors.

MORITO: Same as Goi. Different colors. Change of happi for last entrance.

IKENO: Same as Morito.

HANAZO: Same as Morito except change is made for second entrance.

UJI: Same as Morito.

KESA: Simple kimono with pretty floral pattern, embroidered obi, change

MASAGI: Same as Kesa, different colors.

TAKIKUNI: Same as Nokohi but different pattern, also head scarf.

SUJIKI: First entrance, fancy kimono with floral pattern, bright colors, matching wide obi, parasol. Second entrance, very fancy dance kimono, suggested colors, red and black with gold lamé trim and obi, matching silk fans.

TAKAHIKO: Happi, open kimono, knee-length puffed leg pants. Swords (*at least one*).

YOKINAGA: Same as Takahiko but richer looking. Plus Daimyo's hat. (Looks like smurf hat, only black and backwards).

SHUISHU: Same as Nokohi's first costume but with scarf to cover head, no change. (*If this part is doubled with a Geisha servant, a very quick change is needed after Shuishu's first exit.*)

GEISHA'S SERVANTS: Simple floral kimonos. No change.

NINJA: Black happi, black hoods, black pants, black leg wrap, black tabi (*socks*), swords. No changes.

Scene: URC, a pier with cattails and other bushes extending to stage R to suggest a lake shore. ULC, a willow tree. Stage L, more bushes Entrances are DR, UL, and DL. There is a log DRC just above curtain line.

Music up (*author suggests the last 45 seconds of "Kusimoto-Bushi," a Japanese folk tune*). UNOSUKI is sitting on log. NOKOHI is kneeling on pier washing clothes in lake. After 15 seconds she rises, crosses to DL, pausing to bow to Unosuki and exits as two boys, GOI and TAJO, enter and cross to pier, bowing to UNOSUKI as they go. They begin fishing as MORITO and IKENO enter DR carrying farm tools. They cross, bow to UNOSUKI and continue to DL and exit. UNOSUKI addresses the audience as music fades.

● ● ● ● ● ● ● ● ● ● ● ● ● ● ● ● ● ● ●

UNOSUKI: One of the advantages of advanced age is that no one knows whether sitting about is important rest or laziness. The other is knowledge. Having lived so long I have acquired a great deal of that, mostly about my village and the people in it. There are great stories to be found in such a place, though it may not appear so at first glance. It has not always been so sleepy here. There have been battles fought here, and visits of important people. Great storms have come and gone, and many people have been born and lived their lives and died here, and each is a story. This is true of all places where men dwell. But, this village of Sarusawa is uniqe in one very special way. It was visited by a dragon. How this happened is perhaps the best story of all. It began on a day like today when two small boys, named Goi and Tajo, were fishing in the lake...

GOI: Have you caught something?

TAJO: No, I have a snag. It must be a log beneath the surface.

GOI: There's never been anything there before. It must have floated in overnight. Let me help you.

TAJO: Be careful you'll break the line!

(HANAZO enters and stands DL.)

GOI: Hey, look who's coming from the village. It's the kite maker Hanazo, the one they call Big Nose.

TAJO: Has he got a new kite with him?

GOI: He has a package which is probably a kite...and I've got an idea. They call him Big Nose because he cannot keep out of other people's business. So, what we do is... *(GOI whispers to TAJO.)*

TAJO: Okay...Uh huh...Gotcha!!

GOI: Get ready, here he comes...Don't let him get away! Hold on! Watch out! Play him carefully!

TAJO: He must be the greatest fish in the lake! What a fighter! I can't haul him in! I haven't the strength!

GOI: Let me help; he is so big, he's pulling you in! It's all we can do to hold him! We need a strong man for this! (*HANAZO approaches.*)

HANAZO: What have you got there, boys, a monster?

TAJO: Yes! And he's a real fighter!

HANAZO: Be careful, don't jerk the line like that! You're not playing him right! You foolish boys are going to lose him! Let me help you, I am an expert fisherman!

GOI: I don't know, it takes two of us to hold him. He might pull you in!

HANAZO: You insolent brat! I am as strong as an ox! Now, get back and hold this kite. Give me part of the line, we can pull together!

TAJO: All right! On three! One...two...three! (*TAJO lets go of line, HANAZO falls backward into lake when it breaks. The BOYS jump with glee and laughter, and wave the kite.*)

GOI: The monster has pulled him in!

TAJO: Do you think it will eat him?

GOI: Of course!

TAJO: Do you think he would want us to have his kite?

GOI: Naturally! (*The boys exit laughing as HANAZO staggers from the lake.*)

(*UJI enters carrying sign painted with Japanese characters.*)

HANAZO: Why...you...kite thieves! I'll get even with those twirps. The next kite they buy from me will fall on their heads!

UJI: Isn't it still a little cold for swimming?

HANAZO: Uji, you idiot, I wasn't swimming! I was attacked and thrown into the lake by hoodlums...delinquents of the worst kind...attacked and robbed!

UJI: Robbers! Where? I'll protect you, I'll fight them all! Out you cowards! Fight like men! (*UJI swings sign, knocking HANAZO back into lake.*) Oops, I'm sorry! (*UJI helps HANAZO out.*)

HANAZO: I already chased them off, you fool! Be careful with that thing! You almost took my head off! What is that, anyway?

UJI: It's the sign you told me to make for you to advertise your new kite design.

HANAZO: Let me see. Look at this! Look, you incompenent fool! You've done it wrong! It's supposed to say, "A dragon kite will ascend from this spot on the first day of summer at noon"! You left out the word kite! This says a dragon will ascend, not a dragon kite! You'll have to do it over; it won't do at all!

UJI: But the other words are done so well, couldn't you use it anyway?

HANAZO: Why would I want a sign advertising dragons? I sell kites not dragons!

UJI: You could switch to selling dragons. (HANAZO does a take, throws the sign down, and crosses to log. UJI picks up sign and sets it up, lovingly.)

HANAZO: This village is full of fools and thieves! Every time I even try to talk to anyone I get criticized, insulted, or treated to some really stupid babble. I, who have been to Kyoto, Edo, and Osaka. I should have stayed in one of those cities!

UJI: But, Hanazo, this is your home. Your grandfather was born here, your father was born here, you were born here. You belong here. ·

HANAZO: I belong with people of true taste and refinement, not among country bumpkins! There is nothing here for me.

UJI: Sarusawa has some good points.

HANAZO: Oh yeah, what? It doesn't smell too bad? It's not in the swamp, only next to it? Come on, Uji, show me something good about this village. (KESA and MASAGI enter DL.)

UJI: How about that? Hello, Kesa; hello, Masagi. (GIRLS cross to them giggling.)

KESA: Hello, Uji.

MASAGI: Hello, Hanazo.

HANAZO: Uh, hello.

UJI: Are you out walking alone? You must be careful! Hanazo was just robbed by a gang of hoodlums!

MASAGI: How terrible! Were you hurt?

KESA: Robbers near Sarusawa! How awful! Will you stay with us and protect us?

UJI: Of course! We won't let them harm a hair on your heads.

HANAZO: I don't think you have to worry; I fought them off. They ran away in the direction of the hills. They will think carefully before returning to face me again!

MASAGI: Then we should thank you for making it possible for us to walk safely and enjoy this beautiful day.

KESA: It is so close to summer and the weather is so warm that we decided to wear our new summer kimonos.

UJI: Why Kesa, they are truly beautiful. Did you and Masagi sew them yourselves? You have done a beautiful job of sewing!

MASAGI: Thank you, Uji, we tried to do our best and reflect credit on our village.

UJI: And look at the obis you are wearing! They are so beautifully embroidered.

KESA: That is Masagi's work. She plans the designs as well as sews!

UJI: Look, Hanazo, isn't it beautiful? A work of art!

HANAZO: Yes, it does show some talent, however, in Osaka they are no longer wearing embroidery on their obis. It is out of fashion. To be considered well dressed nowadays the obi should be plain. I suppose you could improve your style a little by removing the more obvious decorations.

MASAGI: Oh!

HANAZO: And the kimono, well, it just isn't up to date. It's well-done for a country girl, I suppose, but it could use some improvements. Maybe a little fuller in the sleeves, then . . .

MASAGI: *(breaks into tears and runs off stage.)* Boo hoo!

HANAZO: What's the matter? Is the girl sick?

KESA: Good-bye Uji. We must go. We will talk to you again when you are in better company! We prefer gentlemen with manners! *(KESA exits.)*

UJI: I don't believe it! You've run them off!

HANAZO: Nonsense! I was instructing them in their finer points of fashion. I simply wanted to improve their taste!

UJI: I think they taste just fine!

HANAZO: They obviously have no appreciation for education! They are perfect examples of people in this village; poor, ignorant, and unwilling to be instructed. *(As he speaks, TAKIKUNI enters with laundry, crosses toward lake, sees sign and stops to read it.)* Maybe it is my duty to be here.

Maybe I am meant to improve these people in spite of themselves. To do that I need their respect. I wonder how I could teach them to listen to me as they should. *(UJI notices TAKIKUNI reading sign and tugs on HANAZO'S sleeve.)* What is it? Can't you see I'm...Well, look at that. I am surprised, there is someone in this village besides myself who can read!

TAKIKUNI: My goodness! I can hardly wait! Uji, Hanazo, did you see the sign? Wht a marvelous thing!

UJI: Yes, it is a well made sign, but..*(HANAZO clamps hand over UJI's mouth.)*

HANAZO: Tell me, old woman, what does it say that has you so excited?

TAKIKUNI: You haven't read it? Come see! It says, "A dragon will ascend from this spot on the first day of summer, at noon." Isn't this the most wonderful thing!

HANAZO: You believe this sign?

TAKIKUNI: Of course, why would it say that if it were not true? I'm off. I must go tell the village about so important an event. *(TAKIKUNI exits. HANAZO releases UJI.)*

HANAZO: What do you think about that?

UJI: Why didn't you let me explain? If people see that sign, they will think it is true and have expectations of a great event which will not happen! They will suffer great disappointment!

HANAZO: I will instruct them myself, since it is my sign . . . *(HANAZO takes out a coin and waves it in front of UJI who reaches for it. HANAZO pulls it away.)* that is, if you swear to keep your mouth shut!

UJI: It is your sign. I suppose I should let you explain it. *(Takes coin.)*

HANAZO: Good, we understand each other. Now keep quiet, here come the villagers. I will tell them the truth but in their disrespectful way, they will believe nothing I say. Then, when nothing happens on the first day of summer, they will finally respect my superiority. *(Villagers, MORITO, UNOSUKI, KESA, MASAGI, NOKOHI, TAKIKUNI, and IKENO enter together and cross to sign, ad libbing excited comments.)*

HANAZO: What is all this ruckus?

MORITO: Takikuni has told us of this marvelous event, and we have come to see for ourselves!

IKENO: Yes, such a great thing has never happened in all Japan, and to happen in our village!

NOKOHI: We will be famous! There will be a shrine here!

HANAZO: Don't be ridiculous. Such a thing will never happen here. A marvelous creature such as a dragon would never choose such an ignorant and isolated village for his ascension! He would choose a place of refinement, like Kyoto or the palace at Edo! *(VILLAGERS react with insulted murmurs.)*

MORITO: Hanazo, you are always criticizing us, telling us that we are not as good as the people in other places. And, now that a marvelous dragon has chosen our village for his ascension, you cannot see, for all of your conceit, that he would not have done so if we were not worthy!

HANAZO: You believe this will happen because of a sign? I tell you it is a mistake or, worse yet, a jest! And, ignorant peasants that you are, you fell for it! *(VILLAGERS ad lib, angrily.)*

NOKOHI: Hanazo, you will be sorry you said that! The day the dragon ascends you will be the one to lose face! *(VILLAGERS exit, ad libbing jibes at HANAZO and excited comments about the dragon. Only UNOSUKI remains watching HANAZO and UJI from behind tree.)*

UJI: You were right. They didn't believe you.

HANAZO: Of course not! They prefer their fantasies to the truth, and they will ridicule the wise man who dares to speak it. If I were you, I'd keep the bargain you made. Keep silent about this or they will revile you as they do me. I will be vindicated, however, on the first day of summer! *(HANAZO exits.)*

UJI: Hanazo is so educated, I guess he is right. But, it seems to me that the truth is so harsh sometimes, and fantasy so inviting. Wouldn't a dragon be wonderful? *(UJI crosses and sits on log.)*

UNOSUKI: *(to Audience)* And so the days passed. The townspeople prepared for the big event by fixing up their village and decorating the lake side. *(KESA and NOKOHI enter, with 6 x 2 inch strips of paper with Japanese writing.)*

KESA: Uji, look! We have made poem papers to decorate the willow tree!

NOKOHI: Almost everyone in town has written one. When the dragon ascends he will look down and see them and know that we are not ignorant, like some people have said.

KESA: Would you like to write one, Uji?

UJI: Me? I....uh...I don't...I'm no poet, Kesa.

KESA: That's the wonderful part! You don't have to be! Just relax and let the thought of the great dragon inspire you!

UJI: Maybe later. *(KESA and NOKOHI cross to tree and decorate. IKENO and MORITO enter and cross to UJI.)*

IKENO. Hi, Uji! You want to help me trim the bushes?

MORITO: Or help me paint the pier? We have already painted and trimmed and decorated the village.

UJI: You sure are going to a lot of trouble. Hanazo says that there will be no dragon.

IKENO: Uji, when are you going to stop letting that know-it-all kite maker do your thinking for you?

UJI: Well...I...but you see...

MORITO: See what, Uji?

UJI: Nothing. *(IKENO and MORITO look at each other and shrug, then MORITO crosses to pier and begins painting while Ikeno crosses to bushes and trims.)*

(MASAGI enters, running to UJI.)

MASAGI: There you are, Uji! I must get your measurements. We are making new clothes for everybody! We will look very nice on the day of the big event.

UJI: But, Masagi, isn't that very expensive?

MASAGI: Yes, but we will make it all back when the pilgrims start coming to visit the shrine.

UJI: What shrine?

MASAGI: The one the town is building to commemorate the dragon's ascension.

UJI: Oh! But...but...but...

MASAGI: Yes, Uji?

UJI: Nothing, Masagi. *(UJI sits, dejected. MASAGI exits.)*

UNOSUKI: Uji kept his bargain of silence, feeling guilty all the while. But Hanazo argued long and loud against the sign. And no one listened.*(HANAZO enters, crosses to UJI.)*

HANAZO: Watch this! *(He crosses to pier.)* Hey, Morito! You have spent a fortune on paint and it's all for nothing. The sign's a fraud! There is no dragon!

MORITO: Hanazo, go stick your nose in someone else's business! Go away! *(HANAZO crosses to tree.)*

HANAZO: You ladies are wasting paper on a tree that no dragon will ever look at!

NOKOHI: Kesa, do you hear a funny noise in the wind?

KESA: I am not sure, Nokohi, but it may be the voice of someone that we are not speaking to!

HANAZO: You'll be sorry! *(Crosses to IKENO.)* Ikeno, you trim bushes so well that it is a shame that no pilgrims will visit this village to see your handiwork.

IKENO: I trim big noses, too! *(IKENO chases HANAZO around stage with the hedge shears.)*

HANAZO: Stop! Get away! You're a madman! Help!

VILLAGERS: *(ad lib).* Get him! Teach him a lesson! Ha ha! *(They stop.)*

HANAZO: You are all fools! I tell you, there will be no dragon!

VILLAGERS: *(in unison).* Hanazo, Shut up!! *(VILLAGERS exit laughing as HANAZO winks at UJI, who is sitting miserably on the log. They freeze as UNOSUKI speaks.)*

UNOSUKI: This continued until the eve of summer arrived. The lake shore was all decorated and the villagers were all at home making the final preparations for the next day's celebration. *(UNOSUKI exits.)*

HANAZO: Look at this, Uji. They have gone completely foolish. They have spent large sums of money on decorations, and food, and clothing. All for nothing!

UJI: Yes, they have great faith.

HANAZO: Faith in foolishness! Not in wisdom. I tried to stop them, you must admit, but they will no longer listen to me. People in Osaka, Edo, or Kyoto would not be so gullible. I'm sure that even the tribesmen of Okinawa would show better sense than the people of this village.

UJI: I feel so sorry for them. Look what they have done. It's all so pretty. They've all worked so hard to fix up the lake shore, and now they've gone home to wait for something that will never happen. I cannot let this go on. I must tell them. *(UJI begins to exit but HANAZO stops him.)*

HANAZO: Tell them what? That you made the sign and are the cause of their expensive folly? That you did not speak up earlier, as I have, and explain? That you let them make fools of themselves for a small gold coin? I wouldn't if I were you! Besides, Uji, they will be just as disappointed today as they will be tomorrow. Let them wallow in their fantasies one more day.

UJI: I wish I'd never made that sign! It has caused so much trouble.

HANAZO: Nonsense, it was a happy accident! *(As HANAZO speaks SUJIKI and two servants enter DR. HANAZO doesn't notice them.)*

HANAZO: This town is made up of unusually ignorant people who are in desperate need of my tutelage. This has happened to prove to them their need to listen to me. I can bring them the wisdom of Kyoto, Osaka, and Edo where people are wise, sophisticated, and have real style!

UJI: Speaking of style, Hanazo, look behind you. A geisha!

HANAZO: I wonder what would bring such a lady to this village.

UJI: Let's offer her our service and find out. *(They cross to GEISHA, who is reading the sign.)*

HANAZO: M'lady, may we be of service?

SUJIKI: Oh, honored sir, if it would give you pleasure you may help me find an inn where I might stay, if this is the village of Sarusawa.

HANAZO: This is Sarusawa. But may I ask what would bring so beautiful a lady to our humble pigsty?

SUJIKI: I am here to improve and perfect my art. Which is, as you know, the art of soothing entertainment.

HANAZO: How could being in this miserable place help to perfect your art?

SUJIKI: Often, in my profession, I am called on to tell a story. It must be a special story to soothe away the cares of my clientele. Such stories are hard to find. So, I have come here from Kyoto to witness the most wonderful ascension of the dragon, so that I might tell the story with proper feeling.

UJI: This might be a different story than you planned!

HANAZO: Shut up, idiot! You give me a headache!

SUJIKI: Oh, let me help you. I can soothe it away. If you please, sit here. *(SUJIKI leads HANAZO to the log. He sits. She signals to her servants who begin playing soft music—flute and an oriental stringed instrument. [The author suggests "Lullaby from Itsuki Village"]. SUJIKI massages HANAZO'S neck and head.)* Is this better?

HANAZO: Oooah! Ahhh ! *(As he moans and groans, he melts.)*

SUJIKI: Wouldn't it be nice to hear a soothing story of a great dragon's ascension as your headache dissolves?

HANAZO: Yes, oh yes! Anything you care to say!

SUJIKI: That is why I have come—to perfect my art.

HANAZO: How could it be any more perfect?

SUJIKI: You are too kind in your praise. I have plans to build a small teahouse here by the lake. There I shall entertain the weary pilgrims with tea and song and the story of the dragon's most marvelous ascension.

HANAZO: You would be with us forever and I could visit you whenever I like?

SUJIKI: But of course, I would be honored if you found my teahouse worthy of your presence.

UJI: What if the dragon does not appear? What if the sign were only a hoax?

SUJIKI: That would be most unfortunate. I would not be able to stay. A village of this size could not support a geisha unless there was a reason that pilgrims from outside would come frequently. I would have to return to Kyoto.

HANAZO: We could build you a great statue of a dragon. You could tell the story of its construction.

SUJIKI: Oh no! A dragon is not just an event to be reported. It is a marvel which must be seen with the heart as well as the eyes. A statue appeals only to the eyes! No, no, no. One must see a dragon live, or hear of it from one who did. Nothing else will do. Now I must go and wait until tomorrow. Which way is the inn, please? (*SUJIKI signals to her servants who stop playing and collect baggage.*)

UJI: That way, honored lady. (Points DL.)

SUJIKI: Thank you, kind sir. I would be delighted if you should come and have tea with me sometime. (*SUJIKI and servants exit DL.*)

UJI: To have a geisha and teahouse in Sarusawa, that is a dream!

HANAZO: Word of that sign has somehow reached Kyoto and that poor lady believed it. Such a trip for nothing. She will, no doubt, tell of the foolishness of our village when she returns to Kyoto. They will laugh at us forever. (*TAKAHIKO enters DR.*)

TAKAHIKO: Hey you, bumpkin! Yeah, you. Come here. Is this the village of Sarusawa where the dragon is to ascend tomorrow?

UJI: This is the village of Sarusawa, but I don't believe a dragon will ascend here.

TAKAHIKO: Oh no? Look, here is the sign! Of course he will! I have come a hundred miles, all the way from Osaka, to see this event. I assure you, I would not do such a thing for anything less than a dragon.

UJI: A wise and educated samauri from Osaka, he would not be so foolish as to believe in something which will not happen.

HANAZO: Shut up, you idiot. Your brains are hay!

TAKAHIKO: What's that?

HANAZO: I said, "Have you a place to stay?"

TAKAHIKO: Not yet. Is there a decent inn in this miserable place?

UJI: There is a small inn in the village with clean beds, and the food is not too bad even though the innkeeper is a fool who believes in the ascension of dragons.

TAKAHIKO: If he believes, he is no fool! Who says it will not happen? *(UJI points to HANAZO.)* Why do you say that? This sign says different.

HANAZO: The sign could be a mistake, or even a hoax.

TAKAHIKO: It better not be! I have traveled long and hard to be here and I would be very angry if such a hoax were played on me. I would feel honor bound to deal severely with the person who would play such a poor joke.

UJI: I'm sure no one from our village would do such a thing, intentionally, but perhaps by accident...

TAKAHIKO: Such an accident should have been reported before so many people were inconvenienced. Such a thoughtless person deserves to pay a heavy price.

HANAZO: Oh, no one here would be so thoughtless!

TAKAHIKO: Then the sign must be real.

HANAZO: Uh, well...I guess...if you say so, then it makes good sense.

TAKAHIKO: Good. I'm off to the inn to celebrate the coming event with good saki! *(TAKAHIKO exits DL.)*

UJI: Saki! Oh no! He will drink much tonight and his mood will not be good tomorrow when the dragon doesn't appear!

HANAZO: I can't believe it—a samauri from Osaka so foolish as to fall for this nonsense. I suppose that all the numbskulls in Japan are not in this village. However, it surprises me that a samauri would be one. *(As HANAZO speaks two NINJA enter quickly from DR. UJI sees them and pulls HANAZO around.)*

UJI and HANAZO: Ninja! *(They fall to the ground in terror. YOKINAGA enters DR and crosses to the prostrate pair.)*

YOKINAGA: Get up! Get up you country fools, prepare yourselves to give directions to the Emperor's representative.

UJI: Who is that?

YOKINAGA: Me, you idiot!

UJI: Yes sir! Sorry sir!

HANAZO: How may we humble villagers be of use to a noble person such as yourself?

YOKINAGA: I am the Daimyo Yokinaga, counselor to His Majesty, the Emperor. I have been sent here to represent His Majesty at the ascension of the dragon. Word of this miraculous event reached the palace at Edo two days ago. I need directions to an inn.

HANAZO: This rumor reached the palace?

YOKINAGA: Rumor?! This had better not be just a rumor for the sake of this village! The Emperor would not like it if his most trusted advisor had wasted days in pursuit of a rumor!

UJI: What if it were just a mistake...or a hoax played on the innocent villagers, and not their fault?

YOKINAGA: Hoax? Innocent villagers? Hah! After careful investigation and examination, I would think that those reponsible would wish that they had never played their little prank!

HANAZO: Careful and complete investigation?

YOKINAGA: To be sure.

UJI: Not stopping until the cultprits are found?

YOKINAGA: Without a doubt!

HANAZO: Absolute retribution?

YOKINAGA: Absolutely!

UJI and HANAZO: The best inn in town is that way. I hope you enjoy the dragon tomorrow!

YOKINAGA: Thank you. *(YOKINAGA and NINJA exit DL. HANAZO staggers to log and sits.)*

HANAZO: Oh, are we in big trouble!

UJI: What do you mean we? This was all your fault. I wanted to explain, but no, you had to be the big shot know-it-all.

HANAZO: You took the gold coin. Our only chance is to keep our mouths shut! We plead ignorance. When they question us, we know nothing...nothing. We cannot tell anyone what we know. There is nothing to tie us to that sign but our own big mouths, so we keep quiet!

UJI: That makes sense. We try to weather the storm. Okay, I'll go along, but I hope you've learned something from this.

HANAZO: I certainly have. When this started, I believed that I was the only intelligent man in our village. Since then I have learned a great truth.

UJI: I hope so!

HANAZO: I was wrong. I am not the only intelligent man in our village. I am the only intelligent man in all of Japan!

UJI: What?!!

HANAZO: Yes, even the Emperor and his advisors fell for this nonsense! And when word of my eloquent pleas for sanity reach the Emperor, he will no doubt retain me to teach clear thinking to his other advisors. I'll take you along as my servant. Wouldn't that be an honor?!

UJI: The samauri's sword couldn't hurt you; your head is already missing!!

HANAZO: It must be my family that has the brains. Not my father's family, they came from this ignorant village, but my mother's people. (*As HANAZO speaks, SHUISHU enters UL behind him.*)

HANAZO: Yes, I remember, when we visited them in their home in the mountains, they all seemed very intelligent. My mother showed good sense when she moved back to live with them. Yes, that has to be it!

SHUISHU: Hanazo, is that you?

HANAZO: Mother? How...when...Why are you here?

SHUISHU: I have walked many miles today from my family's home in the mountains to join you here for this special occasion.

HANAZO: What special occasion?

SHUISHU: The dragon's ascension, of course. Since I am old and I fear I had but one trip left in me, I decided that an opportunity to see such a great sight would be the best way to use it. Besides, it also gives me the chance to see my precious little boy. This wonderful dragon is a double blessing! My how handsome you are!

UJI: This poor old lady, who has traveled all the way down from the mountains, is your very intelligent mother?

HANAZO: *(TO UJI).* Shut up! *(To SHUISHU.)* Mother, what makes you think that these rumors are true?

SHUISHU: It is said in the mountains that even the Emperor has sent a delegation to the dragon, so it must be true! But, if it is not true, then I must return to the mountains and tell your poor old grandmother not to come tomorrow.

HANAZO: Grandmother! Is she planning to come, too?:

SHUISHU: Oh, yes! But if you think that there is any reason why she shouldn't, then you should tell me so I can stop her from taking so dangerous a journey. It's getting dark already.

HANAZO: Mother, you must know that...uh...well, you see...about a week ago...*(UJI grabs HANAZO and moves him D.)*

UJI: Hanazo! Remember? The Emperor's investigation? The samauri? The sword? What your mother doesn't know can't hurt us!

HANAZO: But she's my mother...and my poor old grandmother is coming!

UJI: What would your grandmother think of a grandson being executed for perpetuating a hoax?

HANAZO: This is the second worst day of my life.

UJI: The second worst? What was worse?

HANAZO: Tomorrow! *(He collects his mother.)* Come, Mother, let me take you to my humble cottage. *(They exit DL leaving UJI alone on stage.)*

UJI: *(moving down to log and sitting).* It was just a simple mistake. How could it have gone so wrong? I wish I had never picked up a brush! Everyone will be so disappointed. All they wanted was to be special for a change...to be more than the poor little village by the swamp. A dragon! What an honor! What a fantasy!...Just a fantasy. *(As he continues. SUJIKI and servants enter UL behind him. The servants proceed to the pier where they begin to decorate as if it were a teahouse. They set up a small tea service, Japanese of course, and take up their musical instruments. SUJIKI notices UJI and moves down behind him, overhearing the rest of the monologue.)*

UJI: A dumb, foolish fantasy as Hanazo has pointed out over and over again. He is right, though. The world is not a fantasy. It is cold and hard and very real. No dragon, no fame, no pilgrims, no teahouse...just an ugly little village by a bog!

SUJIKI: Excuse me please, sir.

UJI: Huh? What?

SUJIKI: I am sorry to have overheard your private thoughts. I beg your pardon, but it is my profession to bring happiness, and you look so sad.

UJI: Thank you, kind lady, but there is nothing you can do. I wish there were. My problems will not go away with a song.

SUJIKI: Perhaps then...a demonstration?

UJI: Of what?

SUJIKI: Fantasy and reality.

UJI: You must excuse me. I am uneducated and ignorant. I do not understand.

SUJIKI: Let me show you. (*She moves directly behind him and covers his eyes.*) What is behind us by the lake?

UJI: A pier. An old pier somewhat dilapidated.

SUJIKI: Not a teahouse?

UJI: No, just an old pier.

SUJIKI: Then come and sit! (*Music up. [Author suggests "Kuroda-Bushi," a Japanese folk tune]. SUJIKI leads UJI to the pier where the servants have set up for the tea ceremony. He kneels and she kneels opposite him. She makes and serves tea in an abbreviated version of the tea ceremony. After she has served him and both have sipped tea, she takes fans from her obi and begins to dance. Dance continues until the end of the song. SUJIKI then takes UJI's hand and leads him back to the log. The two servants giggle and exit.*) Now look, Uji. What do you see? An old pier...or a teahouse?

UJI: I...I...I see both! It can be both!

SUJIKI: Then, honored sir, which one is real and which one is fantasy? (*Before UJI can answer, SUJIKI kisses him. He stands speechless as she exits DL to village. He slowly turns and crosses to the pier and sits. UNOSUKI appears UL*)

UNOSUKI: And so Uji sat as the stars rose and a mist covered the lake. He spent the rest of that night in meditation of Sujiki's question. Then morning broke over the lake with an ominous red sun which shimmered and smoked in the mist beneath. The villagers and their guests breakfasted together at the inn and chattered excitedly about the expected event. Hanazo, however, did not take part. Instead he wandered in misery to the lake shore. (*HANAZO enters and crosses toward C. UNOSUKI steps behind tree.*)

HANAZO: What kind of pond scum am I? I am letting my poor old grandmother make a dangerous journey down a mountain because I am too cowardly to tell the truth. I can't; I must go and stop her! (*HANAZO begins exit but UJI jumps up and stops him.*)

UJI: Oh no, you don't!

HANAZO: Uji, I have to!

UJI: I'm not going to let you! The only way to stop her is to tell her about the sign, and she will, no doubt, tell the truth when the Emperor's investigation gets around to her. I have been known as the biggest fool in Sarusawa all my life, but even I can figure out the consequences of the truth coming out now. No, Hanazo, this was your idea, and you will play it out to the end! (*HANAZO crosses to the log and sits.*)

HANAZO: I never intended it to go this far. How did word of this sign reach the mountain? Or Osaka? Or Kyoto? Or Edo? This village must have the biggest mouths in all of Japan! The biggest mouths and the smallest brains!

UJI: It does...when you're here!!!

HANAZO: It was your stupid sign that started all this!

UJI: No, Hanazo, it was your tender pride. Oh, I am guilty of complicity in this, I admit that, but the cause was all you! You always stick your nose where it is not wanted or needed. You always tell everyone that they are wrong and that you know better...you always demand that your opinion be considered the right one...And it never is!!! Did it ever occur to you that you might be wrong? That someone else might have a valid opinion? Have you ever thought about the fact that the people of this village could fish, farm, make pottery, cook, sew, and in general take darn good care of themselves before you came along? I admit that you make a pretty good kite, but in everything else...you are a clod!!! I'm not even sure about the dragon!! Everyone, from the farmers of this village to the Emperor, believes that a dragon will ascend. Only you dispute it. Why should I believe you? You've never been right before, so why now? I'm tired of you bossing me around and telling me what to think! I like Kesa's kimono! I like Masagi's obi! And I like them just the way they are! So, I am going back to town, sit down with my friends, and drink some saki. Then I'm going to come back out here, with everybody else, and I'm going to see that dragon!! (*UJI exits DL. HANAZO watches him in disbelief.*)

HANAZO: It must be blissful being stupid. He's going to see the dragon. He, who made the sign, is going to join all the others in fantasy. (*Yells to wings.*) Drink plenty of saki! You'll need it to help you see dragons!

(UNOSUKI steps from behind tree.)

UNOSUKI: So Hanazo sat, and as the morning sun rose toward its noontime zenith, the people of the village and their visitors began to gather at the lake shore. *(People enter DL ad libbing excited chatter. They gather URC by the pier.)*

UNOSUKI: They were in a festive mood and no one took notice of Hanazo pouting nearby. Neither did anyone seem to notice the dark clouds gathering in the sky. Only Hanazo seemed conscious of a freshening of the wind.

HANAZO: Oh, great! Now it's going to rain! How can this day get any worse? *(There is a flash of lightning and a thunderclap. Startled, HANAZO dives for the ground; the people gasp.)*

MORITO: Look! There at the far side of the lake! Just above the trees! *(More lightning and thunder. The people ad lib lines of astonishment and point toward the UR wing. HANAZO looks up in the wrong direction.)*

HANAZO: What's going on?

NOKOHI: Oh! Look how he flies!

YOKINAGA: It is magnificent!

HANAZO: What? Where?

TAKAHIKO: He's going higher! He's headed for the clouds! *(People ad lib, HANAZO turns and heads for the pier but trips on the log and falls flat on his face.)*

PEOPLE: Oohh!

HANAZO: What? What?

MASAGI: He's gone!

PEOPLE: Aahh! *(People break up into smaller groups and chatter excitedly. HANAZO picks himself up and runs from one group to another.)*

HANAZO: What was it? What happened?

NOKOHI: What do you say now, Hanazo? Mister, there's-not-going-to-be-any-dragon! *(People ad lib laughs and catcalls.)*

HANAZO: I saw nothing!

IKENO: Of course not! Is it not written. "There are none so blind as those who will not see!" *(People laugh.)*

HANAZO: It can't be!

YOKINAGA: But it was! I must return to Edo immediately and report this to the Emperor! (*YOKINAGA and servants exit DR.*)

TAKAHIKO: It was fantastic! A truly great event!

HANAZO: It is impossible!

TAKAHIKO: (*drawing sword and advancing on HANAZO*). Are you calling all of us liars?

HANAZO: (*falling to knees in panic*). No! No! I only meant...I...I...you see...it was my sign!!!

MORITO: What? (*General murmur from people. UJI looks scared and begins trying to slowly sneak off.*)

TAKAHIKO: Aren't you Hanazo, the one who argued against the dragon?

HANAZO: (*weakly*). Yes.

NOKOHI: Look what he's trying to do now! He, who scoffed and laughed at us, is now trying to save face by claiming to be the prophet who wrote the sign! (*Angry murmurs from the people.*)

HANAZO: But...but...no...no...you see...

TAKAHIKO: Well, what do you say? Are you claiming to have written the sign or not?

HANAZO: No! You see...it wasn't like that...it was Uji who wrote the sign! (*A gasp from the people. UJI freezes in his tracks.*)

MORITO: Well, Uji. Is this true? Did you write the sign?

UJI: (*after a pause*). Yes.

IKENO: Uji has been touched by the gods!

MASAGI: Uji is a prophet!

MORITO: Three cheers for Uji! Hip hip hooray! (*The people join in the cheer as they gather around UJI and lift him to their shoulders. They exit DL with Uji, cheering as they go. Only HANAZO, SHUISHU, and UNOSUKI remain on stage.*)

SHUISHU: Hanazo, I am not very proud of you. You behaved very badly!

HANAZO: But, Mother, this dragon business was my idea!

SHUISHU: Son...(*Bonks him on the head with her cane.*)...can it!!! (*SHUISHU exits DL. HANAZO follows, pleading.*)

HANAZO: But...but...I don't understand. It couldn't be! An optical illusion...that's what...or a reflection on the water...or just a cloud...or swamp gas. Mommy!!

UNOSUKI: And that is the tale of the dragon of Sarusawa. But for those of you who wish to know more...the village became famous and people came from all over Japan to visit the dragon shrine. Sujiki's teahouse was very successful. Later she married the great prophet, Uji, and they had many little geishas. As the number of pilgrims increased, the village grew very prosperous and influential. For instance, it became very stylish to wear the kimonos and obis designed in Sarusawa by Masagi and Kesa. And do not feel sorry for Hanazo; his mother finally forgave him. Besides, he grew quite rich selling souvenir kites to the pilgrims. He never gave advice again, and in time his silence won him the reputation of a wise man. And of the dragon...was it real? Or was it only a mass hallucination born of the desires of the people? Whoever is wise enough to answer that is equal to the gods. *(UNOSUKI begins to exit DL. GOI runs out on the stage DR. He does not see UNOSUKI. GOI calls to the wings.)*

GOI: It's all clear!

TAJO: Are you sure?

GOI: Yeah, come on! *(TAJO enters DR laughing and flying a dragon kite. The boys run around the stage with it, laughing. UNOSUKI watches boys, turns to audience, and shrugs.)*

UNOSUKI: Sayonara! *(Music up. [Author suggests "Kushimoto-Bushi"]. Lights fade.)*

End of Play

4

An O. Henry Holiday

or

"The Hobo's Christmas Feast"

by

Ric Averill

Characters

Santa Claus: *(also HOBO BILLY)*
Soapy
Knickers
Top Hat
Duchess
Whistlin' Dick

Production Notes

Santa Claus: *(also HOBO BILLY)*

Soapy: A classic New York Hobo, he's about 35, big and simple looking, warm with a couple of days growth of beard, wears a long, well worn, winter coat and floppy hat. *(Plays guitar*)*

Knickers: A kid, tomboyish, about 12. She is full of energy and vitality; wearing knickers, a scarf and a stocking cap all full of holes.

Top Hap: A theatre Hobo, back alley all the way. She *(or he)* is older, late 40's-early 50's, and gives the impression of having once had class. She wears faded tux with tails, top hat, fingerless black gloves, a slightly stained tux shirt and a makeshift bow tie. *(Plays fiddle*)*

Duchess: A bag lady, late 30's, early 40's. She dresses in layers of brightly colored clothes; a dress covered with skirts and shawls - all bright and clashing - sashes, scarves, belts, bangles, beads and an absolutely ludicrous flowered hat. She is elegant by her own definition.

Whistlin' Dick: A ragamuffin Hobo, about 25. He has a short beard, wears a short-waisted bright coat, dirty shirt, patched pants, bright mismatched socks, big boots with no toes, fingerless gloves and around his neck a great variety of whistles, all of which play different sounds.

An O. Henry Holiday was inspired by the stories of O. Henry and his love The play was also inspired by a PBS vignette featuring a bag lady and a junk man on a date. The junk man picks up the bag lady in his horse and cart and escorts her to a deserted underpass in a big city. They set up for dinner by unloading all the furnishings and trappings from his cart and her bag, setting up a skeletal room in the middle of nowhere. The room becomes a complete interior dining room environment with the city and the busy traffic overpass as a background. In this new environment the two of them become sophisticated and romantic. This play takes place under a railroad overpass in the early 1900's. The Hobos are each distinctive characters, almost clown-like in the clarity of their definition. Each of the Hobos brings a variety of trappings and furnishings with which to decorate a "living room" loosely defined by two old boxcars. By the time the "feast" begins, the trainyard area should look quite festive and the various furnishings and items serve as sets and props for the vignette the Hobos share with Hobo Billy.

In the play, Soapy, the main Hobo, has failed to bring the soap to the feast. He is depressed, expressing to a dimestore Santa that he really doesn't have anything to "give" this Christmas. The dimestore Santa turns out to be the real Claus and, disguised as an ill "Hobo Billy," shows the Hobos that in the giving of the stories and songs that make up their lives, they have more of value to share than they ever realized. As you do this play, enjoy the world of the Hobo, O. Henry and Christmas all mixed into one. The play is dedicated to Michael Helvey, Tommee Sherwood, Chris Johnson, Jeri Standfield, Gail Bronfman, Jeanne Averill and all true Hobos everywhere.

*NOTE ABOUT MUSIC: It is wonderful if the Hobos can provide the music for the play, including accompanying songs and providing incidental music for the "play." However, the play can be done with a "ragtime" piano accompaniment and work just as effectively.

TIME: Christmas Eve, early 1900's

PLACE: A Hobo Jungle under the Railroad Tracks.

PROLOGUE: A New York City Street
> (*Front of main curtain. SANTA CLAUS is standing on a streetcorner with a donation bucket hanging in front of him. He is ringing a bell.*)

• • • • • • • • • • • • • • • • • •

SANTA CLAUS: Ho-ho-ho! Merry Christmas. Ho-ho-ho! Pennies for the poor! Pennies for the poor!!

SOAPY: (*SOAPY bustles past SANTA in a big hurry.*) Sorry, Santa, I can't stop now. I gotta get some soap! Sorry! (*Exits. SANTA is amused.*)

SANTA CLAUS: Merry Christmas to you, fellow. My, my, everyone's in a hurry this time of year. Such a hurry. Soap? Pennies for the poor! (*SOAPY enters again, dejectedly.*) What's the matter, fellow, you look like you just lost your best friend.

SOAPY: Oh, all the stores are closed and now I can't get any soap. Here, you might as well have these.(*Gives SANTA his pennies.*) It's not very much, but it's all I've got. I don't need it now that I've completely failed the others. No soap . . . (*Sighs.*)

SANTA CLAUS: Well, Soapy, what did you need with a bar of soap on Christmas Eve, anyway?

SOAPY: How'd you know my name's Soapy?

SANTA CLAUS: Well, I am Santa Claus.

SOAPY: Oh. Well, you see, every year, a bunch of us hobos get together for a big Christmas Feast.

SANTA CLAUS: Christmas Feast?

SOAPY: Oh, yeah, it's a lot of fun. We all get together and we have the best time. Knickers is there, and Top Hat, the Duchess, there's a bunch of us. We eat and sing and . . . uh-oh, it's already going on now, probably, and I'm supposed to be there cause I'm the host as it's at my place and I didn't even get the soap and they'll probably wish we didn't even have it and . . .

SANTA CLAUS: Hold on, Soapy, you never told me what you needed the soap for.

SOAPY: Well, you see, everybody's supposed to bring something to the Christmas Feast every year, and I bring the soap. It's very important, it's the only time in the whole year we ever wash.

SANTA CLAUS: Ho-ho-ho!!! Ho-ho-ho!!!

SOAPY: I wish I could give you some more money, Santa Claus, but I really don't have anything else to give you. I don't have anything to give anyone. *(Pulls empty pockets out of pants.)* I have to get going, so . . .

SANTA CLAUS: Well, Merry Christmas to you, Soapy, and may it be a special one! Merry Christmas!

SOAPY: Merry Christmas, Santa. *(Exits.)*

SANTA CLAUS: Ho-ho-ho! Oh, Soapy, I know something you don't know. You have a great deal more than pennies to give this Christmas, you do, and I'm going to prove it. Ho-ho-ho!! *(Music of "Christmas is Coming" is heard on guitar as curtain opens revealing the Hobo Jungle.)*

MALE VOICES: *(Sing as lights come up, as a drone to introduce "Christmas is Coming.")*
Christmas . . . Christmas . . . Christmas . . . Christmas . . .

ALL VOICES: *(FEMALE VOICES take up melody over MALE VOICE drone.)*
Christmas is coming, the Goose is getting fat!
Please put a penny in the old man's hat!
If you haven't got a penny, a ha'penny will do,
If you haven't got a ha'penny, then God Bless You!
(Company repeats this backstage music and KNICKERS enters, looking about curiously.)
Soapy!! Soapy!!! Hey, Soap! It's me, Knickers!!
(Sets down her ragbag of props by the fire, checks out the old boxcar.)
Where are you, Soapy? . . . Not here? Drats! I hope he didn't forget us.
Place doesn't look a thing like Christmas
(Sits by fire, pulls out matches and some cut tin stars.)
Well, I can fix that up a bit. First get a fire going, then some decorations . .

VOICES: *(Sing again as KNICKERS lights a fire, then puts up some tin stars on the boxcar.)*
Christmas is coming, the Goose is getting fat!
Please put a penny in the old man's hat!
If you haven't got a penny, a ha'penny will do, If you haven't got a ha'penny, then God Bless You!
(At the end of the song, TOP HAT enters and surveys the scene in a dignified manner, carrying a large suitcase and with a rope trailing behind her offstage.)

TOP HAT: What a dump! This must be the place!

KNICKERS: Top Hat! Top Hat! You're here!!

TOP HAT: And where else might I be, Knickers? I never miss an entrance. And I never miss the Feast. But where is our dear host, Soapy?

KNICKERS: Not here. Yet. But I'm sure he's just getting something in town to make the place look more like Christmas.

TOP HAT: A good idea. I've brought some things along, too.*(Tugs at rope.)* Be a good Santa's helper and help me fetch the door and things I brought for us.

KNICKERS: A door? Maybe it'll keep the cold out! *(KNICKERS follows rope and drags and huffs and puffs a stage door on.)*

TOP HAT: Perhaps, but I suspect that fire you've made will do a better job of that! *(Looks about.)* Ah, what a rustic setting for the annual Hobo Christmas Feast! *(Directing KNICKERS.)* Right there! That's good! And could you bring the other things from the cart there, too? *(Points KNICKERS off stage. KNICKERS sighs and begins to bring on various stage props and furnishings to be used in the plays, starts to set up a "living room.")*

KNICKERS: Where'd you get all the stuff, Top Hat?

TOP HAT: The Victoria just closed a play last night and can you believe it?-they were going to junk these wonderful stage props?! Can you believe it?

KNICKERS: *(Dragging on a fireplace mantle.)* These are great! It'll look just like a real living room. I'm gonna hang out a stocking tonight!

TOP HAT: And maybe you'll get as lucky as I did, Knickers! Look . . . real sugar! Given to me by Mr. Chaplain – for helping him keep folks away from the stage door!

KNICKERS: Can I have some?

TOP HAT: Not now! Some for each of us later . . . and some for the Hobo stew!

KNICKERS: Now you're talking.

TOP HAT: Knickers, be a good lad and fetch the last load-one more should do it-and there's food in the canvas sack! *(Look around as KNICKERS goes off for last load.)* This place is in dire need of some direction on the redecoration! *(Exits, singing of "Christmas is Coming" resumes, KNICKERS and TOP HAT re-enter and sing and decorate. They set out food, silverware, utensils, lamps, holiday greens, etc. As they finish, the DUCHESS enters slowly, peering at them shyly.)*

KNICKERS: *(Notices her.)* Oh, look! It's the Duchess! Hey, Duchess, what are you doing?

DUCHESS: *(Hushes KNICKERS.)* Shhh, no, no! *(Whispers for KNICKERS to come to her. KNICKERS answers in a whisper.)*

KNICKERS: What is it? *(DUCHESS explains a plan for her entrance to the Feast. KNICKERS then executes it.)* Ladies and Gentlemen! Hobos of all cities! Announcing the Duchess of Duquesne!! From High Chicago!

DUCHESS: *(KNICKERS hums and toots a trumpet fanfare. TOP HAT bows and spreads out a "red carpet" for her. DUCHESS whispers to them again and they spring off, bring her an easy chair, put her in it and carry her to a place by the fire.)* My thanks, good subjects. *(They snicker. It is a game they always play.)* It is so delightful to be here on the coast at last. I had a dreadful time getting here! But look, presents from my bag!! For you, Knickers, chocolate from the King of Sweden. And look, Top Hat, for the kitchen I bring celery from the Duchy of Belgium and coffee from the Witch Doctor of Jamaica!! *(Tosses things to TOP HAT, who puts them by the fire.)*

TOP HAT: My thanks, dear Duchess!!

DUCHESS: Not at all! But where is Soapy, our host? Not at his own home?

KNICKERS: I was first and nobody was home when I got here.

TOP HAT: Nor I.

DUCHESS: Nobody home? You mean . . .*(Looks at them and sings.)* Hey ho, nobody home, meat nor drink nor money have I none, Yet I will be mer-er-er-er-ery, hey ho, nobody home! *(They all sing, joining in the round, hop up and decorate until the place really begins to resemble a decorated living room. At end of song, DUCHESS speaks.)* This place gets nicer every year.

KNICKERS: Every minute, I say!

TOP HAT: A perfect place for a soliloquy! To be hungry or not to be . . .

KNICKERS: Food is the answer! I'm starting the Hobo stew! *(Starts to prepare ingredients and cook, then a sharp whistle is heard.)* What was that?

TOP HAT: Someone espies us.

KNICKERS: That's a Hobo Whistle! Someone whistle back!!

TOP HAT: My, I don't whistle well. . .

DUCHESS: Whistling is uncouth . . .*(They look at her.)* But . . . *(She lets out a huge whistle between her fingers. It is answered.)*

KNICKERS: That must be Whistlin' Dick! *(Another whistle.)* Sure enough, it is!! Duchess!! *(She whistles again. DICK enters.)*

WHISTLIN' DICK: Good evening all! Pleased to join your hospitality! Duchess! *(Greets all with handshakes.)* Top Hat! You brought your fiddle. And Knickers, you squirt grow every year, don't you? But look what I got here! All the way from St. Louis I brought it! *(Drags a trash can on.)* The cleanest trash can from Forest Park! And . . . *(Goes off, drags on an old Coca-Cola sign.)* . . . a table to go on it! And finally . . *(Brings on a scraggly small evergreen tree.)* . . . a part of the Forest! A Christmas tree!! *(They set up table and prop up tree beside it.)*

TOP HAT: My, but nothing to eat?

WHISTLIN' DICK: *(Pulls out a string of sausage.)* Just a little top grade Cincinnati Dancing Pig Sausage!! And if everybody's here, then let's open the feast with a song!!

DUCHESS: No! Wait! No songs yet, Whistlin' Dick-Soapy's not here!

WHISTLIN' DICK: But I saw him on the way into town-from the train! He was talking to Santa Claus-in front of the big department store? He must have been going to get something for the feast!

TOP HAT: Well, at least he's coming.

KNICKERS: Hey! Let's surprise him!

WHISTLIN' DICK: Yeah, let's!

DUCHESS: I'm planted and I'm not moving!!

WHISTLIN' DICK: Aw, come on. It'll be a great Christmas surprise.

TOP HAT: Don't be a poop, Duchess.

DUCHESS: Alright, let's hide!! *(They hide just as SOAPY enters, singing to himself.)*

SOAPY: Now bring us some hasty pudding, Now bring us some hasty pudding, Now bring us some hasty . . . *(Notices transformation of house, including the door through which he has just arrived.)* What's this? A door on my humble abode? But it wasn't there when I left. Oh, my. I must be losing my head. *(Checks.)* No, it's still there. But so is everything else. *(Looks about.)* Still there and there and there and there! I've moved uptown without traveling an inch!! And it all looks like Christmas! *(Steps through door.)* Well, here I am, home at last!!

ALL: *(Jumping out from hiding and shouting.)* Merry Christmas, Soapy!!!

SOAPY: *(Jumping back, startled.)* Well, look at you! Will you look at all of you *(Greetings and handshakes all around.)* Gathered here and decorated and everything! Duchess, Knickers, Top Hat, Whistlin' Dick! It's great to see you all-and you've done such things to the place!! But I have some bad news. *(They look at him with anticipation.)* I truly hope you don't think I let you all down. I mean I tried, very hard, and I feel bad because I don't have anything to give all of you but . . .

WHISTLIN' DICK: Come on, Soapy, out with it!

SOAPY: I couldn't get any soap.*(They all stand, nodding heads, evaluating this information, then suddenly burst out laughing and cheering. SOAPY doesn't quite understand their glee.)*

KNICKERS: *(Spitting on her hands with zest.)* Let's get the dinner going!

TOP HAT: *(Pouring drinks into tin cups.)* First, some coffee!!

DUCHESS: Java!

WHISTLIN' DICK: Morning dew!!

SOAPY: *(As they all raise their cups to drink.)* Wait! Just a second. Let's take off our hats. A toast, folks. We must think before we celebrate of all the poor Hobos who don't have a friend or a place to go. The Hobos who may ride a lonely boxcar to a wintry grave tonight! *(Picks up guitar, strums, they sing the old Jimmy Rogers Hobo tune. It is almost magical as it seems to call the real "Hobo Billy" from the inside of the boxcar.)* Ho-oooooo, Ho-oooooo Bo Billy! Riding on a Eastbound freight train, Speeding through the night, Hobo Bill, the railroad bum, Was fighting for his life! The sadness of his eyes revealed, The torture of his soul. He raised a weak and weary hand to brush away the cold.. *(HOBO BILLY - SANTA CLAUS stumbles out of the boxcar wearing a reversible red coat, the inside-out of which is a ragged brown number, and a silly aviator's cap, which is pulled over his white hair and beard. He crosses to the door and begins to knock and cough.)* Ho-ooooo, Ho-oooooo-Bo Billy!

KNICKERS: I think that's sad . . .

TOP HAT: Look! At the door!!

SOAPY: Let him in!

WHISTLIN' DICK: He's a coughin'!

DUCHESS: He's one of us!! Bring him in!! *(SOAPY, TOP HAT, and WHISTLIN' DICK go get HOBO BILLY.)*

WHISTLIN' DICK: What's a matter, fella?

HOBO BILLY: The fever . . . got the Hobo fever. *(He coughs some more.)*

SOAPY: Here, put him in the chair by the fire! *(They escort him to the big easy chair by the fire.)*

TOP HAT: Rub his feet down!

KNICKERS: Give him some of this coffee.

HOBO BILLY: No, no coffee. Sleep . . . Want to sleep!

DUCHESS: Don't let him sleep! It's the worst thing!

KNICKERS: That's right. That's what happened to my poppy!! Fell asleep and then froze to death.

TOP HAT: It happens. The fever gets them sick, then the cold knocks them dead!

WHISTLIN' DICK: Listen, buddy . . . you can't go to sleep! You can't! You gotta stay awake!!

SOAPY: Don't yell at him, Dick. What's your name, Mac.

HOBO BILLY: Billy, Hobo Billy. *(They look at each other.)* But don't bother with me. I'm just an old railroad bum.

DUCHESS: Nonsense. You're one of us. Now, you just drink that coffee. *(They rub him down, give him the royal treatment. He is still coughing, but perks up a bit.)*

HOBO BILLY: That's nice, but I'm still a bit tired.

KNICKERS: Well, you can't sleep! You can eat, drink and be merry with us, but we won't let you sleep.

TOP HAT: We won't sleep either!

HOBO BILLY: Why? Why bother with an old Hobo?

SOAPY: You're one of us, Billy!! We're gonna keep you awake. *(Looks about at others.)* How? *(They all look dumbstruck.)* Wait . . . we'll . . . uh, we'll tell him a story!!

KNICKERS: Everybody likes a good story!

TOP HAT: Yes, like Scherezade!!

DUCHESS: Stories and songs! The Feast entertainment!!

WHISTLIN' DICK: Just like on the boxcars – to stay awake for the next stop!!

SOAPY: Would you like to hear some stories, Hobo Billy? Huh? Would that keep you awake?

HOBO BILLY: A story? Yes, a story would be nice. A Christmas story?

TOP HAT: Of course . . . and see here . . . we could act them out!! After all, I've been around the theatre for years!!

WHISTLIN' DICK: The Hobo Christmas Feast Theatre presents!: *(Blows on* *one of his whistles. There is anticipation, but no story.)*

DUCHESS: What? What does the Hobo Christmas Feast Theatre present? Who's got a story?

HOBO BILLY: *(BILLY coughs.)* It's alright.

DUCHESS: Quickly.

SOAPY: I got a story!! I got one. Remember the Christmas that I didn't make it to the feast? *(They all do.)* Well, I never told you why. Come here. All of you. Tell you what we do . . . *(SOAPY assigns parts, and they all mumble, then slightly rearrange some of the furniture for the "play." BILLY coughs. The Hobos line up; they will provide their own incidental music and act all the parts. WHISTLIN' DICK blows a new whistle and announces:)*

WHISTLIN' DICK: *(Picks up an instrument, then to BILLY.)* Now, you be quiet and listen, cause the Hobo Christmas Feast Theatre Presents, "The Gift of the Magi!" and I'm gonna play the horsey-dee-hoofs! *(He starts playing an overture and the HOBOS set up Jim & Della's little "apartment".)*

THE GIFT OF THE MAGI

(KNICKERS is moving about in the kitchen, preparing coffee She wears a mop head for a wig and is being DELLA, the wife. SOAPY comes in wearing a "costume" vest being JIM, the husband.)

KNICKERS: Good morning, Jim. Coffee's ready.

SOAPY: Morning, Della. My, you look as lovely as ever this fine Christmas Eve morning. *(They embrace. He runs his fingers through her hair.) And I think your hair is even prettier in the Winter.*

KNICKERS; They say the cold air does it good.

SOAPY: Is there sugar? *(As he reaches for the jar, she stops him, concealing the fact that the sugar bowl contains her Christmas money.)*

KNICKERS: No, Jim, now, you know that there isn't. You shouldn't even have to ask. *(She puts the jar aside.)*

SOAPY: Well, never mind that, anyway. Who needs it? *(He pulls out a beautiful watch and looks at it. A factory whistle blows.)* Time to head off for work anyway.

KNICKERS: Jim, I wish they wouldn't make you work on Christmas Eve. It just doesn't seem fair.

SOAPY: May not be, but you know we need the money, with the high rent and all . . . *(He drops the watch, picks it up, replacing it carefully in his* *pocket.)* Oh, my gosh!

KNICKERS: Be careful Your Grandfather would never have given you that watch if he had known how often you would drop it!

SOAPY: Nonsense. Look, it still runs fine. It is beautiful, though, and I will try to be more careful. Well, I must be off. *(He exits. She calls off after him.)*

KNICKERS: Goodbye, Jim. Will you be home at five?

SOAPY: *(Steps back into stage area.)* Oh, I forgot. I may be a little late. I have to . . . uh, stop, uh, well, I just may be a little late. Goodbye, now!

KNICKERS: Goodbye! *(To herself.)* Late? I hope he doesn't have to work too late. Not on Christmas eve. *(Goes to the sugar bowl, opens it, spills money out onto the table and counts it.)* . . . 25 cents. . . 78 cents . . . oh, there's not much here and yet it's all the sugar money from the past two months. $1.87. One dollar and eighty-seven cents; and that's all the money I have to buy a present for Jim. Oh, I did so want to get him that watch chain, but it's nearly $21.00 at the jewelers and I'll never . . . *(TOP HAT enters as the COP, walking past the "house.")*

TOP HAT: Good morning, up there, Mrs. Della!

KNICKERS: Oh, good morning, Officer O'Keefe. And a Merry Christmas to you!

TOP HAT: Same to you, Della. Done your shopping all up?

KNICKERS: Come inside, Officer, and have some coffee with me. I have a question for you. *(TOP HAT enters, sits and has coffee with her.)* Isn't this pitiful. All I have is $1.87 to buy a present for Jim with. Now what can a girl buy with that?

TOP HAT: Oh, lots, I suppose . . . candy, a tie and the like. What were you thinking of?

KNICKERS: I wanted to buy him a watch chain. For the beautiful watch his Grandfather left him. You know the one?

TOP HAT: Now that would be a present indeed. But for $1.87 all you could get would be a pretty string or ribbon for it.

KNICKERS: I know, but I wanted a real chain. A gold chain. Surely you can think of some way I can get enough money?

TOP HAT: Course I can, Della, but every way I can think of I'd have to arrest you for and that's no present to give a fella on Christmas Eve unless, of course . . .

KNICKERS: Unless what?

TOP HAT: (*Reaches out and strokes her hair.*) Well, have you ever heard of Madame Sofronie?

KNICKERS: Madame Sofronie? You mean the wig-maker? But what . . . you mean, sell my hair?

TOP HAT: Well, it was just a thought, and perhaps not a good one as my walk past your window each day would not be so pretty, but it is an idea. (*Finishes coffee, puts down cup and exits.*) Well, I must be on my way.

KNICKERS: Well, goodbye, Officer O'Keefe. And thank you! (*She paces and thinks.*) Sell my hair? Well, Jim would hate that. He loves my long hair but then it would grow back, eventually, and he would have a Christmas gift. I'll do it! (*She walks to "Madame Sofronie's," which is run by the DUCHESS.*)

DUCHESS: Madame Sofronie's! Hair goods of all kinds! Wigs we have here! Fine wigs of real human hair!!

KNICKERS: Madame Sofronie! Madame Sofronie!! Would you? Would you buy my hair . . . I mean all my long locks and tresses? Do you want them?

DUCHESS: (*Examines her "mop" hair as though it were truly beautiful.*) What's a nice girl like you want to sell all that beautiful hair for?

KNICKERS: It's my Jim. I want to get him a present a fine Christmas present. I need to give him a watch chain! Please, how much will you give me?

DUCHESS: Well, I hate to, but it is beautiful hair, and I could use it well. I'll give you $20.00 for it. Today.

KNICKERS: (*Sitting as DUCHESS begins to cut the hair.*) Well, I know it will be worth it. I know just the watch chain I want, and the hair will grow back and Jim will be so happy.

DUCHESS: Yeah, yeah, yeah, yeah, . . . (*Finishes up. Give her the money.*) Here you are-$20.00 and have a Merry Christmas.

KNICKERS: Oh, I will, indeed I will thanks to you!! (*She crosses to "Jewelers," which is set up behind a "counter" by WHISTLIN' DICK.*) There, that's the chain I want, jeweler.

WHISTLIN' DICK: (*Looks her over, realizes it's too expensive for her.*) You got the money? It's an expensive chain.

KNICKERS: Yes . . . well, I have $21.87. Is that enough?

WHISTLIN' DICK: (*Takes the price tag off of it.*) Just so happens, today we have a Christmas Eve special $21.00 even and you take the chain!

KNICKERS: Will you wrap it?

WHISTLIN' DICK: You buy it I wrap it! *(She hands him the money and he quickly puts the chain into a decorated box and hands it to her.)*

KNICKERS: Thank you, bye! *(She hurries home, and DICK exits.)* Well, that's that. Now, I make my hair look as best I can and hope he looks at the present more than at me! Oh, I'm so excited. This will be the best Christmas ever!! *(JIM comes "up" to the apartment, a package behind his back.)*

SOAPY: Della, I'm home!! I'm home!! Merry . . . *(Sees her, steps back, staring, aghast.)*

KNICKERS: Jim, darling, don't look at me that way. I had my hair cut off and sold it because I couldn't have lived through Christmas without giving you a present. It'll grow out again. I just had to do it. My hair grows awfully fast, so say "Merry Christmas," Jim, and let's be happy. You don't realize what a beautiful gift I've got for you!

SOAPY: You've cut off your hair?

KNICKERS: Cut it off and sold it! Don't you like me just as well, anyhow? I'm me without my hair, aren't I?

SOAPY: It's really gone!

KNICKERS: Well, you needn't look for it. I did it for you!

SOAPY: Don't get me wrong, Della. I don't think there's anything in the way of a haircut that could make me like my girl any less. But if you'll unwrap this package I got you for Christmas, you may see why you had me acting so strangely at first. *(She opens it.)*

KNICKERS: Combs! The combs I've wanted so long to put in my hair! Jim, you shouldn't have!! You didn't, they were so expensive and now I've ruined . . .

SOAPY: You've ruined nothing, Della the hair will grow back.

KNICKERS: Yes, you're right. My hair will grow back. but look, here, you've got to see what I gave up my hair for. Open it! *(She gives him his present, he opens it, looks at it, sighs, and then begins to laugh out loud.)* What is it, Jim? What is it? Do you love it? Get out your watch so we can see how it looks!!

SOAPY: Della, let's just put our Christmas presents away and keep them awhile. They are too precious to use just at the moment. You see, I sold the watch to get the money to buy your combs.

KNICKERS: You sold? Your watch? I sold? My hair? *(They both laugh and* *cry at once, giggling and hugging and enjoying the irony. Then:)* Merry Christmas, Jim.

SOAPY: Merry Christmas, Della. *(They lean in close to each other then a loud whistle from WHISTLIN' DICK shatters the mood.)*

End of Scene

A GAME OF CATCH

by

Jack Theis

Characters

Michael: A young man, in his thirties who reminisces of a time when
he played catch with his father. At different points in the play,
Michael becomes himself at different ages.
John: Michael's father, who teaches his son lessons while playing
catch on their front lawn.
Helen: Michael's mother, who tries to understand her husband and
son's complex relationship.
Jim: Michael's neighbor and best friend.
Various other characters appear throughout the play as Michael
reminisces.

Production Notes

Lighting: The lighting in the play should remain relatively simple,
proportionate to the complexity of the set design. In general, Michael
should be the main focus and should have a lone spot during his
monologues. Other spotlight notes are given throughout the play, but
they are not necessary. The games of catch and other scenes in front of
the home should have a warm country day feel to them, generally
getting colder as the play comes to an end. The flashbacks that Michael
has could be made more clear through changes in lighting, but this
again is not necessary. Lighting is most important in the last scene,
where Michael hears of his father's death. Here, the stage should be
completely barren of light, save a spot on him.

Costuming: The following are merely suggestions. The main thing to keep in mind is that these are simple rural people, without any flash. The flashbacks take Michael anywhere from 1960 to 1990, so they should not be reflective of any particular era.

Michael: Basic sweater, khaki pants. He is a professional thirty year old, so his clothes have a hint of yuppiness

John: More rural, jeans and his favorite shirt

Helen: Long, motherly, country white dress

Jim: Basic blue jeans and a T-shirt

Sarah: Long, attractive dress that a 30 year old woman would wear

Coach: Baseball hat, baseball sweatshirt, baseball pants

Mr. Shatzmeyer: Expensive professor-type suit

Guidance Counselor: Sweater, long skirt, sagging knee-highs. Again, these are merely suggestions. The play could plausibly be done with no costuming, minimal lighting, and an empty stage. Everything else is merely scenery.

Set Description: The play is set in a rural town in the country, and almost all of the action takes place on the front lawn of Michael and his parents. A country home could be set up upstage right, and perhaps a white picket fence with a gate could be added downstage to give more of a country flavor. John and Michael have various games of catch on the front lawn, so the stage should be wide enough to allow for a ball to be thrown back and forth.

The play opens with a spot on MICHAEL entering SR and walking to DSC. He is reminiscing: he breathes a sigh, kicks some dirt, glances at the house USR. He turns to the audience, pauses, and speaks.

● ● ● ● ● ● ● ● ● ● ● ● ● ● ● ● ● ● ●

MICHAEL: I used to play catch with my dad right here on this front lawn. He'd stand over there (*points DSL*) and I'd stand right here and we'd just toss the ball back and forth until the sun went down and we couldn't see the ball anymore, or my mother would cry out from that window over there for us to come in and have dinner. Sometimes my friend and neighbor Jim would come running out from his house across the street, glove in hand, asking to play. We'd play running bases or five hundred or pinner or games that we'd just make up. From the time I could first catch a ball until the time I left for college when I was eighteen, I played catch with my father on our front lawn, feeling the ball scorch into my glove, hearing the snap his glove as my throw hissed into it. And I used to listen to his words while we threw the ball, and I tried my best to understand every one. Sometimes, what my father had to say while playing catch out on our front lawn became more like a sermon, but I didn't complain. I was content to be spending time playing catch with my father, a man who I felt I didn't really know. I was being taught a new lesson every time out there. He always could reason with me when no none else could. Well, when I was ten years old, baseball was the only thing I had on my mind. School was secondary. Unfortunately, my teacher didn't feel the same way. One day she caught me reading some sports magazines in class, and she was so mad that I had to bring home a note for my parents from my teacher. I gave it to my mother, and she read it out loud (*HELEN, MICHAEL's mother, enters SR and is slowly spotted as she enters and walks to MICHAEL's left. She holds a piece of paper.*)

HELEN: (*reading the note*) "And remind Michael that he has a test on what we talked about today in school. Signed, Ms. Jones." (*to MICHAEL, DSC*) Well, Michael, I hope you're proud of yourself. Why on earth were you not listening in class? This is the fifth grade, Michael. It's time to get serious. (*JOHN, MICHAEL's father, enters SR and is slowly spotted as he enters. He walks to MICHAEL's right and HELEN hands JOHN the note.*)

MICHAEL & MIKE: My father walked in the room, took one look at the note, and said.

JOHN: Michael, go and get your glove. (*MIKE crosses DSR, walking away from two parents who freeze. Spots on parents fade.*)

MIKE: I knew that we were going out to talk, and I was going to get yelled at, so I dragged my feet when I went to grab my glove. (*HELEN exits SR and JOHN stays in his spot. MIKE grabs two gloves and a ball and brings them to JOHN, SC. JOHN takes his glove and walks DSL. Lights come up, and MIKE is now ten years old.*)

JOHN: (*throws ball to MICHAEL, USR, who catches it, grimaces in pain from the speed which the ball arrived to him.*) How was school today, Michael?

MIKE: (*frightened*) Alright. (*Throws ball back, game of catch continued throughout the scene.*)

JOHN: Do you like fifth grade?

MIKE: (*slowly*) I guess.

JOHN: How about your teacher?

MIKE: Look, Dad, I'm sorry about what happened. I was just bored.

JOHN: Michael, when you are at school, it's time for schoolwork. Not baseball.

MIKE: *(looking down)* I guess. But I need to keep up on the stats, Dad.

JOHN: In the middle of class, Michael? Baseball is one thing, but school is something entirely different.

MIKE: I know, but. . .but I want to know as much as you do about baseball, dad. I want you to be proud of what I know.

JOHN: Michael, I am proud of what you know and what you've learned in school. You'll have time to read all of the scores and stats, but there's a time for everything, Michael. You have to make the best of every situation, because at some point in your life, you'll look back and think "You know, I sure should have done something else there," and then where will you be?

MIKE: *(catches ball, holds it and looks at JOHN. JOHN freezes, lights dim. MICHAEL walks USC. Fade spot on MICHAEL.)* A time for everything. Okay, so my dad wasn't a poet or anything, but it's amazing how much can be done if you just follow those simple words. I mean, if I had only listened to my dad then and taken his words to heart instead of blowing off his words, who knows? *(Spot dims on MICHAEL and he walks back DSR. Lights come up, JOHN unfreezes, crosses to MICHAEL.)*

JOHN: I'll tell you what, if you promise to do well on that test tomorrow, I'll get us tickets to the game on Saturday.

MIKE: What? Are you serious? *(JOHN nods)* Dad, you're the greatest! *(runs and hugs him.)*

JOHN: Alright, now run inside and do your homework. *(MIKE runs off SR. JOHN, kneeling on ground, examines the ball and throws it into glove. His wife, HELEN, enters from house. She is in her thirties, wearing an apron, and seems upset.)*

HELEN: Let me see if I understand this correctly. Our son gets into trouble in school for reading a baseball magazine in class, and instead of a punishment he is going to a game on Saturday?

JOHN: No, Helen, it's not like that.

HELEN: Well then please tell me how it is, John.

JOHN: He just needed to be straightened out, that's all. He'll do fine in school.

HELEN: That's always the answer, isn't it? "He needed to be straightened out." John, when are you going to see that all the problems of the world can't be solved while playing catch?

JOHN: You don't understand. *(Gets up and walks inside.)*

HELEN: No, I don't.*(Lights fade on HELEN and JOHN, spot comes up on MIKE as he enters SR.)*

MIKE: My mother tried as hard as she could to understand, however. But I don't think she ever really understood what the game of catch meant to us.*(Spot on MIKE fades, HELEN meets MIKE SC and lights come up.)*

MIKE: *(whine)* But Ma, just because dad is out of town on a business trip doesn't mean you have to play catch with me out here.

HELEN: No can do, son; I'm taking your father's place out here on the lawn. I used to play catch with your father, you know, early in our marriage.

MIKE: Why'd you stop? *(HELEN throws to MIKE, throw sails over his head offstage right. MIKE runs off to retrieve the ball.)*

HELEN: I think because he was always chasing the ball down.

MIKE: *(returns to his spot and throws ball to HELEN)* Okay, Mom, throw it nice and easy right into my glove.

HELEN: Hey, don't patronize me, buster. I've got a better arm than you'll ever have.*(HELEN once again heaves the ball over MIKE's outstretched glove, and MIKE rushes to get the ball.)*

MIKE: *(returns with the ball)* Look, if we're gonna play catch, you have to throw it on target. Just throw a little softer, okay? *(HELEN throws near MIKE and he catches it. Game of catch is continued throughout scene; HELEN's throws are wild and hard for MIKE to catch.)*

MIKE: Atta way, Mom. *(Catch continues. After five or six throws, HELEN is beginning to get confused about the purpose of the game.)*

HELEN: Is this it?

MIKE: *(confused)* What?

HELEN: I mean, this is it? This is what you and your father have been doing for all these years? *(laughs)* Where's the action? Where's the fun? I mean, watching an actual baseball game is more exciting than this, and watching a game is kinda like watching paint dry.

MIKE: Well, we usually talk.

HELEN: About what?

MIKE: I don't know. Guy stuff.

HELEN: Guy stuff? What's guy stuff?

MIKE: Well, we talk about things that we can't talk about normally. When we play catch, everything seems to easier to talk about, and I can tell him almost anything.

HELEN: I see. *(catch continues)* Anything you want to tell me?

MIKE: No, mom.

HELEN: Alright. Just wondering.

MIKE: *(awkward pause)* Okay. There is something I've always wanted to tell you.

HELEN: Yes?

MIKE: You know, as a mom, you're great. *(MIKE catches one of HELEN's bad throws)* but your throws need some work.

HELEN: Well, you're a great son, but your room needs work. Go inside and clean it.

MIKE: Alright. *(Lights fade and HELEN exits SR. MICHAEL crosses DSC and spot comes up on him.)*

MIKE: My father used to tell me stories of him and his father and how I was the same as my father at my age, and other things that didn't really make sense. My grandfather supposedly played in the big leagues for a couple weeks, and my father loved to tell the stories of what his father told him. By my teen years I had heard the stories so many times that they became almost a little boring. But I never interrupted him, even when he told the story of my grandfather in his major league debut – after I had heard the story in its entirety about ten times before . . . *(Spot fades on MIKE. JOHN enters with glove and stands SL. MIKE crosses to SR and the lights come up on them having catch.)*

JOHN: Alright-pop fly! *(gives MICHAEL a high pop up)*

MIKE: Schmidt is under it . . . and he pulls it down! The Phillies win the pennant! The Phillies win the pennant!

JOHN: Good catch. Say, Michael, did I ever tell you of the time that your grandfather first got into a major league game?

MIKE: *(subtly sarcastic)* No, Dad.

JOHN: Well, it was late in the season of '48, and he was playing shortstop for the Brooklyn Dodgers. Pee Wee Reese was out because he had a sprained wrist, so your grandfather had started and played the whole game for the Dodgers. He hadn't gotten a hit in the game and had made only two small plays in the infield, so he hadn't shown much of his talent to the manager. So it comes to the bottom of the ninth, and the Reds have two men on and two out. The score was tied, so the next run would win the game for the Reds. Big Don Newcombe sets and throws a curveball to Grady Hatton, who pops it up on the infield. So my father runs over towards second base to catch the ball while the runners are speeding around the bases. He calls for it, takes a step back, wobbles, and trips over second base. The ball drops and the Reds win.

MIKE: (*after a pause*) But I don't get it, Dad. Why is this such a great story? He dropped the ball! He was the goat! He blew it!

JOHN: I'm not finished with the story. The next day, after his name was mentioned in the article in the sports section as the "nobody who choked" he was benched by the manager. He put a shortstop in that was worse than my father, and who fumbled every play that came to him. So my father walked over to the manager and pleaded with him, "Ya gotta put me in," he said to the Dodgers manager, Burt Shotton. "No way," old Shotton mumbled. "After yesterday's performance, you should be glad you're still wearing that uniform." So my father gathered up all his courage and said, "But I know I'm better than that. Just give me one more chance. I can do it." So Shotton let him pinch-hit for the shortstop the next inning, much to the displeasure of the fans and players.

MIKE: (*after another pause, with new interest in the story*) And?

JOHN: And what?

MIKE: And what happened when he got to the plate?

JOHN: It doesn't matter. The point was that he didn't give up. In the face of all that was against him, he never gave up, and it that respect, he succeeded.

MIKE: (*frustrated*) But what about what happened? Did he get a hit?

JOHN: Michael . . .

MIKE: That's all that matters. If he got a hit. Did he?

JOHN: Michael . . . Alright, yes, he did get a hit. He smacked a double down the left field line.

MIKE: (*satisfied*) Alright grandpa!

JOHN: (*chuckles to himself, begins to walk inside*)

MIKE: (*pause*) You know, I've never heard that second part of the story before.

JOHN: (*stops walking*) Sorry?

MIKE: Oh . . . nothing. Never mind. Thanks for the catch.

JOHN: No problem. *(Lights fade, JOHN exits, spot comes up on MIKE as he crosses DSC)*

MIKE: My dad told me the second part of that story for a reason. Perhaps it was because it never really meant anything to me until I was that age, which was about fourteen. Mabye I needed reinforcement, some sort of reinvigoration. 'Never give up.' Worthy advice. Anyway, high school came along, and I went to the local public school near my home. When spring of my Freshman year came, I tried out for the high school baseball team. Tryouts were set on a certain Saturday of March. Needless to say, I was incredibly nervous. I had dreaded the coming of that Saturday for a couple of weeks. While lying in my bed the night before, I thought of all the great catches I'd make, all the solid hits I'd have. But when morning came, I felt like I was going to throw up. *(Spot on MIKE fades and lights come up as COACH enters from SL in full baseball uniform.)*

COACH: *(marches to MIKE and yells in his ear)* Son! Where are you tryin out for?

MIKE: Uh . . . second base, sir.

COACH: *(pauses, stares at MIKE)* Then get the hell out there! *(COACH crosses USL and studies players trying out. Lights dim and spot slowly comes up on MIKE)*

MIKE: *(acting out great plays)* I was doing amazingly well. I couldn't believe how well I was fielding those line drives. Every ground ball that came to me at second, I fielded cleanly and without error. I was unstoppable. And then. .I got a pop fly. (acts out pop fly) I drifted back to catch it, towards the left side of the infield. I watched sail higher and higher. and as it came down, I got ready to make another catch. . . and then, all at once, I failed. tripped over second base and the ball landed on my head. *(Dim lights fade out. COACH leaves, shaking his head. MIKE is alone SC, on his knees, with dim spot.)*

MIKE: Dad, when I needed you most, you weren't there. I was beaten, and all that rang through my head was, 'Never give up.' But that could not help me now. I had failed. The game of catch was over.

JIM *(offstage)* Hey Mickey! *(Lights come up, including spot on MIKE.)*

MIKE: My friend Jim from across the street also got into the same high school I did. Jim was a great friend through thick and thin, and he picked me up when I needed it. *(Spot fades and JIM enters from SL. JIM and MIKE meet and sit on front of stage.)*

MIKE: *(to JIM)* Hey Jim.

JIM: Hey Mickey! Why you all down in the dumps? Are you still bummin' about the baseball tryouts last week? Get that monkey off your back, pal! We all make mistakes. Besides, I got news that's gonna make your mouth water.

MIKE: *(interested)* What?

JIM: What?

MIKE: What's the news?

JIM: Oh, no, buddy, news like this doesn't come for free. No, sir, you're gonna have to bargain for this one.

MIKE: Aw, come on, Jim, just tell me.

JIM: Nope, sorry. Must have some kickback.

MIKE: Well . . . How about five bucks?

JIM: And?

MIKE: And . . . an Ernie Broglio rookie card.

JIM: And?

MIKE: And . . . I won't tell your mom where you keep your dirty magazines.

JIM: Alright! Listen, Amanda Richardson is having a party.

MIKE: The Amanda Richardson?

JIM: Yes, the Amanda Richardson. So whaduhya say?

MIKE: I dunno. It seems a little out of our league.

JIM: C'mon, buddy, you only live once. Besides, I here that Sarah's going.

MIKE: *(with new-found enthusiasm)* Sarah Parker? Well, maybe I could stop by.

JIM: Atta boy, Mickey. I know your taste. *(JOHN slowly begins to enter from SR, until he is standing behind the two boys)* She's hot stuff. Nice smile and a great body. Did you see that skirt she wore yesterday? *(chuckles)* And she always wears a tight shirt that shows off her . . .

JOHN: Ahem. *(boys notice him)*

JIM: . . . uh, her startling wit and charm, accented by her plethora of wisdom, and punctuated by her adept style and grace.

JOHN: Ah, yes, Jim. Good save.

JIM: Say, is it alright Mike and I head up to a party at one Amanda

Richardson's house tonight?

JOHN: Well, I suppose. Do you want to go to this party, Michael?

MIKE: Yeah, I guess.

JOHN: Jim, why don't you run home while Michael and I have a game of catch.

JIM: One of the infamous games of catch. I'll see ya, Mickey.

MIKE: See ya, Jim. *(JIM exits)* *(JOHN hands MIKE his glove and they take their places for a game of catch. MIKE is DSR, and JOHN is USL)*

JOHN: Michael, for the last time, can you please tell me how your baseball tryouts were last week. You've been sulking around the house ever since then.

MIKE: They were fine.

JOHN: Well, how'd you do?

MIKE: Fine.

JOHN: Michael, what happened?

MIKE: Well . . . I dropped a pop fly at second base. It was a big embarrassment.

JOHN: How did you do for the rest of the tryout?

MIKE: Alright, I guess.

JOHN: Well, then, I'm sure you've got nothing to worry about. If you did well for the rest of the tryout, any coach with a decent eye for talent would let you on the team. So what's this I hear of a party tonight?

MIKE: Yeah, Amanda Richardson's.

JOHN: Do you want to go?

MIKE: Well, yeah, its just . . .

JOHN: It's just what, Michael? *(no answer)* Is it a girl?

MIKE: Sorta.

JOHN: *(chuckles)* My son is having girl trouble. Just remember one thing when talking to girls, Michael – be yourself. You are the best person you know how to be. *(Lights fade on MIKE and JOHN, JOHN exits SR. MIKE crosses USL and is slowly spotted.)*

MIKE: Well, guess what? I made the baseball team. Of course, I had to go to the coach personally and ask if I could have a second shot, but I made the team. I never gave up. I was beginning to listen to my father.

And I also went to Amanda Richardson's party that night. Sitting at home all day, I got kind of nervous. I mean, this was one of my first high school parties. I almost called up Jim and said that I couldn't make it. But I went, and I met Sarah Parker there. At first, I was afraid to talk to her. I knew that she'd never go for a guy like me. But, as my father suggested, I was myself. I went up to her, introduced myself, and asked her what her name was. And do you know what happened? Nothing,She took one look at me, smiled, and walked away. She saw right through me. Yes, it was a very humbling experience. Now, another time, I was sitting out on my front porch. . .

SARAH: *(from offstage right)* Excuse me? *(SARAH, Mike's age, enters from SR. She is spotted as she enters)*

SARAH: I'm sorry, Mike, but you're not quite telling the story correctly.

MIKE: *(greeting an old friend)* Sarah Parker! How have you been? You look great.

SARAH: Listen, that night at Amanda Richardson's, I met a boy unlike any other that I had ever met. Whereas most boys around that age were thinking about only one thing when they talked to me, you came off as an honest young man who just wanted to talk. For the first time in my life, I was seen as a human being, not some toy that was passed around between buddies. But I was so wrapped up in my conceit that I couldn't let everyone else see me talking to you. Michael, your father's words touched me as much as they touched you, and I thank you both for that. *(she exists SL)*

MIKE: *(left alone)* Why did my father leave me? He left me alone. All alone. Without any help. It all went by so fast. *(looks down, pauses)* You know, when I look back on it, all of high school was a blur. Everything went by so quickly. Before I knew it, I was being handed applications for college. My guidance counselor kept nagging me to keep my grades up, for . . .*(An old, tightly-knit, nit-picky woman in a sweater, a long skirt, and sagging knee-highs walks in from SL and speaks while MIKE speaks. As different characters enter and exit, they are spotlighted when they deliver their lines, and spot off when their line ends)*

MIKE and GUIDANCE COUNSELOR: These grades are going to be looked at by colleges all across the country. You've got to start thinking about the rest of your life! (GUIDANCE COUNSELOR exits SL. A tall, highly-bred, high-chin scholar type enters SR with a book in one hand and pointing violently with the other.)

MIKE: My hardest teacher, Mr. Shatzmeyer, was always on my case about the quality of my English papers. He once said that . . .

MIKE and MR. SHATZMEYER: Your reports are sloppy, incoherent, and a waste of goodpaper. Perhaps this failing grade will set you in the right direction! *(MR. SHATZMEYER exits SR. A short, stocky, powerful man enters SL with a baseball cap on.)*

MIKE: And my baseball coach drove me straight up the wall! When he wasn't having us run sprints, he was barking at players about any trivial thing he could think of. He once yelled at me for dropping a line drive saying that . . .

MIKE and COACH: My own grandmother could have made that play, and she's been dead for sixteen years! Come on, Michael, start playing like you mean it and . . . *(COACH continues as MIKE delivers following line. Eventually lights fade on COACH and he exits SL.)*

COACH: . . . quit playing with your head up your butt! Get some pride and show us what you got and quit being a pansy. I don't play pansies. . .(etc.)

MIKE: *(XDSR, talking over COACH CSL)* The worst part was that this all happened at the same time, and there was no escape. I couldn't avoid everything that was going on in each grueling day. I was lost in the schooling system, with no way out. *(JOHN enters from house and walks DS to the end of the lawn)*

MIKE: But my dad told me something once while we were playing catch on our front lawn that kept me going, and I don't think I could have survived the whole ordeal without it. He said. . .

JOHN: Give every situation all you've got. That way, if you fail, no one can say it was for lack of trying.*(Spots on JOHN and MIKE hold)*

MIKE: Dad – don't leave me.

JOHN: I'm not going anywhere, son.

MIKE: Dad, I can't do it all. I can't handle it. I'm not ready.

JOHN: You're ready. Trust me.*(Spot on JOHN slowly fades. He exits.)*

MIKE: I had to trust him. I had to rely on his word. I had to rely on all his words, ringing in my head. I had to put faith in this game, this stupid little game of catch. For it was no longer a game of catch. No, it was something much more. *(pauses, crosses DSR)* It's a simple game, really, when you look at it. A sequence of throw and catch-repeated over and over again. Its monotony could drive some to boredom, but we played it until the sun went down. Why did something so simple mean so much to us? Perhaps because i'ts kind of like life . . . in a way. I mean, you got the beginning of the game, where you just throw the ball without any meaning; the middle, where you begin to understand what you are doing; and the end, where you hold on until the light is gone. (*Lights come up and MIKE's spot fades as JIM enters from SL*)

JIM: So are you all packed, Mickey?

MIKE: Yeah, just some little things still need to be thrown in.

JIM: Why are you standing out on your front lawn?

MIKE: Well, I'm going to miss this lawn.

JIM: (*pauses*) Are you okay, Mickey?

MIKE: Yeah, I'm fine. Aren't you a little upset about this whole thing? I mean, we're probably not going to see each other for a while, and . . .

JIM: Micks, don't get all mushy on me.

MIKE: I'm sorry. It's just . . . never mind.

JIM: How is your dad?

MIKE: Not so good.

JIM: I'm sorry, buddy. I'm sure he'll turn out fine. Up for a game of catch?

MIKE: No thanks, I'll just stick around here.

JIM: What? Do mine ears deceive me? Mickey no play catch? Alright, bud.

MIKE: Alright, Jim.

JIM: I'll see ya. (*looks at MIKE, pauses and hugs him. He exits SL*) (*HELEN enters from SR, walks behind MIKE, lights dim.*)

MIKE: Will he be alright, mom?

HELEN: (*in tears*) Yes, Michael. He's going to be just fine.

MIKE: We have to do something. He's been in there for an hour!

HELEN: We can't do anything, dear. We have to leave in up to the doctors. (*HELEN puts her head down and freezes. Spot slowly comes up on MIKE as he paces DSC.*)

MIKE: Damn it, why is this taking so long? They've been in there for too long. He's not doing good. C'mon dad. Pull through. You can't leave me yet . . . A doctor! He has news! (*HELEN and MIKE look out at audience. They are both silent for a moment, and then HELEN gives a small sob. She exits SR.*)

MIKE: It's over. The game is over. No more playing catch out on the front lawn. I'm alone now. I have no guidance. I have nowhere to go. What can I do? I mean, what is left? (*Lights fade. Lone spot on MIKE. Slowly,* another spot is brought up on JOHN as he enters SL and walks towards MIKE until JOHN is five feet DSL from MIKE,)

JOHN: *(to Mike)* There's a time for everything.

MIKE: *(looks up; to audience)* But what if I'm not strong enough?

JOHN: Never give up.

MIKE: What if that's not good enough?

JOHN: Always be yourself.

MIKE: And what if I fail?

JOHN: You won't. Always give it your best.

MIKE: *(satisfied)* I will, dad. I will.

End of Play

The Fall of the House of Usher
A Radio Adaptation
by
Dorothy C. Calhoun

Characters

Announcer
Critics
Norman
Usher
Valet
Physician
"Voice"

Production Notes

Playing Time: 15 minutes

Costumes: not required

Lighting: not required

Sound Effects: The sound effects will be an important part of this radio theatre production.

Cast of Characters:

Announcer: a mature sounding and dispassionate voice.

Critics: three distinct voices to represent the various
opinions presented in the script.

Norman: mature, cultivated, sympathetic voice.
Should have the ability to represent the audience's
reactions to the eerie events which he witnesses.

Usher: about the same age as Norman, but tired, sick,
afraid as indicated; "Hollow, melancholy, unreal."

Valet: Old man whose voice should suggest subdued
fear with a touch of unreality.

Physician: Crackling voice with a menacing quality.

"Voice": This should sound like an echo, a hollow, sepulchral
voice. Use an echo mike is one is available. If not, a good effect
can be obtained by having the actor talk across the drum
membrane. The voice should reverberate, fading farther
from the mike at each repetition of a word. This same
"Voice" can do the echoing laughter and (Laughter)

(Hoofs clatter to a stop; bird screeches harshly) The hoofs are, of course,
simulated with coconut shells or rubber plungers. Use them on a
hollow surface. The rhythm should be broken as horse stops. Bird
screech should be like a vulture. Recordings may be secured for this
type of bird sound; or experiment with an actor who may be able to
reproduce the sound. Should be off mike and repeated a few times at
different distances.

(Rings bell) Old-fashioned pull-bell. Should not be an electric bell or a
modern type.

(Slow clatter and crash of bridge . . . horse rattles over it.) Rattle of chains and
dropping of heavy platform will give first effect; then the hoofs on a
hollow wooden surface.

(Key grating, door opens) Use a large key in actual lock that is rusty, if
possible. Door should be heavy, and creak as it opens and shuts. This

will apply in many cases throughout the script.

(Bell begins to toll) Large bell, off mike. Musicians' chimes can be used to advantage, using deep minor notes — two of them slow, regular rhythm. Continue to music.

(Feet on stone descending) Hard-heeled shoes should be used on composition board — slow, ominous tread.

(Hollow clang of iron door opening) Chains and key in a rusty lock add t the effect. Roller skate drawn over an iron plate will give a good effect of an iron door.

(Rising tempest . . . wail of wind . . . rattle of shutters) A thunder sheet and wind machine should be used with wood banged together for shutters. Use small pieces of wood clapped in hands.

(Slamming of shutters) Slam pieces of wood twice. Stop wind and thunder.

(Open window . . . wind machine) Slam wood again, resume wind machine and thunder as before.

(Crackling and ripping and breaking of wood) Use wooden fruit baskets or boxes, breaking them at various distances from the mike until the desired effect is achieved.

(Footsteps up wooden stairs) Same as before, only on a wooden platform. Slow, ominous, approaching the mike from a distance.

(Door crashes open. . . wind screams) Use a heavy door, crashing back against a wall as it opens. Bring up the wind machine to highest peak possible, cut as music comes in.

Music: As indicated in the script, "Danse Macabre" can be used on an organ to advantage throughout the program. A pianist might be able to improvise on the theme, or apply different portions to particular scenes and interludes, or perhaps to compose special themes for the effects desired.

This play is one of a series prepared and featured by the Pittsburgh High School over Station WWSW. This play must not be sponsored commercially.

● ● ● ● ● ● ● ● ● ● ● ● ● ● ● ● ● ● ●

ANNOUNCER: *(Opens cold)* How long has it been since you sat down — alone — with a good book?

ORGAN: *(Up softly with "Memories." Establish first phrase and)*

The Fall of the House of Usher   89

ANNOUNCER: Good books are like good friends — always there — always the same — (*Warm it up.*) They're waiting for you — one of many things waiting for you in your pubic library — if you'll go in — and ask for them.

ORGAN: (*Run up whole tone scale to fanfare and immediately in background as*)

ANNOUNCER: This afternoon (*or morning, or evening*) the . . . . (*Name of group*) brings you fifteen minutes with an important writer. Today we present — Edgar Allan Poe!

ORGAN: (*Continues alone for three seconds at same level.*)

ANNOUNCER: Never was there an author that roused such a storm of controversy. In Europe he was hailed as a genius. In his own land critics have never been able to agree. And the quarrel over Poe still rages. Listen to what critics say about him!

FIRST VOICE: His talent was extraordinary, but he did not give the world one single inspiring thought!

SECOND VOICE: His is the most distinctive art the New World has produced!

THIRD VOICE: Distinctive, perhaps! But it was the product of a sickly body and a diseased imagination!

SECOND VOICE: Poe never discovered the difference between the real world and the world of fantasy!

THIRD VOICE: He fled to dreams to escape from the wretchedness of his life.

FIRST VOICE: Brilliant!

SECOND VOICE: Morbid!

THIRD VOICE: Weird! Wonderful!

ORGAN: (*Crescendo and dim into background as*)

ANNOUNCER: What manner of man was this slender, pallid being, with his high, full forehead and flashing gray eyes? Was he painting a self-portrait when he created the unnaturally sensitive, melancholy Roderick Usher in his masterpiece, "The Fall of the House of Usher?"

ORGAN: (*Continues for five seconds and fades out on cue under ANNOUNCER.*)

ANNOUNCER: The House of Usher, among dank sedges and decaying white tree stems, with the dark lurid waters of a tarn or lake lipping its gray walls.

SOUND: *(Hoof clatter to a stop. Bird screeches harshly.)*

NORMAN: So this is my welcome to the House of Usher — a bird of ill omen! What a desolate spot! No wonder my old schoolmate begs for cheerful society!

SOUND: *(Rings bell, which echoes within the house.)*

NORMAN: *(Calling)* What ho? The House! A visitor to the House of Usher!

VOICE: *(Calling within)* I'll let down the drawbridge, sir!

SOUND: *(Slow clatter and crash of bridge. Horse rattles over it.)*

VALET: *(Within)* A moment, sir! This door is seldom opened.

SOUND: *(Key grating, door opens.)*

NORMAN: I'm Norman Legrand — an old friend of your master.

VALET: Welcome to the House of Usher!

SOUND: *(Bird screeches again.)*

NORMAN: Plague take that bird! I should think your master would have it killed!

VALET: On, no, sir! There have always been vultures here. I'll send a boy for your horse, sir.

NORMAN: *(Going)* Roderick Usher is expecting me, I suppose.

VALET: *(Voice coming from distance)* Oh, yes. He heard you coming two and more hours ago.

SOUND: *(Door closes)*

VALET: This way, please, sir!

NORMAN: *(Bewildered)* You say he heard me coming two hours ago? I don't understand.

PHYSICIAN: *(Squeaky)* Good day, young sir! I'm delighted to see you have come! You will be a comfort to Mr. Usher. He'll soon need comfort, I fear. *(Laughs crackly.)* Heh, Heh! Well, good day, sir — good day.

NORMAN: Who was that fellow who just passed us on the stairs?

VALET: The physician, sir. Down this passage, if you please.

NORMAN: Physician! Is Roderick ill?

VALET: No, It is his sister, the Lady Madelaine . . . . *(Lowering his voice)* She won't be on earth much longer — but it's taken her ten long years to die.

ORGAN: (*Alone for three seconds and fade out under.*)

SOUND: (*Knocking on door.*)

VALET: (*Calling*) Mr. Usher! Your friend has arrived!

USHER: (*Off mike — hollow, melancholy, unreal*) Come in!

VOICE: (*Nearer*) Norman Legrand! Forgive me for not being at the door of my house to welcome you.

NORMAN: (*With effort.*) Is it really you, Roderick? I would hardly know you!

USHER: I do not make a habit of looking into mirrors much, yet I know that I have changed. These pallid cheeks, this hollowed forehead, these lack-luster eyes.

NORMAN: (*Laughing heartily*) Nonsense, old boy!

USHER: It was good of you to come to try to help me. I thought that perhaps a human hand, a warm, living hand — in this house of shadows . . .

NORMAN: Your valet just told me of your sister's illness. I'm so sorry to hear of it.

USHER: Hist! There she is now, passing through the far end of the apartment!

NORMAN: Good heavens! (*Low*) What was it the fellow said? She has been ten years dying? She looks as though she has been ten years dead!

USHER: (*Building*) My last relative on earth, my one companion!

NORMAN: But she's able to be about. The doctors may be wrong.

USHER: No, no — she has steadily refused to give way to the mysterious malady that has wasted her to what you just saw. But at any moment now I expect to hear that she is gone. Did you hear me singing when you came? I was composing her dirge.

NORMAN: Come, come, now, old friend. Why, what a conversation we've gotten into — death and dirges and all that sort of thing — Let's have a livelier air . . . (*Hums gay music.*)

USHER: (*With a cry of pain*) No! No! I can't bear it!

NORMAN: What can't you bear?

USHER: I have a strange affliction, a nervous disorder hereditary to my house. It has made my senses morbidly acute. I can eat only the most insipid food, bear only garments of a certain texture against my skin. The smell of flowers makes me swoon. Most of all I am sensitive to sounds . . . (Low) Yes, I am haunted by sounds no one else seems able to hear. Listen! Do you hear that? That faint rustle?

NORMAN: I hear nothing except your infernal vultures over the tarn.

USHER: I hear the worms, my friend.

NORMAN: Worms!

USHER: Far down in the earth the worms are stirring, gnawing . . .

NORMAN: Oh, I say — you can't hear worms!

USHER: And that's not all I hear. I hear the stones decaying in the walls. I hear my sister's heavy breathing in her room . . .

NORMAN: This is folly, Roderick! You must throw off such thoughts.

USHER: Folly! But I shall perish of this folly one day! I am terrified of terror! There is a doom on this House of Usher, Norman. (Building) That's what I am listening for, the approach of doom!

NORMAN: It's the atmosphere of this place. I felt it myself when I first saw it, and heavens knows I am just an ordinary man and not at all sensitive! You should leave this old house, Roderick. Come with me into the everyday world . . . .

SOUND: (Bell begins to toll, ding— dong — ding — dong.)

NORMAN: What does that bell mean, Roderick?

USHER: It means that lady Madelaine is dead.

VOICE: (Echo) Dead . . . Dead! (Fading) Dead . . .

ORGAN: (Continues along for three seconds then in background as . . . along and out under sound.)

SOUND: (Feet on stone descending for five seconds. Hollow clang of iron door opening.)

USHER: (Echo mike) Madelaine was afraid of open places and the night! She has lived so long inside of these gray walls. She would not have rested easy in her grave! (Whisper.) I would have heard her turning in her grave!

VOICE: (Echo mike — softly) Grave! Grave! . . . (Fading) Grave! . . .

NORMAN: Surely that isn't your real reason, Roderick?

USHER: (In whisper) No, there is another reason, but I — I cannot tell you what it is. It is too terrible.

NORMAN: Well, after all, this vault is no worse than the rooms above. Living in this house is like being buried alive!

VOICE: (Low) Alive! . . . Alive!. . . (Fading) Alive!. . .

USHER: Buried alive! Ah! (Laughs and the echoes catch up his laughter.) Ha! Ha! Ha!

NORMAN: Let's get out of here. I'm chilled through. We'll have a fire in your apartment. Let's go up and — talk of pleasant things!

USHER: (In despair — hollow and echoing) I was wrong to send for you, old friend. You have no place in this house. Go while you can! As for me, it is too late!

VOICE: (Echo mike) Too late! La-a-ate! (Fading) Late!

NORMAN: I can't leave you now. I'll stay. Come, Roderick! The candle burns blue in this fetid air!

USHER: Farewell, Madelaine, Farewell, sister! (Going)

VOICE: Farewell. Farewell-l (Fading) Farewell!

ORGAN: (Up and under as)

ANNOUNCER: (Over) And now a change came over the ravaged countenance of the Master of the House. The pallor of his cheeks grew still more ghastly. He cold not remain still but paced up and down. More than once he seemed struggling to divulge some fearful secret. Then came a night of storm that rocked the ancient House of Usher.

ORGAN: (Swells and fades out under sound)

SOUND: (Rising tempest — wail of wind — rattle of shutters.)

NORMAN: There is no sleep in this house. I may as well give up the effort. That wind sounds like voices! I'll shut the windows!

SOUND: (Slamming of shutters. Wind ceases. Silence.)

NORMAN: If I stayed here much longer I'd be as near the verge of madness as Roderick Usher! My poor old schoolfellow. I'm afraid he's lost. . . .

SOUND: (Knocking of door.)

USHER: Norman! (Off mike.)

NORMAN: (Calling) Roderick!

SOUND: (Door opens.)

NORMAN: So you can't sleep either, my dear fellow. Come in, and we'll keep each other company.

USHER: *(Coming up)* So you haven't seen the illumination! Put out your candle! The light of my house is brighter. I'll open the shutters.

SOUND: *(Opening windows.)*

SOUND: *(Wind machine — laughter.)*

USHER: *(Sound over)* The glow you see comes from no moon or stars. It is the light of the tombs!

NORMAN: Shut that window!

SOUND: *(Windows slammed shut. . . noise out.)*

NORMAN: Come away from that window. Those spectral lights have a perfectly natural origin. They're phosphorescence from the stagnant waters of the tarn! Sit down . . . Let us talk quietly, as we did long ago at school.

USHER: Long ago. I can't remember. . . How can I think of anything when my sister is dead! *(In low, intense voice.)* You saw her placed in her coffin — a year ago — Why do you look at me like that?

NORMAN: The Lady Madelaine died a *week* ago, Roderick!

USHER: A year, a week — it is all the same! I am the last of the race.

NORMAN: *(Urgently)* Not if you rouse yourself! Leave this house!

USHER: No, I must perish! Do you know what I shall die of? I'll tell you. *(Whispering)* Fear! Fe-e-ear! *(Fading)* Fear! . . .

NORMAN: Here is one of your favorite books, "The Mad Tryst," by Sir Launcelot Canning. I'll read and you shall listen. It'll help to pass this dreadful night. *(Begins to read.)* "And Ethelred waited no longer to hold parley with the hermit, but uplifted his face and with blows quickly made room in the planking of the door for his gauntleted hand. And the noise of the cracking and ripping of the wood reverberated through the forest. . ."

SOUND: *(Cracking and ripping and breaking of wood.)*

USHER: Do you hear that, Norman, the ripping of wood, the iron scream of the hinges of the vault? . . . I know what she's doing!

NORMAN: It's nothing. I tell you — nothing.

USHER: Madelaine will be here soon. She's coming to upbraid me for putting her in her tomb so hurriedly. Don't you hear her footsteps on the stair?. . .

SOUND: *(Footsteps up wooden steps.)*

NORMAN: No, no! There is an explanation of this. Believe me. Roderick — *(Broken speech)*

USHER: Listen! Can't you hear the heavy beating of her heart? I tell you that Madelaine now stands outside that door! Don't open that door — Don't — don't!

SOUND: *(Door crashes open. Wind screams.)*

ORGAN: *(Under ANNOUNCER)*

ANNOUNCER: *(Over.)* Who stood behind that door? What happened! If you want a thrilling experience — go to your public library and ask for one of the book by Edgar Allan Poe. The librarian is ready to serve you in many ways — to help you read with a purpose — to help you with your particular job. Ask your librarian about these many helpful services which are yours.

MUSIC: *(Segue into "Memories" — up and under.)*

End of Play

Dorothy and the Wizard of Oz
A Partipation Play
by
Steve and Kathy Hotchner

Characters

Glinda, the good witch of the North
Dorothy and Toto
Scarecrow
Lion
Tin Man
Wicked Witch of the West
Wizard of Oz

Production Notes

Time: The Past

Place: Oz

In this participation version of "The Wizard of Oz," a truculent, spunky Dorothy finds herself over the rainbow confronted by the Good Witch, Glinda, who worries as much about her vegetable garden as she does about Dorothy getting back to Kansas. All your favorite characters are here. Children oil the Tin Man, stuff the Scarecrow and hide Dorothy from the Wicked Witch of the West in a forest they, themselves, create. Toto is here, too—a bit stuffed, but held securely in the arms of a Toto watcher—different children selected by Dorothy to hold Toto whenever his barking gets out of control.

The twist, which we dare not reveal, is what has happened to the Wizard himself. Lots of participation for students in this Hotchner participation play.

The important properties that must be on hand for use by the students
    and players are:

Straw hat and cane for the Wizard.

Medal, diploma and clock heart.

Wizard's hat and spectacles.

Oil can.

Handkerchief.

Broomstick.

Toto [stuffed dog].

Our production of this participation play can be done with few props
    [which are necessary for the action], or, if you desire, more elaborate [as
    in the case of the several signs put up around the theater indicating the
    travels of Dorothy and her friends]. You may prefer to perform the play
    so that the children would use their imaginations [for instance, with the
    Scarecrow's straw, etc.].

Scene: After the audience is seated, GLINDA, the Good Witch of the
    North, enters through the audience with TOTO (a stuffed dog) in her
    arms.

• • • • • • • • • • • • • • • • • •

GLINDA: (to various children in the audience) Is this yours? Is this yours? I
    found this very strange creature lost and wagging its tail. Is this creature
    yours? No? Dear, dear, it doesn't look like it belongs in Munchkinland.
    The Wicked Witch of the East is dead. A strange house came sailing
    through our rainbow and then — swoosh, pop — down came the
    house and landed on the Witch. I saw this creature . . . (Addressing a
    child in the audience.) What did you say it was? . . . You didn't. A dog?
    Thank you. I saw this creature run out of the house. Then a girl climbed
    out and before I could thank her for freeing us from the Wicked Witch
    of the East, she slipped away. Did you see her? Is she here, Munchkins?
    Has anyone seen the girl who came sailing through our rainbow and
    freed all of Oz from the Wicked Witch of the East?

DOROTHY: I'm over here.

GLINDA: Who are you?

DOROTHY: And who are you?

GLINDA: I'm Glinda, the good witch of the North. Are you a witch, too?

Is that how you freed us from the Wicked Witch of the East?

DOROTHY: I'm just a person and I'm lost and you have my dog. You're not going to hurt Toto, are you?

GLINDA: Of course not. I hurt no one. I don't even know how to lose my temper.

DOROTHY: Give him back to me.

GLINDA: (*lets TOTO rub her nose*) I like the way he rubs my nose. What did you say?

DOROTHY: Give him back.

GLINDA: Of course. (*She hands TOTO to DOROTHY.*) Please tell us whether you are a good witch or not?

DOROTHY: I'm Dorothy, and I'm lost and . . . What do I care about your silly questions.

GLINDA: You mean you don't come from Munchkinland?

DOROTHY: No, of course not. I come from Kansas. And I don't know any of you.

GLINDA: (*to children*) We have a problem. (*Back to DOROTHY.*) Then if you don't come from Munchkinland, how did you defeat the Wicked Witch of the East?

DOROTHY: I didn't! The last thing I remember is a storm, a great tornado, and my house hurtling through the clouds, and a rainbow, and . . .

GLINDA: But, Dorothy, you have the red slippers that belong to the Wicked Witch of the East.

DOROTHY: I do? (*Looks down at feet.*) I've never seen these slippers before. (*Hugs TOTO.*) Who are all of you?

GLINDA: They're Munchkins, of course. You freed them.

DOROTHY: From who?

GLINDA: From the Wicked Witch.

DOROTHY: What wicked witch?

GLINDA: (*irritated*) From the Wicked Witch of the East! (*Calmer.*) Oh, I lost my temper. This girl made me lose my temper.

DOROTHY: I don't believe any of you. This is some horrible dream.

GLINDA: (*to children*) Munchkins, I had planned a lovely celebration with songs and dances and . . . I can't stand it when someone won't let me say "thank you." You thank her, Munchkins. I'm very upset.

DOROTHY: I want to go home. *(Thunder. The theater darkens. Enter the WICKED WITCH OF THE WEST.)*

GLINDA: Don't be afraid of her, Munchkins. She can't do anything here.

WITCH: *(angrily shouts)* Who killed my sister? Who killed my sister?

DOROTHY: They tell me I did. But if I did, I don't remember doing it.

WITCH: You? You're a mere slip of a girl. You couldn't have . . . *(Looks down at DOROTHY's slippers.)* There they are! The slippers. You're wearing my sister's slippers! Give those slippers back to me.

GLINDA: *(to DOROTHY)* Don't do it.

DOROTHY: I'm so confused. *(To WITCH.)* I don't like you, I know that. If my house landed on your sister, I apologize, but it's not my fault. I don't like being threatened. So if you want the slippers back, ask for them politely.

GLINDA: *(to audience)* Listen to the girl. *(To DOROTHY.)* You must not give her the slippers.

WITCH: Why, you . . . *(Rushes at DOROTHY and tries to take slippers off her feet. Screams as she touches the slippers.)* Hot coals. Hot coals. So, I can't get them off you.

GLINDA: Told you.

WITCH: *(to GLINDA)* Don't snicker at me. I can control all of Oz with those slippers. But I'll get them. I will. Goodbye, Dorothy. *(To children.)* Munchkins. *(Thoughtfully.)* I wonder what Munchkin meat tastes like. *(Laughs and exits.)*

GLINDA: That does it. This is my territory and if you don't leave this moment, I'll burn you to a cinder. *(Realizes she is gone.)* Gone? Oh. Well, good. She can be so unpleasant. Munchkins, I'm troubled. I've lost my temper twice today. I'm afraid this is not such a great day for Oz after all.

DOROTHY: Please tell me how I can get home.

GLINDA: Home? Oh, I can't do anything about that. Only the Wizard can help get you home.

DOROTHY: What wizard?

GLINDA: The Wizard of Oz. My magic is nothing compared to his.

DOROTHY: But . . . where do I find him?

GLINDA: In the Emerald City. But that would take you through the Wicked Witch of the West's territory. You don't want to do that.

DOROTHY: I'm not afraid of her.

GLINDA: You're not?

DOROTHY: Well, a little. But I have to get home. I'll do anything to get back to Kansas. And no evil witch is going to stop me.

GLINDA: In that case, I'll help you. Munchkins, will you help too? Good. The Munchkins and I will be there whenever you need us. Now I have to go and tend my garden.

DOROTHY: But how do I reach the Wizard? And who will keep me company?

GLINDA: Follow the signs. As for company, who knows? Goodbye. Must snip my roses. Trim my daffodils. And those morning glories . . . (*She exits.*)

DOROTHY: Toto, you won't get lost again, will you? You won't bark and chase squirrels? You will? Yes, I suppose you will. (*To nearest child in audience.*) Would you come with me and hold Toto? Make sure he never gets lost. Thank you. Take my hand. Munchkins, help me follow the signs. Tell me which way I should go. (*Lights darken. Signs that glow in the dark are visible all over the theater.*) Do you see a sign? Where should I go? That way. Thank you. (*As she goes in and out among the audience, SCARECROW enters, lies on the ground, scattering straw all about her/him.*) Do you see a sign? Which way? Munchkin, do you have Toto? Hold onto him tight. (*Lights. DOROTHY is back on stage with TOTO watcher. She stares at SCARECROW.*)

SCARECROW: What are you staring at? Do something.

DOROTHY: You talked! Scarecrows don't talk. (*To children.*) Do they, Munchkins? Toto watcher, I'll take Toto now. Thank you. You can go back to your seat. (*Stares at SCARECROW.*)

SCARECROW: What are you staring at? Don't you have any manners?

DOROTHY: Of course I have manners.

SCARECROW: Then stuff me.

DOROTHY: Stuff you?

SCARECROW: (*pointing to straw*) The straw, the straw.

DOROTHY: Oh. Should we stuff this scarecrow, Munchkins? . . . All right. (*Points to three children.*) Would you help me? And you? And you? . . . (*As the children come on the stage.*) You stuff the arms, and you stuff the belly, and we'll stuff the legs. (*As they work.*) What's a scarecrow doing unstuffed anyway?

SCARECROW: Careful stuffing my belly. I'm ticklish. (*Starts laughing.*) Please. It tickles. Thanks. What's a scarecrow doing unstuffed?

DOROTHY: Yes.

SCARECROW: The crows. I'm supposed to scare crows. (*Laughs.*) Please, I'm very ticklish. I don't like to scare crows. I like to think. I like to solve problems. That's all I think about all day. What I'd do if I had a brain. So, what sort of scarecrow am I?

DOROTHY: A very unusual scarecrow.

SCARECROW: All done? Out of my way. When I'm stuffed I feel fresh as a breeze. Out of my way.

DOROTHY (*to three children*) Better go back to your seats. (*To TOTO.*) Toto, stop barking.

SCARECROW: Here I go. (*He leaps, turns cartwheels, hurls himself down the aisles, taking as many leaps, tumbles, falls as he can.*) Thank you. Thank you. Nothing like being stuffed to make you feel spry. (*Suddenly droops and shakes head sadly.*)

DOROTHY: What's the matter?

SCARECROW: What's the matter? Would you want to go back to scaring crows when there's a universe to explore?

DOROTHY: Do you have to go back to scaring crows?

SCARECROW: What else can I do?

DOROTHY: You could help all of us get to the Wizard of Oz. He's going to show me how to get back to Kansas. Maybe he'd give you a brain.

SCARECROW: (*leaps up and touches toes*) A brain! I could make maps, charter mountains, cross unknown seas, travel to the stars . . .

DOROTHY: Yes, yes, come with us.

SCARECROW: I will. I'll do it.

DOROTHY: There'll be terrible danger. Glinda said we'd have to go through the territory of the Wicked Witch of the West.

SCARECROW: She'll unstuff me for sure.

DOROTHY: Suppose, suppose all the Munchkins promise to stuff you whenever you come unstuffed. Will you do that, Munchkins?

SCARECROW: You promise? You'll put the straw back in my belly without tickling me? Then off to the Wizard of Oz.

DOROTHY (*to audience member*) Here, would you hold Toto and come to the next place with us? He loves to chase squirrels. Which way do we go from here?

SCARECROW: Follow the signs. (*Lights dim. SCARECROW comes to an upside down sign that points to the sky.*) Should we go up there? Up to the sky? Might be fun. No. (*Goes to another sign.*) This way. This sign points . . .West. Here we go. (*TIN MAN enters. Takes his position with ax pointed up and other arm pointed at oil can next to his foot. GROUP comes back up on stage and passes him. They stop when they hear:*)

TIN MAN: (*barely audible whisper*) Help me.

SCARECROW: Did you hear something?

DOROTHY: (*to child holding TOTO*) Quiet, Toto. I'd better take Toto. He's too upset . . . Thank you. (*They move forward a few more steps, then:*)

TIN MAN: Help me.

DOROTHY: I hear something. I think. (*To children.*) Munchkins, did you hear something? Where? (*Sees TIN MAN who rattles out a huge sigh.*)

TIN MAN: Thank you.

DOROTHY: It's alive.

SCARECROW: Couldn't be. Nothing but an old piece of tin.

TIN MAN: (*speaking in throaty whisper until he/she is oiled*) And you're nothing but an old pile of straw.

SCARECROW: Says you. (*To DOROTHY.*) It's alive.

DOROTHY: I knew it.

SCARECROW: (*bangs on chest of TIN MAN*) Hollow. He doesn't have a heart. (*TIN MAN cries in large throaty sobs.*)

DOROTHY: You've hurt his feelings! (*TIN MAN cries terribly.*)

DOROTHY: You insulted him. He may not have a heart, but he has feelings. (*To TIN MAN.*) Don't you?

TIN MAN: (*sighs gratefully*) Thank you.

DOROTHY: Why can you only speak in a whisper? (*TIN MAN tries to speak, then shakes his head.*)

DOROTHY: You can't talk any more? Oh, I see. But you can whisper to me if I come close. (*TIN MAN nods. DOROTHY bends to him and he whispers in her ear.*) He's rusted. Every time he cries, he rusts. And he cries a lot. That's a problem.

SCARECROW: If only I could think. (*Leaps into the air in frustration, tumbles, etc. Smiles.*) The oil can. He's pointing at the oil can.

DOROTHY: Of course. (*Goes into audience.*) Would you oil the tin man? And would you please take this hanky and wipe away his tears when he rusts? (*Leads two children back on stage. They begin to oil the Tin Man.*) First the legs. Then the elbows. Then underneath the arms, and the mouth . . . We've done it. Thank you. You can go back to your seats now.

TIN MAN: Thank you. I'm so happy. I can move. It's been so long. I can talk. I'm so happy. (*Starts to cry.*)

DOROTHY: No, no, don't cry. Tell him not to cry, Munchkins, or he'll rust himself again.

TIN MAN: I can do it. I won't cry. (*Heaves out a few sobs and gets control of himself.*) There.

DOROTHY: Are you sure you don't have a heart? (*TIN MAN taps chest and sighs.*)

SCARECROW: Hollow as a drum.

DOROTHY: Well, you could come along too, couldn't he, Munchkins? You could come with us to the Wizard of Oz and maybe he'd give you a heart.

TIN MAN: A heart! That would be wonderful. (*Cries.*)

DOROTHY: Munchkins, tell him not to cry . . . That better be your job from now on. (*TIN MAN always thanks the children when they tell him not to cry from now on.*) I've never met such an emotional person.

TIN MAN: My parents were the same. They rusted long ago. It's a very sad story. (*Cries.*)

DOROTHY: Munchkins. (*If the Munchkins don't understand, repeat, "Tell him not to cry."*)

TIN MAN: Thank you. I'm all right now.

DOROTHY: (*to child in audience*): Would you come along with us now and hold Toto? (*To SCARECROW.*) Is all of Oz this odd?

SCARECROW: Are you so normal?

TIN MAN: On to the Wizard of Oz. I want a heart.

SCARECROW: A brain.

DOROTHY: And I want to go home. I think.

TIN MAN: (*into audience*) Which way to the Wizard of Oz? . . . That way. (*They make a circle, then come upon two signs. TIN MAN reads:*) "Territory of the Wicked Witch of the West. This way to the Emerald City." Looks like this is the way.

DOROTHY: We're not afraid, are we? Glinda said she'd be there whenever we needed her. So . . . on to the Emerald City.

SCARECROW: This says "forest." I've always wanted to explore a forest. I've spent all my life in the open field. Come on. (*None of them move.*)

DOROTHY: This is silly. What are we afraid of? (*Starts moving.*) Snakes, lions, hippopotomi. Everybody stay close by. It's getting very dark. (*To child in audience.*) Would you rub that spot and make some sunlight for us? (*Child rubs spot.*) Thank you. A patch of sunlight. That's better. We'll all stay close and hold hands and follow this path of sunlight. (*They form a line, holding hands. They weave through the audience, making a circle, come back on stage and when their backs are turned, a LION leaps out and roars terribly. The group jumps back in fear. LION advances, grabs TOTO from Toto watcher.*)

DOROTHY: He has Toto. That's terrible. (*To child.*) Don't feel bad, Toto watcher. You can go back to your seat. (*To audience.*) Roar at him, the bully. He'll think you're a whole herd of lions. (*Audience roars. LION drops TOTO. DOROTHY takes TOTO back. LION backs away, roars, backs away.*)

DOROTHY: (*to audience.*) Thank you. (*To LION.*) Aren't you ashamed, trying to frighten us like that!

LION: I'm a lion. I'm King of the Beasts. And I'll scare anyone, any time, any . . . (*Jumps with a shriek and starts chasing his tail.*) My tail. I'm going to get you this time. You follow me everywhere. Get away!

DOROTHY: You're the silliest creature in all Oz.

LION: Tell it to go away.

SCARECROW: Tell what to go away?

LION: My tail.

DOROTHY: We can't tell your tail to go away. No you go away and leave us alone. I don't like a bully. You nearly scared us to death.

LION: I did?

DOROTHY: Come on, everyone. (*Starts to leave.*)

LION: Wait. Don't leave me alone. I can't stand living in a forest. I get scared.

DOROTHY: You get scared? But you're supposed to be ferocious.

LION: I'm not. I'm nothing but a scaredy cat. I'm scared of my tail and I'm scared of my shadow and I'm even scared of my face. You know what the other animals in the forest call me? You know what a mouse said to my face just the other day? "Scaredy-cat." "Scaredy-cat."

SCARECROW: Then why do you try to scare people?

DOROTHY: And dogs?

TIN MAN: And Munchkins?

LION: I'm supposed to, that's why. That's what my Mom and Dad taught me to do. "A lion's supposed to be fierce," my Dad said to me when I was little. So I've been trying to be fierce ever since. And I'm nothing but mush.

TIN MAN: What a sad story. (*Cries.*)

DOROTHY: Munchkins?

TIN MAN: Thank you.

DOROTHY: We're going to the Wizard of Oz so I can go home and the Tin Man can get a heart and the Scarecrow can get a brain. Would you like to come with us and ask the Wizard for some courage?

LION: Could I? Oh, could I? (*To audience.*) Could I? . . . I love you for this. Thanks, Munchkins. (*Hits his tail.*) What's that? Oh, the tail, the tail. (*Starts chasing tail.*)

DOROTHY: (*to child in audience*) Catch the tail so the Lion won't be afraid. (*A brief chase during which the child tries to catch LION's tail, and eventually succeeds.*)

LION: (*to child*) Thank you. Thanks a lot. You caught my tail.

SCARECROW: Are you all right now, Lion?

LION: I'm all right. I'm all right, but don't call me a lion. I don't deserve the name. I'm a cowardly beast.

TIN MAN: Don't be so hard on yourself. Everybody gets scared. You're just a little bit extreme.

LION: I'm nothing but jelly. But, come on. On to the Wizard. To courage. (*They travel, then:*) Out of the forest! I'm getting out of the forest. Look, a sign. "This way out of the forest." And another sign. "To Emerald City." All we have to do is cross this field and we'll be there. Come on, come on, tail. (*They weave through audience, come back to stage. GLINDA* *enters and is waiting for them.)*

DOROTHY: Glinda! Why are you here? We're in no danger. We haven't since the Wicked Witch. Not once. Have we, Munchkins?

GLINDA: Would I be here if I wasn't needed? Oh, what a silly girl. I have apricots to can, mangoes to squeeze, quinces to pickle. *(Looks toward SCARECROW, TIN MAN, and LION.)* Introduce yourselves.

SCARECROW: *(does a leap and touches toes together)* I'm the scarecrow. Pleased to meet you.

TIN MAN: This is an honor. *(Heaves sob, stifles it.)* I know. Don't cry. It's just that I've never met anybody truly important and majestic.

LION: I'm the cowardly lion. And I'd just like to say that you're a very pretty lady.

GLINDA: I'm glad you've found friends, Dorothy. You're all going to need each other.

DOROTHY: What do you mean?

GLINDA: Not now. That's for later. This is an open field. Too open. And therefore very dangerous if the Wicked Witch should come back for you, Dorothy, and those slippers. Munchkins, I want you to make a deep, dark forest so Dorothy and her friends can hide from the Wicked Witch when she comes. Stand up in your seats and whatever you do, don't move from your seats. Raise your arms like this. You are all tall, rooted trees. Magical trees. Root yourselves. Stand silent, immovable. You, too, big people. And remember, if the Witch comes, hide Dorothy. Good-bye.

DOROTHY: But . . .

GLINDA: Don't worry. I have to shear the sheep. Otherwise they develop a terrible itch. *(She exits.)*

DOROTHY: *(to Munchkins)* Are you really a deep, dark forest? And will you really hide us if the Witch comes? Then, we're safe. Come on, Scarecrow, Lion, Tin Man. *(They begin to wander through forest.)*

LION: This is a nice forest. Nothing to scare you here. Here, Scarecrow, have an apple.

SCARECROW: Don't mind if I do.

TIN MAN: Do I hear a bird? Lovely trees. Lots of green leaves.

DOROTHY: I don't know why Glinda felt she had to help us. This is the most peaceful, safe forest I've ever seen. I think I'll have an apple, too. *(The WICKED WITCH OF THE WEST enters.)*

WITCH: Ah ha! Found you, Dorothy. (*Laughs.*)

DOROTHY: Spread your leaves, Munchkins. Hide us. (*A game of hide-and-go-seek begins. The GROUP moves to one area of the audience. Then, as soon as the WITCH comes out from behind her tree, the GROUP moves to another section of trees. This continues through forest scene.*)

WITCH: Where did she go? Dorothy. I don't want to hurt you, sweet girl. I'll give you a way back to Kansas if you just hand me those slippers.

DOROTHY: She's coming. Let's hide over there. Perhaps I should give her the slippers. She says she'll get me home.

SCARECROW: I wouldn't trust her.

LION: She doesn't sound so awful.

TIN MAN: Maybe all she needs is a heart like me.

SCARECROW: Don't trust her.

WITCH: (*sees the GROUP hiding behind children*) There you are. The little game is over. Why are you unstuffing yourself, Scarecrow?

SCARECROW: What do you mean? (*Takes a fistful of straw and throws it on the ground.*)

WITCH: You shouldn't do that.

SCARECROW: I shouldn't do what? (*Starts unstuffing himself.*)

DOROTHY: Don't . . .

SCARECROW: I can't help it. It's a spell. (*He has unstuffed himself and collapses on floor.*)

TIN MAN: I feel like I'm going to cry. (*He cries and rusts.*)

WITCH: (*goes over to TIN MAN*) Yes, cry, Tin Man. Cry. And now you! (*Points to LION.*)

DOROTHY: Lion, what are you doing?

LION: I'm scared. I can't help it. (*Chases tail.*) Get away, get away. Run, Dorothy, run. The Munchkins will hide you. (*DOROTHY goes and hides behind some big people trees. WITCH realizes she is gone.*)

WITCH: Dorothy, your turn. Come out, dear. I know you are hiding over there. (*Runs and looks.*) Where are you, dear? Come out this instant! You can't hide forever, not from me. (*Laughs.*) I'll be waiting for you, Dorothy. (*Laughs and exits.*)

DOROTHY: Is she gone? Thank you, magic trees. You can lower your branches and sit down. You were wonderful. Straw stuffers, we'd better put the scarecrow back together. Lion, get an oiler and tear-wiper to revive the Tin Man. (*Children help revive SCARECROW and TIN MAN.*)

SCARECROW: No tickling. Thank you. Out of my way. (*Leaps up, falls down, leaps up again.*) Marvelous feeling just being stuffed. Nothing like it. Thanks.

TIN MAN: Are we all here?

SCARECROW: Safe and sound.

DOROTHY: Look. Do you all see that light, that beautiful light? That must be the Emerald City.

LION: That's pretty. I'm going to get courage. I know I am. Look at the pretty purple flowers. Dorothy, I'm going to pick a flower for you. (*Picks flower.*) A pretty purple flower for you, Dorothy.

DOROTHY: Thank you. And one for you, Scarecrow.

SCARECROW: Thank you. For you, Tin Man.

TIN MAN: They're almost invisible. What delicate stems.

LION: I'm sleepy. I'm going to take a nap.

DOROTHY: Me, too. I'm so drowsy. (*Falls asleep with already sleeping LION.*)

TIN MAN: Something's wrong. We shouldn't be falling asleep.

SCARECROW: Don't get so . . . (*Yawns.*) . . . For a person with no heart, you sure . . . (*Yawns.*) . . . have a lot of . . . (*Yawns.*) . . . feelings. Nighty-night, Munchkins. (*He is asleep.*)

TIN MAN: It's a spell. The flowers. I can't stand it. It's a spell to make us sleep forever. (*Cries.*) I can't stop crying. These are my best friends and they're all asleep. Forever. None of us will ever wake up. (*Sobs.*) I'm rusting. Call . . . you know who . . . (*The children are given a few beats to call GLINDA. Then GLINDA enters whether they have called her or not.*)

GLINDA: This is the third time. I've helped all of you three times. Very upsetting. But that's for later. What happened? (*Asks specific children in audience to tell her what happened.*) I should have known. This isn't my territory. My powers are very, very weak here. Well, we'll just have to break the spell. (*To all the Munchkins.*) Start shivering, please. We must fill the meadow with cold. Shiver. Rub your arms like this. Good . . . cold, cold.

LION: (*wakes up first*) I'm freezing.

SCARECROW: (*leaps up and does some knee bends*) Getting a bit nippy if you ask me.

DOROTHY: I wish I had my coat. Glinda!

GLINDA: *(to two children)* You'd better oil the Tin Man and wipe his eyes . . . Thank you. Are all of you listening?

DOROTHY: How did we fall asleep? How did we . . .?

GLINDA: Please. You have a lovely, curious mind, but not now. I have something important to say. And, Munchkins, you must listen, too. I can no longer help you.

DOROTHY: Why?

LION: Don't you like us anymore? Is it me? I'll leave and you can help the others.

TIN MAN: *(crying)* We need you. I'll stop.

GLINDA: I could only help you three times. The first was when I turned your slippers into hot coals. The second was when I made you into magic trees, Munchkins. And the third time was just now. This is not my territory. I have no more power here. If I stay a minute longer, the Wicked Witch of the West will destroy me.

DOROTHY: But . . .

TIN MAN: Aren't you our friend?

GLINDA: You have each other as friends. Munchkins, do you want to stay here and help them when they need you? Decide. I can no longer help you. Go to the Wizard of Oz. He'll help you. Goodbye. Good luck. *(Starts to exit.)*

LION: Come back, please.

GLINDA: You're on your own. My rabbits call. Must feed the chickens.

DOROTHY: But . . .

GLINDA: You're on your own. *(And she is gone.)*

LION: On our own?

SCARECROW: No one to protect us.

TIN MAN: Just the Munchkins and us, and . . .

LION: We're all alone. I can't stand it. I'm going back to the forest to chase my tail. *(DOROTHY has separated herself from the group and is staring at a brilliant green light. TIN MAN and SCARECROW stop the LION from leaving.)* Hands off me. Hands off me. I'm not a brave lion. I know when I'm licked. We've got nobody on our side. We're out of Glinda's territory and we're inside the Wicked Witch of the West's domain. Let me out of here. Let me out.

DOROTHY: Look, Lion. There.

LION: What What is it?

DOROTHY: The Emerald City. Please don't desert us. You think you don't have any courage, but I know you do. We're almost there. And somewhere inside that beautiful green new city is the Wizard of Oz. The Wizard of Oz. Think of it. The most powerful person in this whole land. Please come with us.

LION: I'll come with you, Dorothy. Just for you.

DOROTHY: Thank you.

TIN MAN: Oh, that was such a beautiful speech. All right. I won't cry. But I'm very moved.

SCARECROW: (*leaps up and lands next to Munchkin in audience*) I'm feeling smarter already. To the green light and the green city and a brain. (*They travel.*)

DOROTHY: So many streets. Which one do we follow?

SCARECROW: That one. It has more jewels.

TIN MAN: Here we are. This must be the place.

LION: What a beautiful palace. I wish it weren't so big.

SCARECROW: A city to explore. A whole city. Think of it.

VOICE OF THE WIZARD: I am the Wizard of Oz. (*Lightning. Thunder. Horrible music.*) Not that music. Horrible music. Can't ever find the right dials. Don't go away. Let me try again. (*Silence, then:*) I am the Wizard of Oz. Who are you? You You. [Ordinary voice back.] This is hopeless. (*The WIZARD comes out of the light booth. He is an old man dressed in a tattered blue robe covered with stars. He hobbles down the aisles on a cane, wears a straw hat that falls off constantly, talks as he walks, blows his nose, coughs.*) Chilly in the palace. Got a cold last week. Hello, Dorothy, Munchkins, Tin Man, Scarecrow, Lion, Toto. Knew you were coming. But I can't help you. What can I do? Wicked Witch of the West just flew over Emerald City before you arrived, told us she'd rule all of Oz as soon as she got your slippers, Dorothy. Scared everybody in Emerald City inside their houses. (*Sits down and blows nose.*) Sorry. Know what a disappointment this is to all of you. Fake, fake, fake.

DOROTHY: Toto, stop barking. You . . . you can't be a fake. You must have some powers.

WIZARD: (takes out telescope) I own a good telescope.

SCARECROW: But if you're not smarter than we are . . . then . . . there's no hope.

WIZARD: Wicked Witch of the West called my bluff. I'm just an old carnival man.

TIN MAN: But Glinda's magic has run out, and . . . you were our only chance to . . . oh this is . . . Thank you.

DOROTHY: You should be ashamed of yourself.

WIZARD: I am.

SCARECROW: I'm not going to give up. I don't care if I don't have a brain. I can think my way out of this. We can all think, right, Munchkins?

LION: Maybe I don't have any courage, but I can fight with the best of 'em. I'm scared.

TIN MAN: I won't cry. I have feelings even if I don't have a heart. I'm very moved.

DOROTHY: I won't give up either. Now you, you must have some powers.

WIZARD: I'm a fake, I tell you. And I don't think well with a cold.

LION: (lifts WIZARD up and carries him down aisles to light booth, or chases him to light booth) Now I'm King of the Beasts and I'm mad. And I'm telling you, Wizard, we need your help. Anything. Even if it's not magic. You go in that . . . that . . .

WIZARD: Light booth. Plain ordinary light booth.

LION: . . . and think of something you can tell us. (LION throws WIZARD inside light booth, goes back to stage. WIZARD mutters over the microphone, starts pushing various dials.)

WIZARD: Could give you some red lights. Very pretty effect. Or an earthquake. Have an earthquake here somewhere. Wait a minute. The broomstick. The Witch's broomstick. If you capture her broomstick, she has no power. So all you have to do is go into her territory and storm her castle and get the broomstick. How's that? (Opens light booth and sticks head out.) Can I come out? Was I a help?

DOROTHY: I'm scared. I don't know if I can do that. Munchkins, do you want to go with us and try and capture the Witch's broomstick and . . . do you?

LION: My knees are shaking. I'll do it if you do it, Munchkins.

SCARECROW: I don't mind telling you I'm a little frightened myself.

TIN MAN: Well, if we all stick together, we can do it.

WIZARD: I'll follow you with my telescope. Give you thunder and horrible music when you need it. Good luck.

DOROTHY: Don't go yet.

WIZARD: *(returns to light booth. His voice is fading)* 'Bye, 'bye, Munchkins. Good luck to you all . . . Got to get to work . . . Too many switches and dials . . . Too many . . . *(He is gone.)*

DOROTHY: We're on our own again. Let's hold hands tight. Everyone take a deep breath. Here we go. *(They exit. Blackout. Then they return, still holding hands. Lights. LION shaking. SCARECROW alert. TIN MAN shaking. They are all moving very slowly, almost on tiptoe, afraid to make a sound.)*

LION: Oh-oh. Don't like the feeling of this place. Not a tree, not a bush.

TIN MAN: Not even a weed. Just a cold, lonely wind.

SCARECROW: *(as light gradually darkens)* It's getting darker, but the sun was just out.

DOROTHY: Wizard, Wizard, are you there? Can you hear us?

WIZARD'S VOICE: . . . Just a second. Need to focus the telescope. Have you. Where'd the sun go?

DOROTHY: We don't know. It's getting darker and darker. Please try and find some sunlight for us.

WIZARD: Done. Don't worry. I'm the Wizard of Oz. Fading out for now. Be back with sunlight.

SCARECROW: Dorothy! Trees, the Munchkins. The magic trees.

DOROTHY: Munchkins, stand up. Spread your arms. You're trees, deeply rooted trees. Stay still. Don't move from your seats. *(Each of the group moves in separate directions.)*

LION: Dorothy, where are you?

WITCH: Over here

LION: Can't find you.

DOROTHY: Lion, Lion, where are you?

WITCH: Behind a bush.

DOROTHY: Scarecrow?

SCARECROW: Here.

WITCH: Here, Over here

DOROTHY: Wizard, hurry, it's getting darker each second.

SCARECROW: Too many voices. Inky blackness. Thick as soup. Tin Man, where are you?

TIN MAN: Over here.

WITCH: Over here.

LION: Nobody panic. I'm here. Nobody panic. *(Goes to closest child in audience.)* Come here and give me a hug.

SCARECROW: Dorothy.

WITCH: Dorothy?

TIN MAN: Dorothy?

WITCH: Dorothy?

DOROTHY: Over here. Over here! *(DOROTHY backs toward exit. WITCH grabs her and they exit.)*

TIN MAN: Dorothy?

SCARECROW: Dorothy?

WIZARD: Found it. Found the sunlight.

SCARECROW: Thank you, Wizard. Dorothy, Tin Man, Lion, where are you? Sit down, trees, so we can see each other.

LION: Over here.

TIN MAN: Over here. *(They run together and embrace.)* I'm so happy. We're safe. But where is Dorothy? What happened?

SCARECROW: *(picks one child)* Tell me what happened?

WIZARD: Terrible. Found the sun too late. Too late. Too late as always. Just a fake. No good to anybody . . . fading out . . . deeply embarrassed. *(Fades out.)*

LION: Guess it's time for me to be brave. The Witch shouldn't have done that. We're going to rescue Dorothy. *(To children.)* You, and you, check the Scarecrow. Make sure he's tightly stuffed. You, and you, make sure the Tin Man is nicely oiled . . . Thanks. You can go back to your seats. Come on. To the castle. And when I get hold of that Witch . . . When I get hold of that Witch . . . I'll tear her to pieces. I'll make her wish she hadn't taken on the King of Beasts. I'm mad. And when the King of Beasts is mad, there's no stopping him. (*GROUP exits. Static. Wizard's voice as lights black out.*)

WIZARD'S VOICE: Wizard here. Hang on, Munchkins. Have some light for you soon. Just getting my telescope in focus. Have the Witch's castle for you in a second. Got it. Got the castle. Big place. Funny. Not a guard in sight. Not the way it usually is. (*WITCH and DOROTHY enter and take positions. DOROTHY is on a stool. WITCH is combing her hair.*) Fading out for now. Be here if you need me.

WITCH: There, there. Beautiful hair. Soft. Silken. Tell the Munchkins you're all right.

DOROTHY: I am all right, Munchkins. She doesn't seem like a bad Witch.

WITCH: Of course I'm not. Tell them what I did for you.

DOROTHY: She gave me this dress. She fed me hot chocolate and biscuits with honey.

WITCH: You see. "Wicked Witch of the West." Glinda calls me that becausae she's jealous of my power. I mean Dorothy no harm. Wouldn't you be angry if someone killed your sister? Even if it was an accident?

DOROTHY: It's not my fault my house landed on your sister. I'm very sorry.

WITCH: Of course you are. This whole thing has been a terrible misunderstanding. I'm not angry. I just had to get you here so you would listen to me. All I want are the slippers that belonged to my sister and now belong to me. Please.

DOROTHY: (*starts to take the first slipper off, then hesitates*) Why are you acting so sweet to me? Why am I feeling so terribly anxious to do whatever you want me to do? Is this a spell?

WITCH: Give me the slippers, Dorothy, and you will be back home before you can count to three.(*The GROUP enters, and comes up aisles toward WITCH and DOROTHY.*)

DOROTHY: I don't know what to do. I'm feeling a little dizzy.

WITCH: Give me the slippers, you stupid girl!

SCARECROW: Don't like it. No guards. Should be guards. Could be a trap.

TIN MAN: Even if it is, we've got to save Dorothy.

LION: Just let me at her, let me at her.

WITCH: Welcome, friends. Don't be afraid. The door's open. You're expected.

DOROTHY: *(embraces everyone)* I'm so glad to see you all. Toto, stop barking. Lion, you're so brave.

LION: Think I'm afraid of her. I'm not afraid of anything. Put up your dukes, put up your dukes. *(Circles WITCH boxer style.)* I'm not afraid of you. I'm the King of the Beasts. *(Roars. WITCH jumps.)* Got her on the run. Let's get out of here. She's nothing but mush. Wicked Witch of the West. Ha!

WITCH: Look at your tail now, Lion.

LION: What are you talking about? What are you talking . . . Where'd that snake come from? *(WITCH makes hissing noise.)* Where'd that snake come from? Oh, no! Hissing at me. *(LION chases tail.)* Stop hissing at me. *(He runs in circles, faints from exhaustion and fear. The WITCH turns toward TIN MAN.)*

WITCH: Isn't this sad, Tin Man? I have you all under a spell. Doesn't it make you want to cry? Doesn't it make you want to weep?

TIN MAN: I'm sorry, Munchkins, but you can't help me this time. I'm under a spell. *(He cries, rusts.)*

WITCH: Look at your friend, the Scarecrow, Dorothy. See his straw.

DOROTHY: Don't you come near him.

SCARECROW: It's all right, Dorothy. I'm not afraid of her. I know what you're doing. You can't frighten me. I'm smart.

WITCH: Give me those slippers, Dorothy, or I will have to turn your scarecrow into a bonfire.

SCARECROW: Don't listen to her. She's not so powerful.

WITCH: *(holds up her hand and balances an imaginary flame on the tip of her finger)* See the flame, Scarecrow. Blue and orange. Pretty flame. Watch the flame, Scarecrow. Watch the flame.

SCARECROW: I'm feeling kind of hot.

DOROTHY: Wizard, Wizard, are you there?

WIZARD: . . . Thunder. No, that's music. Horrible music. Music having any effect?

WITCH: Watch the flame, the dancing flame. Soon your straw will begin to smoke.

DOROTHY: Oh, Wizard, horrible music doesn't help.

SCARECROW: Maybe if I unloosen my collar.

WITCH: The flame, Scarecrow, the flame.

WIZARD: Wish I could make it rain . . . Used to have rain. No, that's an earthquake . . .

DOROTHY: Rain! Munchkins, we'll make rain. *(WITCH keeps repeating "The flame, the flame." SCARECROW is riveted to her.)* Lift your arms above your heads and then make the rain come down. Shake the raindrops from your fingertips.

WITCH: Don't do that. Stop that, Munchkins, sweethearts. Please stop making that rain.

SCARECROW: I felt a drop on my nose.

WIZARD: How about a thunderstorm . . . *(Sound of storm.)*

LION: *(wakes)* My tail's a tail again.

WITCH: I didn't mean to lose my temper. I won't hurt the Scarecrow. I don't want those slippers. Just stop the rain, please.

SCARECROW: The flame is out. She doesn't like the rain. Keep it up.

LION: *(washing his face)* Nothing like raindrops to freshen you up.

DOROTHY: Make it pour, Munchkins.

WITCH: I don't want the slippers. I don't care about them. Stop the rain. I can't take water. I can't abide water. *(Shrinks herself up and crawls toward exit.)* Melting. I'm melting. So horrible to melt. Soon I'll be nothing but . . . *(Exits.)* . . . a puddle of rain. *(Silence.)*

DOROTHY: Stop the rain, Munchkins. Go see what happened to the witch, Scarecrow. *(He goes out and returns with the Witch's broomstick.)* Well? Is she alive?

SCARECROW: *(grins and leaps)* The Wicked Witch of the West is dead. Or else she's alive in a puddle of rain. Which would be just fine with me. Never knew a puddle of rain that could harm you.

DOROTHY: Thank you, Munchkins. Would you oil the Tin Man? Move his arms. Tin Man, is everything all right?

TIN MAN: Yes. I'm very moved. Thank you. You can go back to your seats.

DOROTHY: Well, we got the Witch's broomstick. Weren't we terrific? Now the Wizard can send me home.

WIZARD: . . . Wizard here . . . Is it raining yet? Can't see what's happening down your way, Munchkins. Telescope broke . . .

DOROTHY: The rain's come and gone, Wizard. The Munchkins made the rain. And the Wicked Witch of the West is nothing but a rain puddle.

WIZARD: Too late again. Fake, fake, fake. Tried to help . . . Wish I was a real wizard.

DOROTHY: You did help. You gave us the idea to make the rain. And you are a real wizard. I just wish you wouldn't mutter so much.

WIZARD: Can't help it. Been alone in this palace too long. Well, got a surprise for you, Dorothy, Tin Man, Lion, Scarecrow.

LION: A surprise. I love surprises. What is it?

WIZARD: Come back to the Emerald City. Right to the palace. Go along.

TIN MAN: Won't you tell me what it is?

WIZARD: No, the surprise is between the Munchkins and myself. Hurry. *(GROUP exits.)* Change of light first . . . Sun is going down . . . End of the day in Oz . . . Coming, Munchkins . . . Need your help for the surprise . . . Be there in a . . . *(Light booth opens. WIZARD hobbles out with medal, watch and diploma bunched in one hand. As he hobbles down aisles toward stage, picks three children.)* Need you to hand out a diploma to the Scarecrow. Thinks he's not smart. Silly, silly. Come along. Would you give the Tin Man a heart? Pretty, isn't it? Tick, tick. Tick, tick. Come on now. And you give the Lion this medal. Four-star General for sure. Rest of you don't say a word when they get back to Emerald City. Come on. Let's stand here. *(He is on stage.)* Hold the surprises behind your back. Here they come. Enter, Group. Come on stage.

DOROTHY: Here's the Witch's broomstick, Wizard. We did it.

WIZARD: Knew you would.

LION: Oh, please. I can't stand the suspense. Give me my surprise.

WIZARD: Scarecrow first. Go ahead, Munchkin. Present your diploma to the Scarecrow and shake his hand.

SCARECROW: The Himalayas are the highest of all mountain ranges with Mount Everest being . . . I have a brain!

WIZARD: You had one all the time. Here, Munchkin. Present the heart to the Tin Man. Though why you need one with all your crying is beyond me. Hold it up to his ears so he can listen to it. Tick, tick.

TIN MAN: *(listens)* I'm so deeply moved. *(Starts to sniffle.)* I know.

WIZARD: Come forward with the medal, Munchkin. For you, Lion. Got it from an old war hero when I was a Kansas man. Put around his neck, Munchkin. (*LION kneels down. Lets child put medal around his neck.*) Now you got your courage, Lion. But you had it all the time.

LION: (*hugs child*) Thanks.

WIZARD: That's the surprise. Go back to your seats, Munchkins. I did something right for once.

DOROTHY: Kansas.

WIZARD: What?

DOROTHY: It's time for me to go home. But I don't want to leave Oz and all of you. I don't know how to go home anyway.

GLINDA: (*enters*) Cucumbers blooming. Butterflies dancing. What a day, what a day. Silly girl, you can go home now if you wish. You tap those slippers three times. You get the Munchkins to close their eyes, you wish, and you're home.

DOROTHY: Glinda, why didn't you help us? The scarecrow could have died, and the Munchkins, and . . .

GLINDA: (*pats DOROTHY's cheek*) You all did just fine. You didn't need my magic. Not even once. Well, Dorothy. Are you ready?

DOROTHY: To leave Oz? Now?

GLINDA: The sun is setting. It's a fine time.

DOROTHY: But . . . (*Goes to SCARECROW.*) I'll miss you.

SCARECROW: I'll miss you too, Dorothy.

DOROTHY: And Tin Man. Don't cry. I don't know how you'll ever get through a day in Oz without rusting.

TIN MAN: I'll use a handkerchief. (*SCARECROW hands him a hanky.*) Thank you.

DOROTHY: And Lion. (*Hugs him.*) You won't chase your tail anymore, will you?

LION: I'm the King of the Beasts. I'll miss you. We'll all miss you.

WIZARD: Me too.

DOROTHY: You're not a fake. You helped us. I just wonder if you know which dial is which sometimes.

WIZARD: A gadget man. I'm just a gadget man.

DOROTHY: I think you're a real wizard. Don't you think he's a real wizard, Munchkins?

WIZARD: I wish I was a real wizard. But once a carnival man, always a carnival man.

DOROTHY: Glinda, can't you do something for him?

GLINDA: *(WIZARD hangs head down)* You do make very pretty sunsets. And I like your thunder. When it doesn't come at breakfast. Very well. I know what you need. A wizard's hat. That straw hat is ridiculous.

SCARECROW: Give it to me. I'm partial to straw hats.

GLINDA: Certainly. *(Turns to child in audience.)* Give this to the Scarecrow, please. *(She is rummaging in bag.)* Here, Munchkin. Put this one on the Wizard. *(Child puts WIZARD's hat on him.)* And these spectacles on his nose. Never known a real wizard without spectacles. Thank you. Go back to your seat. Now you're a real wizard.

WIZARD: Deeply grateful. You sure I'm a real wizard?

GLINDA: We'll soon see.

DOROTHY: I don't want to go home. I don't want to leave Oz.

GLINDA: But you have to, dear. You can return, of course.

DOROTHY: I can? And see everyone again? Everyone?

GLINDA: The next time it rains in Kansas, come outside the moment the rain stops and the sun peeks through the clouds. Find a rainbow, stare hard, and you'll be back in Oz before you know it.

DOROTHY: Just come outside when the rain has stopped, when the sun peeks through the clouds, stare into a rainbow very hard, and I'll be back?

GLINDA: *(nods)* Ready?

DOROTHY: I think so. Tap my slippers three times?

GLINDA: That's all.

DOROTHY: And I'll be back in Kansas.

GLINDA: I wish you'd trust me.

WIZARD: Just a minute. *(Hobbles quickly down aisles.)* Hold on. Don't move. If Dorothy's going home, I want to give her something special. Don't tap those slippers until I tell you I'm ready. *(He enters light booth.)*

DOROTHY: Goodbye, Scarecrow, Tin Man, Lion, Glinda, Munchkins. Toto, we're going home.

GLINDA: Ready, Wizard?

WIZARD: Almost. Let me find the right switch. Yes, yes, should be just right. Goodbye, Dorothy. *(Blackout. In the darkness, DOROTHY says:)*

DOROTHY: Goodbye. *(ALL exit.)*

GLINDA: Tap, tap, tap and she's gone. *(The WIZARD makes a rainbow. [A rainbow can be made out of cloth and pulled across the stage.] As the rainbow unfolds, we hear the WIZARD.)*

WIZARD: Did you like that rainbow, Dorothy? Best I've ever made. Goodbye, Munchkins. Wizard of Oz . . . fading out.

End of Play

8

Alice in Wonderland
An Adaptation
by
William Glennon

Characters

Alice
White Rabbit
The Mouse
Fish Footman
Frog Footman
The Duchess
The Cook
The Cheshire Cat

Production Notes

The production requires props, not scenery, and can be played against a neutral background or lighted cyc.

To the Producer:

Originally this script was written to be performed by eight actors as the "Wonderland Group" plus Alice. However, in the first production, I used thirteen, plus Alice. (One actor played the Mouse, the March Hare, and the Mock Turtle; Fish Footman and Frog Footman doubled as the Playing Cards during the croquet game; the Dormouse and the Gryphon were doubled. Further doubling is possible and in keeping with the original intent).

The actors should be numbered for the roll call in the opening and lines distributed as desired, with Number One more or less in charge. Group activity, however, is the basic idea—much like the Commedia d'elle Arte—a planned outline filled with spontaneous moments.

123

Our company carried a few props on with them, and found the others in the wings. Placards, for example, were carried. They were decorated with question marks, exclamation points, and patterns, to arouse curiosity. Later they doubled as the opening to the garden and the door to the kitchen. For the croquet game we used short sections of a picket fence as a "boundary" and the stools seen earlier were turned over so roses could be inserted in the holes drilled in the legs. The fence went on to make a witness box for the tral which also had small ladders instead of thrones for the King and Queen. We had a stylized stove in the kitchen scene and a coat rack big enough for the Cheshire Cat to curl up on, but mostly the "scenery" was sparse.

Our company wore tights and collared smocks to begin with. Midway through Act One nearly everyone was in full costume. Suggestions of the costume would be just fine, though. That approach goes along with the idea of spontaneity and inventiveness, whatever it takes to help Alice—and the audience—enjoy her "turn."

William Glennon

ACT ONE

SCENE: The ACTORS enter through the house as the lights dim. As they walk down the aisles, they are talking with each other about their predicament. Anxious to do "Alice in Wonderland," they have found they lack an Alice. They have all opted for the other parts it seems. The audience hears snatches of their exchanges.

• • • • • • • • • • • • • • • • • • • •

ACTOR: Imagine. Without the White Rabbit, yes. We could skip that part. The Mock Turtle, you bet. Cut that scene. But no Alice? Impossible.

ACTOR: Why didn't you agree to be Alice?

ACTOR: Because.

ACTOR: Because why?

ACTOR: Same reason as you. I like my own part.

ACTOR: Well, it's not "The Mad Hatter in Wonderland" or "The Queen of Hearts in Wonderland." It's "Alice in Wonderland." (*Etc.*)

ONE: (*LEADER, now at front of house near apron*) Now, now, now. We've got a little stumbling block, true, but we've been in worse pickles.

TWO: Name one. (*ACTORS are now sitting on apron, leaning on it, standing on edge of stage, etc.*)

ONE: Well, let's see.

TWO: You can't do "Alice in Wonderland" without an Alice. So let's give up. (*ACTOR with highest number suddenly discovers the slit in curtain. He's curious and slips through.*)

ONE: Perhaps someone's reconsidered. That's a possibility. Let's count off again.

TWO: We've counted off and counted off and counted off and we're still in the same pickle. It's not a possibility.

FIVE: Actually we're in a theatre.

SIX: Good place for a story.

TWO: We're in a pickle in a theatre and there isn't going to be a story. Face it.

ONE: Now, now. Let's hear it! Count off! I'll start things rolling. One! (*And he names the part he's going to play.*)

TWO: (*unhappy*) Two. (*And his part. The roll call continues until all the parts have been named with the exception of the ACTOR who went in back of curtain.*) See? We may as well pack up and go home. No Alice, and that's that.

SEVEN: No Wonderland.

EIGHT: Bother.

ONE: Aren't we missing a part?

TWO: Of course! Alice! How many times must you be told?

ONE: No, someone else . . .(*ACTOR returns from behind curtain. He is excited.*)

ACTOR: Listen!

ONE: Oh, yes, there he is. And you're going to be . . . uh . . .

ACTOR: Listen. There's a girl. (*Giggles.*) A girl. Just behind this thing. (*Curtain.*) And she's sitting there doing nothing.

ONE: Nothing?

ACTOR: Well, daydreaming, maybe.

ONE: That sounds promising.

ACTOR: And she's young and pretty and just perfect for you-know-who. (*A murmur.*)

TWO: But she's not one of us.

ACTOR: Well, she could be, couldn't she?

TWO: But she won't know what to do.

ACTOR: That's never stopped you.

ONE: Now, now, now. Mustn't bicker.

ACTOR: Come on. See for yourself.

FIVE: We could help her, you know, along the way. We know what to do. Sort of.

ONE: She can certainly help us.

ACTOR: Let's give it a go! Shall we?

ONE: Well, I see no reason why we can't at least look at her.

FOUR: No reason at all. So let's look.

TWO: How do we get rid of this thing? (Curtain.)

ONE: Blow it away. (*ALL take in deep breaths and blow. The curtain rises. ALICE is seated center, daydreaming. They seem to like her. Quietly they tiptoe from the house to the stage, passing far right and left. As they move, ALICE speaks and ALL freeze.*)

ALICE: What a lazy day. With nothing to do. Perhaps I should have followed my sister when she left. "Come along. Back to the house and I'll fix you some tea. Don't you want some tea, Alice?" (*ALL heads turn quickly to her. They are amazed.*) "Not yet, dear sister. I'm going to stay here for a while. By the stream. In the sunshine. I'll have my tea later, thank you." (*She sighs. They look at each other, bright-eyed.*) Oh, I do wish something unusual would happen. (*ALL snort softly and move quietly to set up necessary props.*) Something very unusual.

ACTOR: Unusual!

ACTOR: (*as they place stools around ALICE*) And fun.

ACTOR: Can't wait!

ACTOR: Ready. (*ONE mounts a stool at UL, raises his arm with extended finger and then drops finger as a signal to begin. ALICE doesn't quite hear the following but senses something.*)

FIVE: The White Rabbit hurries for fear he'll be late . . .

EIGHT: Imagine his fate if he makes the Queen wait!

SIX: Down in the ground where the hole goes so deep . . .

THREE: The tumble is liable to put you to sleep. (*ALL giggle.*)

THIRTEEN: You'll fall at a speed that will make your ears sing,

ONE: Past curious whatchamacallits and things,

EIGHT: Past orange marmalade in a jar on the shelf,

TEN: Past mirrors that smile when you smile at yourself. (*ALL giggle.*)

SIX: Past odd little doors and a window or two,

FIVE: Perhaps you'll encounter a picture of you!

THIRTEEN: Down deeper and deeper and deeper you'll go,

SIX: Down deep in the rabbit hole, head over toe;

THREE: You'll fall to a place so unusually gay,

EIGHT: It's terribly likely you'll hear yourself say:

ONE: It's bewitching, beloved, beyootiful and . . .

ALL: Grand,

ONE: So wondrously wonderful, your . . .

ALL: Wonderland!

THREE: So becoming, befuddled, beguiling and . . .

ALL: Grand,

ONE: So wondrously wonderful, your . . .

ALL: Wonderland! (*They cup hands over faces, open hands and call softly.*) Alice! (*ALICE looks about as if she's almost heard them.*) Alice! (*She smiles.*) (*WHITE RABBIT has donned ears, a waistcoat and has a watch. He now leaps from behind the GROUP.*)

ONE: Now.

RABBIT: (*hops DL*) Oh my ears and whiskers, I'll be late!

ALICE: Sitting on a wooded bank, one can occasionally expect a white rabbit to scamper by. Curious though, when the white rabbit is wearing a waistcoat, carrying a watch and is able to speak. Late? Late for what?

RABBIT: Now where's the hole? I must find the hole! It will never do to keep the Duchess waiting.

ACTOR: That's my part!

ACTOR: Sh!

RABBIT: Oh, my dear little paws and fur, I can't find the hole! If I'm late getting home, I'll be late for the Duchess, and if I'm late for the Duchess, I'll be late for the Queen's croquet game. And if I'm late for the Queen's croquet game she'll chop off my head! *(The OTHERS have formed a human "rabbit hole" at left, with signs identifying it as such. One says "Rabbit Hole," the other, "Enter Here." They get these props from the wings—or perhaps have carried them on.)*

TWO: *(holding sign "Enter Here")* Ahem!

THREE: Do you think she'll follow?

ALICE: I think I'll follow. *(Rises and crosses to hole.)*

ONE: I think she'll follow.

ALICE: Odd. I never noticed this rabbit hole before. *(The OTHERS form a tunnel above the hole.)* Very curious. *(Reading signs.)* "Rabbit Hole" "Enter Here." Well . . . I'm not exactly a rabbit, but . . . *(She enters.)*

SIX: There she goes! *(The "tunnel" moves, with ALICE inside it, to center, where it becomes the circular wall of the hole through which ALICE is falling. The actors face ALICE in a tight circle, their arms over their heads.)*

THREE: Down deeper and deeper and deeper she'll go.

ONE: Down deep in the rabbit hole, head over toe.

ALICE: *(rising and swaying, as though she is falling as the OTHERS kneel)* I must be nearly to the center of the earth. *(They rise again and she drops out of sight.)*

TEN: She'll fall at a speed that'll make her ears sing . . .

TWO: Past curious whatchamacallits and things . . .

ALICE: *(rising)* I keep falling past the most curious things . . .

SIX: Past orange marmalade in a jar on the shelf . . .

NINE: Past mirrors that smile when you smile at yourself.

ALICE: *(rising)* A mirror smiled back at me. Nothing curious there, but if I keep falling this way, I shall surely land on the other side of the world where people have to walk on their heads, and that will be extremely curious.

ONE: Is she nearly there?

ACTOR: Almost!

ALICE: *(rising)* I wonder what Dinah, my cat, would think of all this.

Such a fall, I dare say, would probably cause her hair to stand on end. What's the White Rabbit going to be late for? The Duchess? A croquet game?

RABBIT: The White Rabbit hurries for fear he'll be late. Imagine his fate if he makes the queen wait!

ALL: She's almost there. Thump! *("Hole" splits apart. The ACTORS scatter about.)*

ALICE: *(on the floor)* Didn't hurt at all. When I get home I'm going to fall down the stairs just to show how brave I am.

ALL: Oh?

ALICE: Three stairs to the landing. *(She rises, looks about and crosses DR).* Well, I wonder where I am now. And where's the White Rabbit, I wonder . . .

ALL: *(overlapping her)* Wonderland . . . Wonderland . . . *(They are forming a door at center.)*

ALICE: *(overlapping)* I wonder where this goes. *(On hands and knees, looking through tiny doorway.)* Why, there's a garden! *(SEVERAL behind doorway hold up roses.)* A lovely garden . . . with fountains! *(ACTOR runs to left of door and squirts water.)* But I shall never be able to go through this little doorway. I'm much too big.

ALL: Tsk, tsk, tsk.

ALICE: Oh, dear, what a pity I can't just shut up like a telescope. Considering what's happened so far today, I don't really think shutting up like a telescope is all that impossible. *(She leans on a crate upon which has been placed a little bottle and a sign "Drink Me.")* Drink Me." Hmmm.. Wonder if I should. I seem to be wondering quite a bit today. I wonder .

ALL: *(overlapping)* Wonderland! Wonderland!

ALICE *(overlapping)* I wonder . . . Well, it isn't marked "poison" and that's a good sign. It's a sensible rule to avoid anything marked poison." Yes. Hmmm.

ALL: Hmnmm!

ALICE: *(rises)* Just a little bit. *(She drinks.)* Mmmm. Tastes like a mixture of cherry tarts, plum pudding and buttered biscuits.

ALL: Mmmmmm!

ALICE: *(drinks)* Very nice. Very nice, indeed. *(Slide whistle. The door grows larger as ALICE "shrinks.")* Well, here goes the telescope again! Mustn't shut up too far or it might be like a candle going out. And I don't want to go out. Then I'd never get through to that lovely garden. *(The bottle is replaced by a piece of cake with sign "Eat Me.")* "Eat Me!" Oh, I do love currant cake. *(She eats some of the cake and begins to grow as the door grows smaller.)*. Well, I never! A bit of currant cake and I'm back to normal size, or maybe even bigger. *(She checks the opening.)* Yes, bigger. Now I shall never get through to the garden. Never, never never. *(She cries.)* First, I'm as tall as a house, and then I'm as small as a mouse. It's getting curiouser and curiouser. Indeed it is. I must stop crying though, especially since I can't remember why I started. Oh, yes! The dear garden with flowers, *(Garden appears.)* and fountains, *(Fountain appears and squirts water, and shrugs.)* I shall never see. *(She cries again. TWO ACTORS hand her water soaked handkerchiefs with which she wipes her eyes and then wrings them out.)* And where's the White Rabbit? How rude of him to vanish. He must have known I was following him. How very rude. Besides, I don't know where I am or where I'm going or how to get there! *(She "shrinks" again; the door grows.)* I'm . . . I'm . . I'm shutting up again! I'm shrinking! And I didn't eat a bit or drink a drop. It must be in my system. *(A long piece of blue silk is taken from the costume of one of the actors. FIVE ACTORS sit on stools placed in a semicircle around two stools and make waves with the long piece of silk, and the other props are taken off.)*

ALICE: I must run. I don't know where or why, but I must run! *(She does, until she "slips" and falls into the pool of tears. She is on her knees behind stool at right with stomach on stool and making swimming gestures with arms. She tastes water.)* Why, it's salt water! *(ONE, wearing mouse ears, "swims" toward her and leans over a stool, "swimming?")*

ALICE: Excuse me.

MOUSE: Why? What'd you do?

ALICE: I didn't do anything.

MOUSE: Then what do you want to be excused for?

ALICE: I don't want to be excused for anything, really.

MOUSE: In that case, I would advise you not to say "Excuse me." *(He starts away.)*

ALICE: Please don't swim away.

MOUSE: I can't swim in one place.

ALICE: *(noticing him for the first time)* Why, you're a mouse.

MOUSE: No comment.

ALICE: Can you tell me where I am?

MOUSE: You ought to know. They're your tears, not mine.

ALICE: My tears? *(Looks around.)* Amazing.

MOUSE: Big tears, I'd say. You must be quite blubbery.

ALICE: Don't mice cry?

MOUSE: Not this much. It would take me a hundred years to cry a pool this size.

ALICE: I must tell Dinah.

MOUSE: Who's Dinah?

ALICE: Dinah's my dear little cat.

MOUSE: A cat! *(He gasps, holds nose and "dives" under.)*

ALICE: Oh, I'm sorry. I don't suppose we should talk about cats.

MOUSE *(coming up, gasping for breath)* I wasn't.

ALICE: But Dinah's such a sweet pet. I'm sure you'd take a great fancy to her. She purrs *(ALICE purrs.)* and washes her face with her paws, and she's such a great one for catching . . . uh oh . . .

MOUSE: She's a serpent! *(He "dives" again.)*

ALICE: I beg your pardon.

MOUSE: *(up again)* Pardon granted.

ALICE: Good. Now how do we get out of here?

MOUSE: Try swimming to shore.

ALICE: What'll I find there?

MOUSE: Depends on which shore you swim to. *(Giggles.)*

ALICE: Well, I'm looking for a white rabbit.

MOUSE: Why?

ALICE: I followed him and poof! he vanished.

MOUSE: A likely story.

ALICE: I believe he was on his way to a croquet game.

MOUSE: That so.

ALICE: You think I should attend the croquet game, too?

MOUSE: Did she invite you?

ALICE: Who?

MOUSE: The Queen.

ALICE: No. But I have a feeling that's where I'm going.

MOUSE: Better see the Duchess first.

ALICE: Where can I find her?

MOUSE: Where she lives, of course. But don't say I told you. I don't care to have my head chopped off.

ALICE: Neither do I.

MOUSE: Well, that's what she'll do, you know.

ALICE: Who? The Duchess?

MOUSE: No, the Queen. She's uncommonly fond of beheading people.

ALICE: That's very . . . rude.

MOUSE: Try telling her that.

ALICE: One can't go about chopping people's heads off. It just isn't done.

MOUSE: Just isn't done! (*He swims away and the pool of tears follows him. All stools and props are struck.*)

ALICE: Wait! I've several questions I want to ask you. It's impolite to swim away when I haven't finished . . .(*RABBIT appears at right.*)

RABBIT: Mary Ann! What are you doing in the tub with your clothes on?

ALICE: Mary Ann!?

RABBIT: Don't call me "Mary Ann." I'm not Mary Ann. You're Mary Ann.

ALICE: But . . .

RABBIT: No "buts" about it. Run home this instant and fetch my white gloves and a fan.

ALICE: (*indicating "soaked" dress*) Look, I'm rather wet . . .

RABBIT: If you run fast enough the wind will dry you off. Quickly! I'm late! I'll need my white gloves for the croquet game . . . it's one of her new rules . . . and the fan for the tea party, if she's in the mood. Hurry! (*Crosses to left.*)

ALICE: Which way?

RABBIT: (*turns*) Which way? Which way indeed! No idle questions! Off with you! (*Looks at his watch.*) Oh, my wrinkly nose and pointed ears! Look at the time. (*Starts off at left.*) I'll meet you there promptly. (*Turns.*) On the dot! (*He is gone.*)

ALICE: I'm not Mary Ann. I'm Alice, I think. And I haven't the faintest idea where home is, his home or mine. Perhaps if I run far enough, I'll find one of them, though it wouldn't surprise me very much if I didn't. *(She smiles.)* It's like a game without rules. *(As ALICE runs in place, facing left, SEVEN, THIRTEEN and TWELVE run from left to right, one at a time, carrying signs: A tree, a bush, another tree.)*

ALICE: *(after watching signs)* Everything's so curious, and getting curiouser all the time. *(She "loses" ground, and TEN runs on from left as FISH FOOTMAN. They run toward each other and stop at center.)*

FISH: *("acting" grand, but with a twinkle)* You see this handsomely engraved invitation, I suppose?

ALICE: Yes, I do.

FISH: Well, it's not for you. So stop your whining.

ALICE: I beg your pardon.

FISH: That will do no good whatsoever. I'm not in a position to grant pardons.

ALICE: The very idea.

FISH: That's it! The very idea! You seem rather bright but your hair wants cutting.

ALICE: Personal comments are not in very good taste.

FISH: And good taste is just what we'll have when the tarts are ready.

ALICE: What tarts?

FISH: *(he hops to other side of her, making fish noises)* I know you know the invitation is for the Duchess to attend the croquet game and have a tart with the Queen afterwards.

ALICE: It is?

FISH: The Queen of Hearts, she made some tarts, all on a summer day! And so forth.

ALICE: Yes, I've heard that before.

FISH: Of course you have . . . I just said it! If you'd cut your hair you'd hear better. That's only common sense.

ALICE: Has anyone stolen the tarts?

FISH: Not yet. We've got to run. Quickly!

ALICE: Why?

FISH: To stay in the same place! *(They run in place toward left. THIRTEEN, SEVEN and TWELVE enter right, running. TWELVE carries fancy tops for easels on which placards were placed in house, which are soon to become the double doors to the DUCHESS' house.)*

ALICE: I don't want to stay in the same place, if you don't mind.

FISH: But, I do mind. Faster! *(THIRTEEN and SEVEN break and run to fetch "doors." They construct the doors at upper right.)*

ALICE: We don't seem to be getting anywhere.

FISH: Faster! Faster!

ALICE: *(losing ground and backing to DR)* I do wish we could have a little rest.

FISH: *(stops running and ALICE catches up to him DL)* Stop!

ALICE: *(looking about)* We don't seem to have moved at all. We're in exactly the same place.

FISH: Would you have it otherwise?

ALICE: Well, in my country, when we run fast we generally get somewhere.

FISH: Time for knocks on the door.

ALICE: What door?

FISH: There. *(He goes to door, pantomimes three knocks on door. THIRTEEN and SEVEN, behind doors, say "Knock" each time FISH pantomimes a knock.)*

FISH: Hark ye! Hark ye! Open ye! An invitation from the Queen. *(FROG steps through doors as they are opened.)*

FROG: The Frog Footman, servant to the Duchess, at your service.

FISH: The Queen invites the Duchess to a game of croquet and dearly hopes she can make it or else.

FROG: I see. *(Sneezes.)*

ALICE: Bless you.

FISH: *(to FROG)* Pay no attention to her. She's waiting for a haircut.

FROG: It's not her turn.

FISH: I know it, but she kept screaming at me. *(ALICE smiles but sobers when they look at her.)*

FROG: *(to ALICE)* The Duchess is not fond of people who scream. She's highly sensitive to screaming.

ALICE: I didn't scream and I'm not waiting for a haircut.

FISH: Why do you need a haircut?

ALICE: I don't need a haircut.

FISH: See? She makes no sense at all.

FROG: None whatsoever.

ALICE: I think you're trying to confuse me.

FROG: The Duchess is very sensitive to confusion. *(To FISH.)* I'll give her the invitation and pray I don't get hit with a pot.

ALICE: The Duchess might throw a pot at you?

FROG: Of course not. But the cook will. *(FROG, in a series of mechanical motions takes the invitation from the FISH. Then he motions FISH out of the way. The door opens, he waves at ALICE and disappears. All through the preceding, he makes frog noises.)*

ALICE: A strange household, I'd say.

FISH: Please don't expect me to stay. She'll need cherries for the tarts. *(He starts to run backwards.)*

ALICE: If you run that way, you can't see where you're going!

FISH: I know. Makes for surprises. *(He continues backwards.)*

ALICE: Perhaps this is where I'm supposed to meet the White Rabbit on the dot. *(She goes to door. ONE [LEADER] enters and goes to FISH.)*

ONE: *(loud whisper)* She's doing just fine, isn't she? And having fun, too.

FISH: *(still on the run)* Wait'll she meets the Duchess.

ONE: And her cook! *(They exit.)*

ALICE: *(pantomimes knocking the way FISH did)* May I come in? *(Lights flash and horrible vocal sounds are heard as ACTORS set scene for DUCHESS' house.)*

DUCHESS: *(singing)* Speak roughly to your little boy, And beat him when he sneezes; He only does it to annoy, Because he knows it teases.

COOK: *(rushes to DUCHESS and joins in)* Wow! Wow! Wow! *(She returns to stove.)*

DUCHESS: I know a million verses to that song and I hate 'em all. *(She sneezes.)*

ALICE: Bless you. (COOK *places a pot over her head, hits it with another, and sinks behind the stove.*) Well, I never!

DUCHESS: Living backwards, that's what does it. (*The BABY cries violently. It is VOICE of an ACTOR off left.*) What's the matter with you? Want a good bouncing? (*She bounces the baby mercilessly.*) There! That ought to do it! PIG!

ALICE: I don't like to interfere . . .

DUCHESS: Piggy pig pig! Dance me a jig! Pour on molasses, And call it a wig! (*Sneezes.*)

ALICE: Bless you! (*ALICE sneezes.*) Bless me!

DUCHESS: What a terrible conversationalist you are, and that's a fact. Try the soup.

ALICE: The soup? Oh, all right. (*COOK sneezes.*) Bless you. (*DUCHESS snorts.*) Blessing people after they sneeze is a form of good manners.

COOK, DUCHESS, CAT: (*together*) Do tell.

ALICE: (*trying to be pleasant*) There may be too much pepper in the soup. (*COOK, insulted, shrieks and runs out with a metallic crash to punctuate her exit. ALICE watches her go then notices the CAT on the coat rack. He chuckles and grins.*) Gracious! What an unusual pussycat. Are you smiling, Kitty? (*CAT chuckles.*)

DUCHESS: It's not a smile, it's more of a grin. PIG!

ALICE: Pig? Please, are you addressing the cat or the baby or me?

DUCHESS: (*for an answer, tosses the BABY in the air*) Pig! Pig! Piggy! Pig! Pig!

ALICE: Oh. Please don't think me forward, but is there a reason for the cat to grin like that?

DUCHESS: Certainly. He's a Cheshire Cat and that's why.

ALICE: Really?

DUCHESS: I said it, so it's so.

ALICE: Dinah doesn't grin.

DUCHESS: That's her problem.

ALICE: But Dinah's a cat, too, my cat, my dear little kittypuss. (*Another horrible crash off at right.*) And frankly, I'm wondering how I can get back home and see her right now.

DUCHESS: Stop wondering. If you were living backwards like me, you'd be home last Wednesday.

ALICE: But I'm not living backwards. I'm living forwards.

DUCHESS: The mess people make of their lives. But there's no time for tea. (*This is said as if ALICE had asked for tea.*)

ALICE: I didn't ask for tea.

DUCHESS: I expect I'll need white gloves and a fan.

ALICE: Oh, yes, that's right. I wonder, Your Highness, if you could tell me how to get to the Queen's croquet game.

DUCHESS: Certainly. I could tell you. But then I could choose not to tell you. You see my position? (*COOK enters, rushes to stove and bangs pots and pans mercilessly.*)

ALICE: Do you think the Queen will object to my company?

DUCHESS: Nothing to fret about even if she does. She'll only behead you.

ALICE: (*crossing to DUCHESS*) Only?

DUCHESS: Tell you what. We'll make a game of it! After she has you beheaded, I'll box her ears. There, now, won't that be fun?

ALICE: No.

DUCHESS: There are two things I can't abide, and the other one is rudeness.

ALICE: Forgive me, I don't wish to seem rude, nor do I wish to be beheaded.

DUCHESS (*leaping up*) Run! We've got to run! Quickly! Run! (*COOK, holding pots and pans, and DUCHESS, holding baby, run to apron. ALICE follows after being given a couple of pots to carry.*) Faster! Faster! No talking or singing or arithmetic! Run! (*As ALICE loses ground, COOK and DUCHESS stop and resume positions.*)

ALICE (*panting*): I don't believe we got anywhere.

DUCHESS: Of course not!

ALICE: We're in exactly the same place.

DUCHESS: Thank heavens!

ALICE: But so is the cat and he didn't run. He didn't even get up.

DUCHESS: (*leaping up and tossing baby to ALICE*) Here! I must ready myself for the Queen's croquet game! (*As DUCHESS runs out L, COOK searches wildly for something to hit her with. After DUCHESS has passed,*

COOK swings at the air with a pot, then throws it after her, picks up another pot and runs off L. CAT vanishes behind his curtain.)

ALICE: Well, I never! They might have said "good-bye." (*CAT reappears by opening the curtain in front of his shelf. COOK and DUCHESS run on and crowd around ALICE and say "Bye-bye" and then disappear off R, COOK chasing the DUCHESS.*)

ALICE: Whatever am I to do with this dear little baby? (*BABY cries.*) There, there! I certainly shan't treat you as roughly as the Duchess did. (*He cries horribly, then the cries change gradually to oinks.*) Now, now! Rock-a-bye-baby . . . what a strange looking child. (*She is unsnapping its dress.*) I do believe he somewhat resembles a . . . (*Oinks are quite discernible as such.*) . . .PIG! (*SEVEN runs on from L, attaches dog leash to PIG and pulls it off L as RABBIT runs on from R.*)

RABBIT: There you are! Don't bother to explain, there isn't time! Just make certain you fetch my white gloves and fan and meet me on the dot. And remember, Mary Ann, there is absolutely no time for a haircut! (*He exits L with BABY's dress.*)

ALICE: I think I need a little help.

CAT: (*opening his curtain*) Tell me what happened to the baby?

ALICE: (*crosses to CAT*) It turned into a pig.

CAT: I thought it would. Are you having a good time?

ALICE: I'm a little confused. Between smiling and frowning sort of.

CAT: What's a dog do when he's happy?

ALICE: Wags his tail.

CAT: And when he's angry

ALICE: He growls.

CAT: Now you take me. I wag my tail when I'm angry and growl when I'm happy.

ALICE: I call that purring.

CAT: Call it what you like. It's all part of the nice madness.

ALICE: I am having a good time. It's all so . . . unusual.

CAT: That's what you said you wanted, you know—something unusual to happen.

ALICE: Yes, I did. You heard that?

CAT: Are you going to play croquet with the Queen?

ALICE: I think so.

CAT: Good. I'll see you there. Or perhaps you'll see me there. You never know.

ALICE: It's all one and the same. That's the rule.

CAT: You're catching on.

ALICE: I'm trying.

CAT: By the way, did you say the baby changed into a fig?

ALICE: No, I said "pig."

CAT: I knew it was one or the other. (*Looking up.*) In that direction lives a Hatter and (*Looking down.*) in that direction lives a March Hare. Maybe one of them can help you. They're both mad, you know. (*He vanishes.*)

ALICE: Well, I expect the only thing to do now is . . .run! Faster and faster! (*As ALICE runs in place, the kitchen set is struck and the tea party is set up. Before the scene change is completed, ALICE stops running and speaks.*)

ALICE: Oh dear! I'm so tired, I've just got to sit down for a while. (*THIRTEEN places stool behind her; she sits.*)

ALL: (*they are lined up along tea party table. Each says one word*) And—how—long—pray—tell—do—you—intend—to—rest?

ALICE: Oh, I'd say about ten minutes. (*The ACTORS sigh and pose with folded arms to wait as the curtain falls.*)

End of Scene

9

Uncle Vanya

by

Anton Chekhov
An Adaptation by Loraine Cohen

Characters

Sonya

Production Notes

The setting for this play is the country estate of Serebrayakov in Russia in the late nineteen hundreds where several people have been living quietly, if not exactly, joyfully. Vanya has been managing the estate when Serebrayakov brings home his new wife, the exquisite Elena. Elena's presence acts as a catalyst, bringing to sharp focus the unhappiness and meaninglessness of all their lives. The frustrations seethe for awhile, then build into an explosion and when Elena leaves, everything settles back into the outward calm of before. Nobody takes any positive action to change their lives and this is the pathos of the play.

In the following scene, Sonya, the plain daughter of Serebrayakov is agonizing over her life and her unrequited love for Astrov, a friend of the family's, who is also her father's doctor. The Monologue has been put together with several shorter speeches of Sonya's throughout the play.

SONYA: He has consented to have supper with us and stay the night and he did let me serve him a bit of cheese from the sideboard. His soul and his heart are still hidden from me; but why do I just now feel so happy? And when I implored him not to drink any more, he didn't. I said to him that it was so unbecoming to him. I said, "You are refined, noble and have such a gentle voice. More than that," I said, "You are like nobody among the people I know, like nobody else—you are beautiful!" Was it the wrong moment for just that? But he did understand when I reminded him that he always said that people don't create but merely destroy what's given to them from above. Then why, why, must he destroy himself? He did understand because he began to talk about his work and his feeling of tenderness for the peasants. And he was so right about the intelligentsia. He said they tire one. They have shallow thoughts, shallow feelings. And those that are clever and more important, he said are hysterical, absorbed with analyzing themselves. They whine, they despise everything, they slander people cruelly and when they don't know what kind of a label to stick on someone's forehead, they say, "He's an odd one, odd!" And they think the Doctor's odd because he loves the woods, and because he doesn't eat meat. He's right, there is no longer any spontaneous, pure, free kinship to nature or to people . . .

Oh, he's so wise, so wise. And yet—yet he didn't understand when I told him about a younger sister. Oh how terrible it is that I am not pretty. I know I am not pretty, I know, I know. Last Sunday as we were leaving church, I heard them talking about me and one woman said: "She is kind, generous, but it's a pity she is not pretty." Not pretty. I have such a silly face. And here he is, gone, and I keep hearing his voice and his steps, and when I look at a dark window I see his face there. Oh, I'm so ashamed, I must seem so silly.

And he is clever. He can do anything, is able to do anything. He heals the sick and he plants woodlands—When he plants a little tree, he is already dreaming of the happiness of mankind. Such people are rare, one must love them. He drinks, he is sometimes rude, but what harm is there in that? A genius in Russia can't be as spotless as a saint. What a life he leads! Impassable mud on the roads, frost, blinding snow, enormous distances, people crude and wild, poverty all around, diseases. In such a setting it would be hard for anyone who works and struggles day after day to keep himself steady and sober at forty. And just now he's so sad because one of his patients died under chloroform.

Nobody listens to him. They find his work with the trees so monotonous. I've heard Elena say so. And yet he's already received a bronze medal and a diploma for his planting of new wood plots. He petitioned not to have the old ones destroyed. If they would only hear him out they would agree with him completely. He says that forests adorn the earth, that they teach a man to understand the beautiful and inspire him to lofty moods. Forests soften a severe climate. In countries where the climate is mild, you spend less effort in the struggle with nature, and so man there is gentler and tenderer; people are beautiful there, lively, easily excited, their speech is exquisite, their movements are graceful. Their sciences and art blossom, their philosophy is not gloomy, their relation to a woman is full of exquisite nobility . . . .

Oh-h-h, how I long to be pretty, and I know I am not. When a woman is not pretty they tell her, "You have beautiful eyes" or "You have beautiful hair." Oh, I have loved him now for six years, loved him more than my own mother; every minute I hear his voice, feel the touch of his hand; and I watch the door waiting: It always seems to me he will be coming in. He is here every day now, but he doesn't look at me, doesn't see me. It's such agony! I haven't any hope. I often come to him, start talking to him, look into his eyes. He doesn't see me. I have no more pride. Everyone knows I love him, even the servants know. And he—he never notices me.

These sad autumn roses. Winter will be here soon and they will all be gone. Perhaps then, Uncle Vanya and I can get back to work. All the hay is mowed, it rains everyday, everything is rotting, and Uncle Vanya and everyone here is occupying themselves with illusions. The farming has been neglected completely. I'm the only one that works and I have no strength left.

And in the long evenings, we can sit together and do our work, translating and copying papers. It's a long, long time now we haven't sat together at this table, Uncle Vanya and I. There seems to be no ink. And we must take care of all the bills too. Work will save us. We must live, we shall live. We'll live through a long, long line of days, endless evenings; we'll bear patiently the trials fate sends us; we'll work for others now and in our old age without every knowing any rest, and when our hour comes, we'll die humbly and there beside the coffin we'll say that we suffered, that we cried, that we felt bitter, and God will take pity on us, and you and I, Uncle, darling Uncle, shall see life bright, beautiful, fine, we shall be happy and will look back tenderly with a smile on these misfortunes we have now—and we shall rest. I have faith, I believe warmly, passionately . . . (Kneeling with Uncle Vanya's picture which she has taken off the desk)

We shall rest! We shall hear the angels, we shall see the whole sky all diamonds, we shall see how all earthly evil, all our sufferings, are drowned in the mercy that will fill the whole world. And our life will grow peaceful, tender, sweet as a caress. I believe, I do believe . . Poor, dear Uncle Vanya, in your life you haven't known what joy was; but *(through her tears)* wait, Uncle Vanya, wait . . . We shall rest . . . We shall rest . . . We shall rest.. . .

End of Scene

10

The Magic Wood
by
Ric Averill

Characters
Rebecca Carson
Charity Carson
Giles Carson
The Redcoat
The Owl
Robin Hood
Friar Tuck
Sheriff of Nottingham
Sister Merry Mirth

Production Notes

Cast of Characters

Rebecca Carson: A young girl, 10, who is lazy, tomboyish and bookish.

Charity Carson: Her Mother, soft and comforting, occasionally cajoling.

Giles Carson: Her Father, shy, caring nervous, but brave.

The Redcoat: A smooth, crude, and brash villain.

The Owl: A wise old bird.

Robin Hood: The aloof, noble and clever "king" of Sherwood Forest.

Friar Tuck: His cleric, a blustery, clumsy, gregarious man.

Sheriff of Nottingham: The slimy, evil, conniving arch enemy of Robin Hood.

Sister Merry Mirth: Friar Tuck's daffy sister, a nun, captive of the Sheriff.

Cast may be doubled as follows:

GILES/FRIAR TUCK

REDCOAT/SHERIFF

CHARITY/MERRY MIRTH/OWL

The original production was done with these doublings in mind and the reflections of these characters between the two worlds is intentional.

TIME: 1779 and 1191, a blustery October evening.

PLACE: A New England Village, The Magic Wood, Sherwood Forest and the Castle of the Sheriff of Nottingham.

SETTING: The play should be done on a unit set so that the action is never interrupted. The set can "wrap" around the audience in an "L" shape if the playing space allows. If this is done, the Stage Right side should represent 1779 New England and be done in browns, blues and greens. This playing area needs a small jail cell made of logs, with a barred window and a huge lock far Down Right. Center Right is an interior cut away of a cottage, dressed like a Puritan kitchen with a small loft bed and a broom closet. There is a table, plank seating on barrels and a fireplace with an iron kettle on it. Behind all is a forest which should become very dense at the junction of the "L". At this center juncture there is a strange tree with what appears to be two trunks. The trunks intertwine at about five feet high, forming an arch below them. Perched above the arch is an OWL, whose eyes can light up and who can become animated and speak. This is the center of "The Magic Wood." The Stage Left side should represent 1191 Sherwood Forest and Nottingham Castle and be done in silvers, blues, and greys, including the trees. The silver forest grows less dense and encompasses a clearing Center Left. The far Down Left side of the side features a wall and the cutaway of a castle tower. There is a tapestry hung near a huge cell up a set of stairs "in the tower" with barred windows and a huge lock.

• • • • • • • • • • • • • • • • • • •

REBECCA: You there! Stand aside! (*REBECCA sets down the book and candle and reads a moment more, then hops up and grabs the plank. She sets it between the two barrels, picks up a broomstick and holds it like a staff.*) I intend to cross first, tall stranger, so you'd best stand aside! (*As she talks, an eerie light creeps up on the Sherwood Forest set. ROBIN HOOD is discovered in the same position as REBECCA. He mimes what she is doing.)* Oh, so you thinks to cross first? Then it's my quarterstaff you'll be feeling against the side of your head! *(She starts to cross plank, does fight with imaginary "Little John", ROBIN mimes the same.)* Take that! You'll feel a sound drubbing before I'm through with you!

CHARITY: *(From offstage.)* Rebecca! Rebecca, is that floor scrubbed yet? What are you doing?

REBECCA: *(Looks off, as does ROBIN.)* Ignore the voice from yon distant castle. Back to our buffet *(There is more fighting.)* You are quite powerful, sirrah! Thou shouldst be one of my Merry Men. Whoa. . . . *(She slips, tumbles, as does ROBIN.)* Ooops! See, thou hast verily knocked me flat and given me a drubbing.

CHARITY: *(Enters.)* I'll give you a drubbing, young lady! I thought I told you to get this floor scrubbed. What is this mess?

REBECCA: *(She shrugs, ROBIN shrugs and walks off. Lights fade on Sherwood Forest.)* Sherwood Forest?

CHARITY: Sherwood Forest indeed? Books again? *(Picks up the book, "Robin Hood")* Robin Hood. Why don't you read a story that's of some use? A book where there is a heroine who spends time scrubbing floors — like Cinderella. Then you could play Cinderella and get the floors scrubbed at the same time.

REBECCA: Mother. You don't understand. Cinderella hardly has adventure. I like adventures so that's what I read.

CHARITY: Not when it's time to scrub the floor. Finish your chores and you may read a bit more before bedtime.

REBECCA: I don't want to. I'm at a really good part, Mother. Little John beats up Robin Hood and then Robin Hood gets him to be one of the Merry Men!

CHARITY: That's hardly the best way to make friends, Rebecca. Do as I say and scrub this floor!

REBECCA: Not now. I'll do it later.

CHARITY: Later is bedtime. Do your chores now!!!

REBECCA: You can't make me!

CHARITY: Why, if your Father were here . . .

REBECCA: Well, he's not! He never is!

CHARITY: You're right. So since he's not here I guess I'll have to make a worker out of you . . . *(She walks toward REBECCA, a shot rings out.)*

REBECCA: (*Running into her mother's arms.*) Mama!

CHARITY: There, there, it's all right, dear. It's all right. Hush, baby. This war is getting far too close.

REBECCA: If Father coming home?

CHARITY: Yes, dear. He'll be home soon, God willing.

REBECCA: Why do they have to fight, Mama? Why does Father have to be a Minuteman?

CHARITY: Sometimes I wish I could make better sense out of it, Rebecca. The King is unjust, taxes are high . . . But you should love it, dear. War is, after all, a great adventure.

REBECCA: Not when it's your Father they're shooting at.

CHARITY: I know, sweetheart. Now, hop up to your bed and see if you can get some sleep.

REBECCA: I wish father would come home soon. (*She falls asleep*)

CHARITY: (*Starts to scrub the floor.*) It isn't fair, you know, Giles. Whatever it is you fight for, it isn't fair to the children, you know . . . (*She hums lullaby and scrubs as lights dim down on her, up on the outside area. A shot rings out, footsteps are heard. GILES enters, looking about.*)

GILES: Whoa, Thomas, it's my place. I'll catch up with you at the Adams farm. (*GILES knocks on the door.*)

CHARITY: What? Who is it? Who comes calling so late?

GILES: Just a country lad, looking for the milkmaid I spied down by the kirk.

CHARITY: Giles, is it you? (*She flings open the door, gives him a big hug.*) Giles! Oh, Giles!

GILES: Hush, and calm down. The Redcoats are right behind us . . .

CHARITY: Rebecca. Your father's. . .

GILES: Don't wake the child, Charity, it'll be harder on her that I have to move on — and I must go quickly. The men await me up at the Adams' farm. The Redcoats occupy the village now. If any of us get caught as stragglers we'll be locked up there. Are you all right?

CHARITY: I sure could use a man around again . . .

GILES: I'll be back soon, I promise, if we push them back, we'll . . . (*A shot rings out. REBECCA slowly starts to wake up, looks around disoriented. THE REDCOAT enters at the same time, looking roughly around.*)

THE REDCOAT: I heard something over here, Peyton. Go on up the road, I'll look about for stragglers. *(He goes up toward door.)* Ho! Open up in there! *(He hits door with rifle butt. REBECCA wakes up.)*

CHARITY: Quickly, Giles, in the broom closet! *(GILES starts for the broom closet, gets in as REBECCA, rubbing her eyes, comes down from loft. REDCOAT bursts through door.)*

THE REDCOAT: All right, you won't open up, you got something to hide?

REBECCA: *(Simultaneously spotting her Father.)* Father?

CHARITY: Rebecca. Shhh. . . . .

THE REDCOAT: I ain't yer Father, little girl, but I'm glad to know he's here. Out of the way! *(Shoves CHARITY aside, approaches broom closet.)*

CHARITY: You get out of my house! Get out!

THE REDCOAT: Ye a rebel, too, lady? Off me! *(He swings his arm, knocks her over.)*

REBECCA: Father! Mother's hurt! Help!

GILES: *(Comes out of closet, grabs for the REDCOAT)* You blasted beast! I'll. . . .

THE REDCOAT: *(Holds him at gunpoint.)* What'll ye do, traitor? Go to town with me, if ye value life!

REBECCA: Let him go! *(She runs to kick the REDCOAT.)*

GILES: Rebecca, you stay back. See to your mother! Sir, if you've harmed her, you'll wish you were never born.

THE REDCOAT: Don't curse me, Yankee. I wish that already!

REBECCA: She's breathing. I think she's all right. Father?

GILES: Go into the woods, Rebecca! Go to the neighbors and tell them what's . . . *(REDCOAT hits GILES with the butt of his gun.)*

THE REDCOAT: Quiet, fool! *(Turns to girl, she backs away, afraid.)* You heard him, urchin. Get to the woods! Can't do a thing here. Go to the woods. But remember — it's a cold October night and the Magic Wood is haunted, little one, haunted by demons and wraiths. Get out!

REBECCA: Let my father go!! *(REDCOAT growls at her, she screams and runs out, disappears in forest. REDCOAT throws water at GILES who slowly come to.)*

THE REDCOAT: Hop to, rebel! It's off to jail. Ye want your daughter to

The Magic Wood 149

tell the others you've been caught, eh? And just who are ye anyway?

GILES: Not one of the King's Own, that's all I'll say, Redcoat.

THE REDCOAT: March! (*REDCOAT marches GILES out and toward the jail, Right. CHARITY, wakes up, shakes head, looks about and dashes out the door.*)

CHARITY: Giles! Rebecca!!! (*She disappears in forest. REBECCA wanders back on, looks about the woods fearfully.*)

REBECCA: Thomas. Psst. Grandfather Adams. Mrs. Wilson? Where are you? Father's been taken. (*As she whispers this, the woods seem to whisper back. Other actors provide VOICES.*)

VOICES: Father's been taken. Father's been taken.

REBECCA: What? Who's there.?

VOICES: What? What? Who's there? Who's there? Who? Who? Who . . .

REBECCA: Please, help, I . . .

OWL: (*Eyes lighting up.*) Who, who, who . . .

REBECCA: Oh, it's you, old Owl. I thought I heard voices.

OWL: Oh, you probably did.

REBECCA: What? You talk?

OWL: Only if you listen.

REBECCA: Is the forest haunted then?

OWL: Does it seem so?

REBECCA: A bit.

OWL: Ah — it is a bit, I'd say. But what is troubling you so?

REBECCA: My Father. He's been taken by Redcoats. I need help, but I can't seem to find my Father's friends. I can always find the path in the daytime.

OWL: Tis a strange night. What will you do about your father?

REBECCA: I'd like to set him free.

OWL: And how might that be done?

REBECCA: If I were Robin Hood, I'd just go challenge that Redcoat and fight for my Father. (*REBECCA tries to free her father, but the REDCOAT has him locked up and holds the keys. She is chased back to the forest and again meets the OWL.*)

[. . . ed. note: In the play, this action could be pantomimed . . .]

REBECCA: I wish Robin Hood were here right now.

OWL: Hmmm, and what would you do for him?

REBECCA: Do for him? What do you mean?

OWL: You would have him free your father. What would you do? What have you ever done to free anyone else?

REBECCA: What are you talking about?

OWL: Something about your human Golden Rule, I think. But don't bother about that. If you really want to find Robin Hood, simply walk under this tree. (*The tree begins to glow and change colors. REBECCA is spooked.*)

REBECCA: Under there?

OWL: Yes. What you seek is there, as well as what you need. But remember this — you can't come back until you are ready.

REBECCA: But . . .

OWL: Just think of it as an adventure.(*The OWL's eyes go out. The music builds, the glowing tree becomes even stranger.*)

REBECCA: An adventure. But Owl, Owl? What do you . . . an Adventure. (*She steps through the archway formed by the trunks and falls to the ground. There is strange music. She stands up as lights become silver, blue and grey on Sherwood Forest. She is awestruck.*) An adventure. (*REBECCA hears singing and hides as ROBIN HOOD and FRIAR TUCK enter singing roughly and exercising Macho Tricks.*)

REBECCA: (*Stepping out from behind a tree.*) Robin Hood. Friar Tuck. I'm so glad I found you!

ROBIN HOOD: (*Looks her over, then looks at TUCK. ROBIN uses some "high English" like thees and thous in moments of formality and passion. Otherwise, he speaks like a reasonably normal hero. TUCK also follows this convention.*) What, ho, Tuck! Dost thou know this little girl?

FRIAR TUCK: Don't think so, Robin.

REBECCA: No, No, you don't know me, but I know you.

ROBIN HOOD: Very strange.

FRIAR TUCK: (*Referring to her gingham dress.*) Why dost thou wear a tablecloth wrapped around you, girl?

REBECCA: No, it's my dress, you see. You have to help me save my father.

ROBIN HOOD: Ah, now we're getting somewhere. Your father knows us?

REBECCA: No, my Father's been captured by Redcoats, and he's a leader of the Minutemen and . . .

ROBIN HOOD: She's deranged, Tuck.

FRIAR TUCK: Now, listen, little chuck, there is a nunnery down the road. They'll feed you and pray for you and . . .

REBECCA: I don't want to go there. I want you to help me. Please, come with me. You'll see.

ROBIN HOOD: Begging your pardon, young lady, but as you insist upon knowing me, perhaps you also know that I am quite busy. Right now, the good Friar and I were on our way to relieve the Sheriff of Nottingham of a certain captive he has. So, if you don't mind . . .

REBECCA: Oh, I know all about that — fighting the Sheriff, robbing from the rich and giving to the poor . . .

ROBIN HOOD: I don't like to call it robbing, exactly.

FRIAR TUCK: We simply transfer wealth. Now if you would simply transfer yourself out of our way, we may proceed to assist my dear Sister Merry Mirth.

REBECCA: But you have to help me. I've come all the way from New England!

ROBIN HOOD: New England? New? England? She is deranged, Tuck.

FRIAR TUCK: Yes, it's certain, unless . . . (He whispers to ROBIN HOOD.)

ROBIN HOOD: Oh, yes, quite possible. Little girl.

REBECCA: Rebecca, my name's Rebecca.

ROBIN HOOD: Little Girl, you say you know all about us . . . and the Sheriff?

REBECCA: Oh, yes. The Sheriff lives in Nottingham — in a big castle — and he's always doing terrible things and he hates you because you're so clever and he doesn't want you to marry Maid Marian and . . .

ROBIN HOOD: Yes, Tuck, you must be right. The girl is a spy. Shall I pin her to yon tree with arrows?

REBECCA: I'm not a spy!

FRIAR TUCK: Robin, I hate to leave her out here. Let's tie her in a meal sack and catapult her over the castle walls. Much more merciful.

REBECCA: I'm not a spy. I'll prove it. You come with me into the Magic Wood and we'll go under the tree and you'll see how my Father is held captive by someone just as bad as the Sheriff. Please.

ROBIN HOOD: What a winning way she has, Tuck.

FRIAR TUCK: All right, little girl.

REBECCA: Rebecca.

FRIAR TUCK: We'll follow you into your Magic Wood.

ROBIN HOOD: *(Pulls dagger and leans down right next to her.)* But listen to me. If thou art a spy for the Sheriff a-leading us into a trap, thou wilt be very, very sorry for it. Lead on.

REBECCA: It's this way. See, the Owl's eyes light up and . . . The tree looks . . . *(Nothing is quite as strange as it should be. There is no lighting change and the OWL is stock still.)* . . . and you walk under this funny tree here and . . . and now you're in my time, which is later than your . . . *(They do, nothing happens.)* . . . I don't know why it didn't work.

SHERIFF OF NOTTINGHAM: *(Leaps out from behind a bush, sword drawn.)* Ah-ha! I thought I heard a screeching and leeching! Robber! You are mine now!

ROBIN HOOD: She was a spy! Tuck, take her and beat her! As for you, Nottingham, you're naked without a few dozen footmen! En Garde!

REBECCA: But I'm not a spy!

FRIAR TUCK: Quiet, little one. It's not polite to make noise when the masters duel. Just sit by me. *(They sit and watch. The fight goes back and forth briefly, neither getting the upper hand, then ROBIN HOOD suddenly knocks sword from SHERIFF's hand.)*

ROBIN HOOD: There! Thou art disarmed! Next time thou surprisest me, thou shouldst just go ahead and stab me in the back, like the little girl who led us to you.

SHERIFF OF NOTTINGHAM: Next time, I shall hang you from the tallest gallows!

ROBIN HOOD: *(Holding the SHERIFF at bay.)* Ha! Tuck, didst thou beat the little girl?

FRIAR TUCK: Uh, well, actually, I, uh, taught her a lesson, yes, I did. *(Looks at REBECCA, urging her to conspire with him.)* Didn't I?

REBECCA: I suppose.

ROBIN HOOD: Sheriff, I don't know what made you venture so far from your own castle walls. I'm surprised to see you so bold. Tuck, let's see if the good Sheriff can find his way back, without the use of this little spy. *(He grabs the SHERIFF's tunic and pulls it up over his head. TUCK ties it up. They turn him around three times and send him on his way.)* There!

SHERIFF OF NOTTINGHAM: You can't do this! I hate this. I hate you! When I get back, I'll show you no mercy! Aargh! *(Bumps into a tree and walks off.)*

ROBIN HOOD: Tuck, let's follow the dear Sheriff and see where he keeps your Sister Merry Mirth! Saving her is the day's true work! *(He exits.)*

FRIAR TUCK: I don't now who you are, little girl, or where you come from, but the Sheriff of Nottingham is evil company. You should find something better to do with your little life than to work for him. *(He exits.)*

REBECCA: But I don't work for him. I don't! I . . . I want my Father. Why did I come here? Why? *(She sits and starts to sob.)*

OWL: *(The OWL's eye's light up.)* I believe it had something to do with getting help.

REBECCA: Oh, you're a lot of help. Why couldn't I go through the tree to my own time?

OWL: It wasn't time. You're not ready.

REBECCA: I am too. You're not any help at all. And neither was Robin Hood. He wasn't at all what I expected.

OWL: I don't think you were what he expected either.

REBECCA: It's not my fault the sheriff happened to be there. Wait a minute, the sheriff. Maybe he'd help me save my father.

> [. . .In the play REBECCA returns to the castle and pleads with the SHERIFF to help her. He says that he will on the condition that she help him. Much to her surprise, this "help" includes scrubbing the Castle floor. While doing this chore, REBECCA finds the innocent SISTER MERRY MIRTH locked up in a cell. She returns to ROBIN HOOD and they devise a plan to trick the SHERIFF, retrieve the key to the cell and free MERRY MIRTH. This action could be pantomined . . . .]

REBECCA: We've done it! Robin Hood! Friar Tuck! We've done it! *(As SISTER MERRY MIRTH and REBECCA run out of Castle into woods!)*

SISTER MERRY MIRTH: You mean you did it, Rebecca. All I did was eat gruel and giggle.

ROBIN HOOD: What's this? You did do it. *(Coming out of woods with*

154   *The Magic Wood*

TUCK.)

FRIAR TUCK: Sister!! Sister Merry Mirth! Sister mine!

SISTER MERRY MIRTH: Oh, Friar Tuck, holy little brother! It's so good to see you.

FRIAR TUCK: You look lovely, my sweet. You must come join our band!

SISTER MERRY MIRTH: Oh, I will. Is the food good?

FRIAR TUCK: Indeed it is for I am the cook! Come, I'll fix you some roast mutton right away. Robin, Rebecca, will you join us?

ROBIN HOOD: *(Looking seriously at REBECCA.)* Not now, Tuck. I believe that I have another adventure in store. Rebecca's father is held prisoner .by the Redcoats.

FRIAR TUCK: Oh, yes, well, don't be long. Come, Sister, let's to camp. *(They exit arm in arm, laughing and talking.)*

REBECCA: You mean you really will help me?

ROBIN HOOD: Dost thou doubt my word? I told you that if you helped me, I'd help you. You have saved Tuck's sister. *(He kneels and bows to her.)* I am your vassal. We two shall not be parted until your father is freed of whatever imprisons him. Lead the way.

REBECCA: The last time I tried to go through the Magic Wood, I couldn't.

ROBIN HOOD: Thou didst not have me with thee.

REBECCA: But I did. See, here's the tree . . . . *(The OWL lights up.)* And the Owl, you see, the owl?

OWL: Who?

ROBIN HOOD: *(To OWL.)* You. She wants to know if I see you.

OWL: Do you?

ROBIN HOOD: Of course I do. Though I'm not used to talking to uncivilized creatures.

OWL: Nor I.

REBECCA: Oh, owl, we want to go back to my time! Robin Hood is going to help me save my father.

OWL: I suggest you go!

REBECCA: You mean it will work this time? The archway is ready for me?

OWL: Or you are ready for it. Now go — go through the Magic Wood. Your Mother is looking for you! (*Lights go out. Weird tree lights come up. REBECCA takes ROBIN's hand and they go through.*)

REBECCA: You see, Robin Hood. We're in my time now.

ROBIN HOOD: This is New England?

REBECCA: Yes, isn't it lovely? (*We hear gunshots and weird sounds, wind, storm.*)

ROBIN HOOD: Yes, lovely, though cold, I might add. Where is your father?

REBECCA: Just a little ways down this road, past my house . . . see? There! (*They approach her log cabin, ROBIN is impressed.*)

ROBIN HOOD: You live here?

REBECCA: Yes, with my Father and Mother. It's not a Castle, but it's really quite nice . . .

ROBIN HOOD: (*Peeks in, looks at book, picks it up.*) What is this? What strange language and these pictures . . . (*He drops the book, surprised by what he sees.*)

REBECCA: It's all right. That's you! That's a book about you, see?

ROBIN HOOD: Perhaps you are not deranged. Perhaps I am deranged! (*CHARITY pops out of the broom closet and smashes a frying pan over ROBIN's head. He slumps to the ground.*)

CHARITY: There! Take that! Don't you come bothering my girl again, Tory!

REBECCA: Oh, Mother! Look what you've done. You've buffeted Robin Hood! You've knocked him out. Mother, he's here to help us.

CHARITY: Rebecca! What are you talking about? Here, give me a hug!

REBECCA: (*As they hug.*) Mother. This is Robin Hood. Look, see the picture. (*ROBIN begins to stir.*)

CHARITY: He may think he's Robin Hood . . . (*Raises pan.*)

ROBIN HOOD: Listen, Lady, I'll think I'm whoever thou wants me to be, just don't hit me with the pan again.

REBECCA: Robin, are you all right?

ROBIN HOOD: If I'm Robin, which even I am beginning to doubt, I'm sure I haven't had so sound a drubbing since Little John knocked me off the log with his staff.

CHARITY: He talks like Robin Hood.

REBECCA: It doesn't matter what you think, Mother. He wants to help us save Father.

CHARITY: But where is Father? I've been looking all over for you!

REBECCA: He's in the jail in town. Are you all right, Robin? Can you fight now?

ROBIN HOOD: Not her! But perhaps your Redcoat. Let's go free that father of yours!!! *(They leave the cottage, make their way through the Forest as the key theme plays. They come to the jail and face the REDCOAT.)*

REBECCA: *(Steps forward first, MOTHER and ROBIN HOOD behind her.)* Stand and deliver!

ROBIN HOOD: *(To CHARITY.)* That's what I always say.

THE REDCOAT: What? I though I told ye to get lost in the Forest, Little Girl! Out of here!

GILES: Rebecca, is that you?

REBECCA: This time I have help, Redcoat. I've brought my Mother . . .

THE REDCOAT: Oh, I surrender right now.

REBECCA: And I've brought Robin Hood!

GILES: Charity, what's gotten into her?

ROBIN HOOD: *(Jumps forward.)* Adventure, dear sir! That's what's gotten into your daughter!

THE REDCOAT: That's cute. Ye're a pretty peacock of a solider.

GILES: Rebecca, have you gone quite daft? Who is this friend of yours in the strange clothes?

REBECCA: I haven't gone daft, Father! I've gone quite sane. We've come to rescue you, just as I rescued Sister Merry Mirth. You've got to do what you know is right — and when you do, there's others will help. You know that. That's why you fight the King!

GILES: I guess I do. But be careful, this Redcoat has a gun!

ROBIN HOOD: Enough talk! Action makes adventure! En Garde, Sirrah!! *(He draws his sword and slashes the air.)*

[ROBIN and the REDCOAT taunt each other and begin an elaborate swordfight. The REDCOAT suddenly bears down on ROBIN HOOD and slashes sword from his hand.]

REDCOAT: There the adventure is over!

REBECCA: *(She holds up the key that released SISTER MERRY MIRTH.)* Not so fast, Redcoat! I, uh, I have the key!

REDCOAT: *Key? (He turns and looks, ROBIN rolls and grabs his sword back.)* Nonsence! No one has the key, for there is a key for that key and a key for that!

ROBIN HOOD: What does it matter Redcoat, for you have me to face again now!

REDCOAT: Little girl! Ye'll have me to reckon with when I finish with this knave!

CHARITY: Is it really the key, dear?

REBECCA: Oh, I don't think so, it's just the key I used to save Sister Merry Mirth when I was . . . it's the key I got from the Owl . . . it's . . . . it's worth a try!

(ROBIN and The REDCOAT have been fighting low-key, so to speak, during this, so that when she gets ready to open the door, they have fought out of sight. The key opens the lock.) It works! Father, you're free! [. . . The family is reunited. ROBIN bows to the girl's clever and adventuresome spirit. He invites the very able REDCOAT to go back in time with him and become one of his Merry Men – Will Scarlett. REBECCA returns home with her family and picks up the book . . .]

And yet another worthy Yeoman joined his Merry Band! *(Lights dim down on tableau, she is reading her book and laughing.)*

End of Play

11

Scraps

by

Tagore J. McIntyre

Characters

Pete
Mary
Dillon
Tim
Benny Yellowfeather
Mr. Conway
John
Jimmy
Marlinda
Mr. Tillinig

Production Notes

Place: The playground of a school on the edge of an Indian reservation.

Characters:

Pete, a well-liked Anglo boy

Mary, an Indian girl; Pete's friend

Dillon, an Indian boy; Pete's friend

Tim, a quiet, thoughtful Indian boy

Benny Yellowfeather, an Indian boy with problems

Mr. Conway, the playground duty teacher

John, a disliked Indian boy

Jimmy, a slightly retarded Indian boy; John's brother

Marlinda, a tough Indian girl

Mr. Tillinig, an insensitive schoolteacher

Other students may be in background

Scraps requires a cast of ten (*six boys, two girls, two men*) with extras as desired.It is morning. PETE, MARY, and DILLON are playing basketball. TIM sits on the bleachers. BENNY sits nearby watching. DILLON makes a basket.

● ● ● ● ● ● ● ● ● ● ● ● ● ● ● ● ● ●

SCENE ONE

PETE: Hey, Tim! Want to play basketball?

TIM: No, thanks! I'm drawing a picture.

PETE: Okay! Hey, my ball.

JOHN: (*approaches the group*) Hey, you guys! I'll give you this Coke if you let me play.

MARY: Go away, Boney.

DILLON: Yeah, get outta here, Boney!

PETE (*secretively*) Mary, my watch says that there's only ten minutes until the bell rings. Get the Coke from John and he won't play very long anyway!

MARY: (*back with group*) All right, John, you can play for the Coke. (*Takes Coke from JOHN.*)

CONWAY: (*walks up holding a book which he has been reading while standing*) Boys, there is a teachers workshop still going on in the cafeteria. You'll still get to play for, maybe, another half hour, and I'll still be your duty teacher.

PETE: (*glances at MARY*) Okay, thanks, Mr. Conway. (*MR. CONWAY walks away reading his book.*)

JOHN: Well, let's play!

PETE: Oh, I don't want to. (*Group breaks up.*)

JOHN: (*looks confused, then angry; yells at his bigger brother who has been standing by himself*) Jimmy, Jimmy, come 'ere. Beat this guy up for me. He won't let me play. I gave him my Coke.

JIMMY: (*strolls over, hands in his pockets, grinning*) Why aren't you dummies lettin' my brother play?

DILLON: Hey, John, why do you always have to call your big retarded brother?

PETE: (*to JIMMY*) For one thing, we're not dummies, and for another, this guy's a pest. Just like your stupid friend, Benny Yellowfeather.

JIMMY: Yellowfeather's not my friend, joker. Give back the Coke John gave you.

PETE: Sure, why not? Who wants a Coke from a wino's kid? (*Throws Coke toward JOHN. It falls and squirts on the ground.*)

JIMMY: (*faces PETE, ready to fight*) Stupid! I'm gonna beat you up!

PETE: (*laughs*) Come on, man, I don't want to——.

JIMMY: Chicken!

DILLON: He's not a chicken. He doesn't look like you.

JIMMY: Shut up!

DILLON: You shut up!

JIMMY: Make me!

DILLON: Give me some wood and nails. I'll make you so this reservation will have two blockheads! (*Looks at others for laughter.*)

JIMMY: (*turns to fight DILLON*) I'll show you, Big Mouth!

DILLON: I wouldn't try anything, Wino. Here, I got something for you. (*Punches Jimmy in the stomach.*) It's called a Navajo punch! (*JIMMY starts to cry.*) Want me to do it some more, Retard? (*JIMMY runs offstage. JOHN runs after him, his head down.*)

BENNY: (*approaches from the bleachers*) Can I play with the ball?

MARY: Benny Yellowfeather, get out of here!

PETE: Come on, Benny, and let you kick it out in the trees? No way!

BENNY: (*whining*) I won't.

PETE: Listen. This ball belongs to Mr. Tillinig, right?

BENNY: (*looking bored*) Uh-huh.

PETE: And I'm the one who took it from the class to play with, right?

BENNY: Yeah.

PETE: If you lose it, who's gonna pay for it? You already have a record of losing balls!

BENNY: (*getting mad*) I won't lose it!

PETE: Okay. (*Bounces the ball to BENNY.*) But you know what will happen if I end up paying for Mr. Tillinig's basketball! Come on, Mary, Dillon. Let's go somewhere else. (*All three walk downstage and BENNY tries to shoot baskets upstage. MARY and DILLON look at PETE questioningly.*)

PETE: Well, if we play, John will want to play.

MARLINDA: (*rushes up to DILLON, her hands on her hips; looks mean*) Hey, Dillon, I heard that you said something bad about me! (*MARY and PETE step back.*)

DILLON: Hey, I didn't say any—(*MARLINDA socks him in the mouth.*)

MARLINDA: Jimmy told me! He don't lie! Now listen up. I just want you to remember that I don't want to hear nothin' from you. (*Stomps off.*)

DILLON: (*rubbing his mouth*) I don't either!

PETE: Where's my ball, Benny?!

BENNY: (*ignores what PETE said*) Hey, Rich Boy, you're getting fat, you know that? You might rip those new pants you got on!

DILLON: Who's getting fat?

BENNY: Ole Pete.

DILLON: Well, compared to you, he's—

PETE: Cool it, Dillon. I'll settle this. Benny, you want your face turned inside out? At least I don't have a washrag on like you do!

BENNY: Just kidding, P-Pete.

PETE: Now, where's the ball?

DILLON: (*grinning, looks at the others*) I suppose it went out to lunch!

BENNY: Oh, I forgot. I left it out by the basketball goal.

DILLON: (*points over to the goal*) Really? I don't see any ball! (*Runs over to the goal, searches area, comes back.*) No ball!

PETE: Now you've done it this time, Yellowfeather! You've lost another ball, and this time it's on me!

BENNY: (*shrugs*) You can't prove it to Tillinig! Ha! Ha! Ha! (*Benny tries to run off, but DILLON grabs him. TIM closes his drawing pad, gets up, walks toward the others.*)

MARY: (*to BENNY*) We'll get you for this!

DILLON: We're gonna beat you up if you don't tell Tillinig you're the one who lost the ball. And you have to pay for it!

BENNY: Not me! You checked it out.

PETE: *(shoves him)* Look, creep. You're the one in trouble whether you like it or not. Right, Dillon? *(Bell rings. MARY and DILLON nod in agreement as they hurry to the classroom.)*

SCENE TWO A dreary classroom.

TILLINIG: *(wringing hands, biting lips, but trying to smile)* Are all the balls in the ball box?

BENNY: No! Pete lost the basketball.

TILLINIG: *(surprised)* Peter, did you lose the basketball?

PETE: No, Mr. Tillinig, Benny did!

TILLINIG: Now. Wait just a minute. Who lost the ball, Ben?

BENNY: Pete. He took it out.

TILLINIG: Who lost the ball, Peter?

PETE: *(rolling his eyes)* Benny.

TILLINIG: Come here, boys. You will both get swats.

DILLON: Wait, Mr. Tillinig! It's Benny's fault! I saw the whole thing!

TILLINIG: Now, Dillon, tell us what happened.

DILLON: Well, you see, Benny wanted to play with the basketball that Pete took outside. So Pete let him. Then Benny lost the ball.

TILLINIG: Oh, I see. Ben, come here. Now you're going to tell the class the truth, right? *(BENNY shrugs.)* Did you do what Dillon said?

BENNY: No.

TILLINIG: Okay. Are there any other witnesses besides Dillon?

MARY: I saw it too. Benny is lying!

TILLINIG: Okay, Ben. Did you do it?

BENNY: *(lowers his head and smiles)* Yes.

TILLINIG: Whoa! Now, you just said that you didn't do it. Now, did you do it or not?

BENNY: Yeah, I did it!

TILLINIG: Okay, come here, Peter. *(PETE walks up.)* Now, Ben, say you're sorry!

BENNY: *(mutters)* Sorry. *(Class smirks and giggles.)*

TILLINIG: *(looks at BENNY)* Well, let's see. That'll be sixteen dollars and ninety-eight cents for the basketball.

PETE: *(walks back to his desk, next to Dillon's)* Thanks for the backup. That was a close one!

DILLON: Look at Benny. Wonder what he's gonna say now!

BENNY: *(waving his arm)* Mr. Tillinig, you know what Pete did? He smashed John's Coke all over the ground!

TILLINIG: John should know better than to bring a Coke to school.

BENNY: But—but—

TILLINIG: No buts! Peter is not in trouble. Now, we're going to have art. Tim, get the drawings that we drew last week out of the cabinet.

TIM: Okay.

TILLINIG: Okay, here is some tape. Put your pictures on the wall. *(Everyone does. Tim's picture looks like this: Sun is shining behind some mountains; silhouette of two boys fighting. TILLINIG points at Benny's picture.)* Who's that? Fat Albert?

BENNY: *(angrily)* No!

TILLINIG: Well, I don't know! I'm not supposed to, am I?

TIM: I like the colors in your picture a lot, Benny.

BENNY: *(turns around, startled)* You do?

TIM: What's that in her hand?

BENNY: It's a board.

TIM: What is she going to do with the board?

BENNY: *(makes a face)* What does anybody do with a board? *(Walks away.)*

TILLINIG: Okay, put the art stuff away. *(Everyone does.)* Okay, take out your math books, please. *(JOHN takes out a little car and starts to play with it; the others take out their math book. TILLINIG stares at JOHN)* Take out your math books, please! *(JOHN doesn't hear him and keeps on playing. TILLINIG grabs the car and throws it away.)* You act as if you're still in kindergarten!

JOHN: Hey, that was my brother Ralph's car! He'll beat me up if he thinks I lost it!

DILLON: Well, then, you can tell your brother that you owe him a new car, Monkey! (*Class laughs; DILLON looks around, happy. JOHN starts to cry.*) I said Monkey, not Crybaby! (*Class laughs again.*)

TILLINIG: Enough is enough. (*Frowning.*) Okay, John, get out your math book. Page two forty-six. Benny! Paper costs a lot of money. Stop wasting it. That's three pages you've wadded up. (*JOHN passes a note to TIM. PETE sees it and grabs it.*)

PETE: Mr. Tillinig. John just passed this note.

TILLINIG: Let's see. (*Opens it; reads it silently.*) Ben, come here and read this to the class.

BENNY: (*scared*) "Tim, I hate Mr. Tillinig. Do you? Yes. No." (*Class is silent; some mouths drop open.*)

TILLINIG: (*sarcastically to BENNY*) Well, this is a fine work of art, John! Tim, what is your answer?

TIM: (*speaks calmly*) You know the answer is no. I would have told you myself if I had got the note.

TILLINIG: Okay, for writing the note, John, you don't have to work anymore. (*JOHN looks at TILLINIG in awe.*) Instead, you can go to the principal's office with a note that says for you to get three swats and for you to sit in the office. (*Writes the note.*) Well, you'd better be on your way. (*JOHN leaves the room.*) Class, do your math.

SCENE THREE   Classroom, after math.

TILLINIG: Close your math books. You may have free time now.

PETE: Hey, Tim, let's play checkers.

TIM: All right. (*BENNY hears that PETE wants the checkers, and runs to the shelf and gets the game.*)

PETE: (*grits his teeth*) Tim and I want to play checkers! Could we play with them?

BENNY: Shut up! I got the checkers first!

TIM: Well, Pete, do you want to draw?

PETE: *(glares at BENNY)* Yeah, I guess so. *(TIM gets paper and hands some to PETE.)*

TIM: Here's some paper.

PETE: Thanks. *(There is a knock on the door. TILLINIG answers it.)*

CONWAY: It's time for Jimmy to come to special ed.

TILLINIG: *(chuckles mockingly)* Jimmy. It's time for special ed! *(Most of the class laughs. JIMMY gets up, his head down, and walks out the door.)*

TIM: I'm going to draw Batman fighting the Penguin. *(Everyone else is doing something, but BENNY is standing up holding the checkerboard. TILLINIG is grading the math papers.)*

MARLINDA: *(to BENNY)* Hey, clown, who do you think you are—the big checker sheriff of the class?

TILLINIG: *(holds up a paper)* Well, Ben, you've done it again.

BENNY: What?

TILLINIG: You should know. You've done it a hundred times. How did you ever get in this grade anyway?

DILLON: *(to MARY)*: Yeah, I wonder how he got in here myself.

MARY: Me too.

TIM: *(shows PETE his picture)* Finished.

PETE: That's a great picture!

BENNY: *(walks over)* That's a dumb picture! *(Bell rings.)*

TILLINIG: *(looks happy)* Time for recess!

(All go outside except TILLINIG.)

SCENE FOUR   Playground, Kids are playing.

PETE: *(walking)* Tim, that was really stupid of Benny to say that. He's dumb!

TIM: Yeah, maybe. But I think he was just mad about what happened today. He's usually—

PETE: Why do people act dumb like that?

TIM: When I act dumb, it's usually after my mom and dad had a fight.

PETE: You're not dumb. Haven't you noticed the way he acts? First he lies. Then he tells the truth. I guess you're going to say his parents do the same thing.

TIM: I wasn't going to say that. I don't know why anybody does anything. *(JOHN comes out of the principal's office. BENNY goes up to him.)*

BENNY: How many swats did you get?

JOHN: Shut up! You don't have to tell the whole playground, do you?

BENNY: Hey, I didn't— Oh, go flush your head down the toilet! *(Starts to walk away.)*

JOHN: If I did that, my head would look like yours! *(Hurries after BENNY.)* Who do you think you are, the president? I saw your dad hanging around the bar last night.

BENNY: What were you doing there, waiting for your mom?

JOHN: *(yelling)* Well, you look like a monkey! If a monkey came to your house, your mom would think it was you. If you even have a mom!

TIM: *(looks really upset)* I'm going back to the room, Pete. See you later.

BENNY: *(in John's face),* Shut up! Your mom is so fat she looks like Porky Pig! She's always stuffing her mouth! No wonder you're just a bag of bones! Your mother eats all your food! *(JOHN and BENNY start fighting; a crowd gathers around them.)*

SCENE FIVE   Classroom.

(TIM and TILLINIG are seated at their desks.)

TILLINIG: Why don't you want to play outside?

TIM: *(drawing)* 'Cause there's a fight.

PETE: *(rushes in)* They got some more guys in the fight!

TILLINIG: I'd better check this out. You guys have so many problems. *(Looks annoyed.)* Where is the duty teacher? Probably out reading a book!

PETE: *(looks undecided about staying or going, then walks over to TIM)* What are you drawing?

TIM: Just garbage.

PETE: Garbage? Looks like people fighting.

TIM: Well, that is garbage! Don't you see how much garbage is in people's lives? No, you wouldn't. You're just— Sometimes I feel like punching someone. But I won't. My people weren't like that. But they changed when you treated them like scraps!

PETE: Hey, why are you getting so mad? I didn't do nothing.

TIM: You say you didn't.

PETE: Well, I'm going to go see how the fight's going. (*Leaves the room.*)

(*BENNY marches into the room alone; starts writing all over the blackboard, nasty things, a picture showing a noose around someone's neck.*)

TIM: (*softly*) You really hurt bad, don't you.

BENNY: (*turns around as if he were going to fight TIM, but he starts crying and shouts*) I hate everybody! My mom and dad got divorced. My mom hits me every time I go home! She yells at me. Everybody here is— I do everything wrong— (*Breaks down.*) Nobody cares!

TILLINIG: (*enters the room; looks angry*) Benny Yellowfeather! Get out here! You are going with me to the principal's office. Right now! (*BENNY gets up, squints, and stares at TILLINIG; he saunters to the door and then rushes out. TIM stares at the chalkboard and what BENNY wrote and drew; his mouth drops open and then he rushes out the door. He does not see JOHN approaching. JOHN stares at TIM who is chasing BENNY. TILLINIG stands looking confused; he stares at chalkboard, appears to be thinking about it.*)

SCENE SIX   Outdoors.

(*TIM chases BENNY.*)

TIM: Wait! (*BENNY doesn't stop, so TIM runs up and grabs him. They both fall to the ground and wrestle.*)

BENNY: Go away! You're just like everybody else! No one's my friend!

TIM: Benny, I'm your friend!

TILLINIG: (*runs up and, grabbing their shirts, pulls them apart*) I'm sick of you young punks fighting all the time! I don't know what your problem is, but you're going to the principal's office right now!

TIM: Mr. Tillinig, you don't understand—

TILLINIG: I understand more than you do! I've been here thirty years! I was here when the parking lot was a playground, and I saw the gymnasium being built too. You can't tell me what's going on! (*They* *walk to the principal's office at the side of the stage; they go inside.)*

JOHN: *(rushes up to PETE)* Pete, you know what? Tim and Benny just got sent to the principal's office by Mr. Tillinig! He said they were going to get swats! Hey, Jimmy, Tim and Benny are in the principal's office to get swats! *(Kids crowd around office, waiting. TIM and BENNY walk out.)*

BENNY: *(softly to TIM)* Y-you shouldn't have got a swat. You didn't deserve it. *(TIM smiles at BENNY and lowers his head. BENNY looks around and kicks a stone.)* Thanks.

(TIM and BENNY slowly walk away.)

End of Play

Winnie-in-the Citie

A New Pooh Adventure

by

Migdalia Cruz

Characters

Winnie-the-Pooh
Piglet
Rabbit
Eeyore
Owl
Tigger
Kanga
Roo
Christoper Robin
Ricardo Rat
Rolando Roach
Rita Roach
Gates Gator
Felicia Feline
Mugs the Pug
Tina Robinson

Production Notes

TIME: The present.

PLACE: A Forest far from a City, and A City far from the Forest.

Characters

THE FOREST:

WINNIE-THE-POOH—A bear of very little brain, who is still very smart. A warm heart, a good soul. He likes to snack on honey and condensed milk every chance He gets.

PIGLET—His best buddy. A little pig with a lot of bravado and no courage—until it really matters.

RABBIT—A very clever rabbit who's good at getting out of scrapes but loses his patience easily.

EEYORE—An existential donkey, who expects the worse but is happy to be included in the best.

OWL—An animal noted for his wisdom—but he's not as smart as He pretends to be, He just uses a lot of big words. Good at making signs.

TIGGER—A bouncing tiger who is very friendly but doesn't know his own strength. Only eats malt powder.

KANGA—A nurturing Kangaroo mom. Sensible, loving, mature.

ROO—KANGA'S baby. Curious and fun-loving. Knows how to swim. Sleeps through the whole adventure.

CHRISTOPHER ROBIN—A little boy with a bad haircut. But he loves his animals . . .

THE CITY:

RICARDO RAT—A rodent who's tired of people running from him. Tough, but with a good heart.

ROLANDO ROACH—An insect with a past. Fast-moving, but slow-thinking.

RITA ROACH—ROLAND's sister. Has a crush on RICARDO. Very smart, but acts dumb.

GATES GATOR—An albino alligator that has survived a flushing, to flourish in the sewers of the City.

FELICIA FELINE—An alley cat with attitude and style.

MUGS THE PUG—A pug-faced street dog. Lives on scraps. Everybody thinks he's scary, but he's really very gentle.

TINA ROBINSON—A tough but sweet little girl with a great haircut, but no friends. Always wanted to go to the country, but since she's broken her leg, her friends decide to bring the country to her.

SCENE ONE

In the Forest. POOH and PIGLET are making a trap for Heffalumps.

WINNIE-the-POOH: This is a perfect trap, Piglet. Finally, we'll get to see the very fierce Heffalumps up close! Aren't you positively positive, excitementwise?!

PIGLET: Very fierce, you say? I—I thought it was only semi-fierce...

POOH: Well, I don't know for sure for I am only a bear of very little brain, but I seem to recall Owl saying that the Heffalump was most definitely fierce.

PIGLET: Oh...Well, you know, I just remembered something I forgot. I best go home and see to it immediately.

POOH: I'll go with you. Maybe we can stop by Rabbit's house and see if he has any tea for us? Rabbit is so good about having things to eat.

PIGLET: But who will watch the trap?

POOH: The trap will watch itself, I think. No one ever bothers a trap except the one you want trapped in it. Let's go. (*POOH takes PIGLET's arm and THEY skip off towards RABBIT's house. Suddenly, RICARDO and ROLANDO step in front of them blocking their path. POOH and PIGLET have never seen such animals, so THEY turn and run in fright. But are again blocked by RICARDO and ROLANDO.*)

RICARDO: Don't be in such a hurry, my fine furry fellows. Is this how you forest folk treat visitors?

ROLANDO: Yeah. Don't youse have a Welcome Wagon, or somethin'?

PIGLET: Oh, my goodness! The heffalumps are here and they are not in the trap! What should we do, Pooh?

POOH: Let me think...They don't seem that fierce, really. Maybe a song. Animals are always soothed by the sound of a good song...(*HE sings.*)What ho! What hey! What a very perfect day! To take a walk—or swing on trees—or talk to strangers just like these!

ROLANDO: I din't know youse types was into rapping. Cool!

RICARDO: Yep. This is the one alright! (*HE opens a burlap sack.*) Get in, bear.

POOH: Yea! An adventure! Come on, Piglet.

PIGLET: No-no thanks. Uhm, I'll just stay here in the forest. The boring old forest. I don't deserve such adventure—

ROLANDO: Get in, pig. Or else.

RICARDO: He's not the one she wants, but he may as come along for the ride. (*RICARDO and ROLANDO laugh sinisterly. POOH laughs too.*)

POOH: Come on, Piglet. This is going to be fun!

ROLANDO: (*Picks up PIGLET and places him in the sack.*) In you go, buddy.

RICARDO: Time to high-tail it, Rolando. Back to the citee, where the lady rats are prettie.

ROLANDO: And where men are men and bears are (*Searching for a rhyme*) pens? No, bears are fens? Ricardo, I can't think of no rhyme.

RICARDO: That's because you are a roach. Come on!

ROLANDO: (*Under his breath*) What does being a roach have to do with anything? I like being a roach . . . (*ROLANDO and RICARDO laugh as THEY exit. EEYORE and RABBIT enter, having witnessed the scene from far away.*)

RABBIT: Oh, dear! Oh, dear! They've kidnapped our friend.

EEYORE: Friends. I mean, they got Piglet too didn't they?

RABBIT: What do you think they want with them? I mean, if I was going to kidnap someone, I'd pick someone elegant, intelligent, handsome...

EEYORE: I guess they just couldn't find me and settled for them...What should we do?

RABBIT: Find Christopher Robin! He'll know what to do. (*THEY cross to CHRISTOPHER ROBIN's door. OWL is putting a sign up on the door that reads "GON TWO WOL'S HOWS BIG SOREE BAK SON."*)

RABBIT: Owl! We're so glad to see you! Have you seen Christopher Robin? There's a terrible emergency! Pooh and Piglet have been stolen!

EEYORE: Yes. They meant to take me, I think. But my luck being what it is, well, they got those two instead. Oh, dear. What a day this is turning out to be.

OWL: Can't you two read? He's at my house. We're having a soirée.

RABBIT: What's that?

EEYORE: Are there refreshments?

OWL: Yes, of course. What else would there be at a soirée?? (*THEY cross to OWL's house, in the crook of a tree.*)

CHRISTOPHER ROBIN: *(Appearing at OWL's front door)* Hallo! Here for the party?

RABBIT: Party?! Well, why didn't he just say so? Owl, you are very frustrating sometimes, always using unnecessary words. Soirée indeed!!

EEYORE: We bring bad tidings. Two of our own are gone. Stolen by animals we've never seen in this forest before. It is a definite emergency. At least, I think so, not that you all ever seem to care what I think, but—

RABBIT: They've taken Pooh and Piglet, to where we do not know.

KANGA: *(Sticking her head out of OWL's door)* Taken them! Oh, dear! We must do something. Oh, Roo! Roo, dear! Oh, thank goodness he's still alseep. If someone took my Roo I would—*(SHE begins to cry.)*

CHRISTOPHER ROBIN: There, there, Kanga. Roo is safe in your pouch. No need to fret about him. But we must have a plan!

OWL, RABBIT & EEYORE: *(In unison)* Yes!!

RABBIT: But what? We don't know where they went...or why.

OWL: This is most perplexing. Perhaps I had best interject or intercede or inter-something. I'm best at that.

EEYORE: Perhaps we should all have a sandwich and a think. I'm feeling rather weak.

OWL: Can't waste all that food. Pooh would understand. It's only civilized really.

CHRISTOPHER ROBIN: I wonder what Pooh is doing right now...

TIGGER: *(Rushing in and bouncing on EEYORE making him fall over)* What did Tigger miss? Got any Malt extract?

EEYORE: It's is indeed a very miserable day. Didn't you see me standing here, Tigger?

TIGGER: *(Bouncing on him again)* You my friend. I always bounce my friends, Eeyore.

EEYORE: Yes. The mixed blessing of friendship.

(Lights cross to a warehouse in the City, the home of RICARDO and ROLANDO.)

SCENE TWO

In the City. POOH and PIGLET are trying on some hip-hopish city clothes with ROLANDO and RICARDO.

ROLANDO: These guys are never gonna pass. They're just too . . . nice.

RICARDO: They gotta pass. We gotta get 'em to, Miss Tina. She won't feel better until we do.

ROLANDO: You really love her, huh?

RICARDO: She was my friend when nobody else would be. Do you understand friendship, Rolando? Well, that's a foolish question. I mean, can a roach understand love like a rat can? I am ponderous of such things, my friend.

ROLANDO: Yeah, of course, uhm, it's like a big cheeseburger somebody fergot to chow and throws it out by mistake, and uhm, it tastes really good when you find it all fresh like that!

RICARDO: That's almost right. (*To POOH and PIGLET who are trying on outrageous hip-hop outfits.*) How you doing there, animals of the "P" persuasion.

POOH: I like these new whatchamacallits!

RICARDO: Clothes. We call them clothes.

PIGLET: I don't like mine. They hang down all funny.

ROLANDO: That's how they're supposed to be, piggy.

PIGLET: (*With all the dignity HE can muster*) That's Piglet, Mr. Heffalump.

RICARDO: What's all this heffalumpy-stuff? I'm a rat. He's a roach. Get over it.

ROLANDO: Yeah. Get over it. (*RICARDO shoots him a disapproving look.*) I mean, do what he says.

RICARDO: Put on your hats and let's go.

POOH: Where is it we are going, if may be so bold to ask?

PIGLET: Yes, and I ask even more boldly. Where??

RICARDO: You guys talk funny. Guess that's what happens after all those years in the forest.

ROLANDO: Spooky.

RICARDO: I kinda like it.

ROLANDO: (*In a small voice*) Yeah, well me too.

POOH: Why do we have to wear these—glows. Not that I'm complaining. I love a good game. But I'm just a curious bear.

RICARDO: We gotta bring you past some tough guys. They'd tear you apart if I let 'em. But don't worry. Just stick by us. It's a big city, and it's easy for a guy to get lost—if you know what I mean.

POOH: Yes, absolutely!

PIGLET: *(In a whisper to POOH)* What do they mean?

POOH: I have no idea.

PIGLET: I'm terrified!

POOH: I'm not! *(HE sings.)* I love the Citie, where heffalumps rule. I love the Citie, it's like going to school!

PIGLET: Even school would be better than this.

POOH: Don't be such a piglet. Adventure is good for you. Christopher Robin taught me that—Oh . . . I miss him.

ROLANDO: You got friends? Ricardo, this guy's got friends. What if they come lookin' for him?

RICARDO: They won't come. They don't know where to look.

POOH: What's the address here, Mr. Heffa—Mr. Rat?

RICARDO: Call me Ricardo. Mr. Rat is my father.

POOH: Oh . . . So what is the address?

ROLANDO: 1625 Anywhere Street.

POOH: What an exciting address!

PIGLET: I think they're not really telling the truth, Pooh. We're gonna be here forever! *(Beginning to sniffle)* I want to go home.

POOH: Don't worry, Piglet. I have a plan.

ROLANDO: What are you twose whispering about?

PIGLET: Nothing, Mr. Heffe—

ROLANDO: That's Rolando to you.

RICARDO: And to everybody else too—that is your name. Stop joking around. We're outta here.

POOH: What?

ROLANDO: That means we're going.

POOH and PIGLET: *(Together)* Ohhh . . . *(THEY exit. Lights cross to OWL's soirée. Everyone is eating and thinking.)*

SCENE THREE

In the forest. At OWL'S soirée. KANGA sniffles. OWL is flipping through big books. RABBIT sits thinking hard. CHRISTOPHER ROBIN stands thinking hard. EEYORE eats.

EEYORE: That was delightful.

KANGA: How can you eat at a time like this?

EEYORE: It's after two. A perfectly fine time for a snack—

CHRISTOPHER ROBIN: She means how can you eat when our dearest friends are who knows where doing who knows what.

EEYORE: Oh. *(Pause)* Good point. But I always think better on a full stomach. Doesn't everyone? *(The OTHERS nod NO.)* Oh.

RABBIT: If only we could find some tracks. Trail them. Hunt them down. Get on our horses and—

OWL: Aren't you forgetting something? We're animals not cowboys.

RABBIT: Oh. Right. Well. We have to think of something.

OWL: Do you remember what they looked like?

RABBIT: Of course.

OWL: Then we can make corposite sketches of the criminals and that, yes, that, is our first step in apprehending the porkertrators.

RABBIT: You mean the thieves, right?

OWL: Yes, of course. Your vocabulary is really growing nicely, Rabbit.

RABBIT: Who will do the drawing?

KANGA: Christopher Robin. He writes the best.

EEYORE: I happened to get an "A" in art. But no one bothers to ask me, do they?? What else could I expect from such a bunch of forestdwellers.

TIGGER: You draw Tigger? I bounce for you.

EEYORE: *(As TIGGER bounces him onto the ground again.)* NO!!! Why me? Why Oh why me?

OWL: You must help in the description, Eeyore. You're invaluable.

EEYORE: Hhumph! That's what I thought. There was one with a really long, meaty-looking tail and whiskers. And the other one had six legs and antennas.

RABBIT: The tailish one was dark gray. And the six-legged one was a shiny brown color—like my cousin, Small, the beetle, but bigger.

CHRISTOPHER ROBIN: (*Getting his pencil and paper ready*) Alright! Say that again—but slower. (*As EEYORE begins again, CHRISTOPHER draws.*)

EEYORE: One . . . had . . . a . . . really . . . long . . . meaty–tail . . . (*Lights cross to the City.*)

SCENE FOUR

In the City. GATES GATOR, FELICIA FELINE, and MUGS the PUG, sit on garbage cans waiting for RICARDO and ROLANDO. FELICIA and MUGS play a game of bottlecaps to pass the time.

GATES: Where are those guys?

FELICIA: Come play with us, Gates. You never want to play bottlecaps anymore. Ping! Ooh! I won!! Give me a kiss, Mugs.

MUGS: Yuck! The Mugs kisses no cats. You got that?

FELICIA: Oh, c'mon, Mugs. You know you can't resist me. (SHE purrs.) How about that, Mugsy-Pugsy??

MUGS: Stop it, Felicia. I'm concentrating.

FELICIA: Why? You lost already.

MUGS: Stragedy. For the next game. (*The sound of footsteps.*) Here comes somebody. Look fierce! (*GATES, FELICIA & MUGS try to look their meanest. POOH sees them first.*)

POOH: Oh, fun! A face-making contest! Didn't I tell you this was going to fabudabulous, Piglet!?

PIGLET: Those are the three scariest things I've ever seen. What are they??

RICARDO: Those are my homies. My brothers. My best mates.

PIGLET: Let's run for it, Pooh. They might not notice—

ROLANDO: Stay right there, piplet.

PIGLET: I won't even bother to correct you, since I know you are just trying to taunt me. And listen, my six-legged friend, it will simply not work.

POOH: Piglet! You spoke up for once. I'm so proud.

PIGLET: You can only push a pig so far.

GATES: Who are these guys? Dinner?? (HE laughs at his own joke.) No. But seriously, y'all, who are they?

RICARDO: New guys on the block. It's okay. They're small, but cool. I'm bringing them over to see Tina.

GATES: What does she want with those two?

RICARDO: I don't know. I mean, I wish she just wanted, I mean...never mind.

MUGS: Can I take a bite outta one?

RICARDO: Chill out. Down, boy.

FELICIA: My hero! You never say that to me.

MUGS: Down, Felicia. You're giving me a rash. (HE scratches emphatically.)

GATES: You're changing, Ricardo. Used to be just you and me, chilling in the sewers. Climbing up people's toilets for fun. What happened?

RICARDO: Can't be a gangster forever. I got responsibilities now.

ROLANDO & MUGS: (With exasperation) Women.

FELICIA: I think it's cute. Tina's a lucky girl.

POOH: (Going over to GATES and poking him) Excuse me, Mr. Uhm, whatever you are, but what are you?

GATES: Funny you should ask. (HE raps.)

Say hey! Say, Hey

I'm Gates the gator from Bayou Larue.

Say ho! Say hey!

I was brought up North to be with you.

Say hey! Say ho!

A simple-minded tourist flushed me down the loo.

Now I'm a bad and beautiful gator of the streets.

Watch your back and mind your feet.

Say hey! Say ho!

Say hey! Say ho! (POOH joins in on the last Say Heys.)

POOH & GATES: Say hey! Say ho! I'm/He's Gates the gator from Bayou LaRue. Say ho! Say hey! I/He was brought up North to be with you. Hey! Hey!

GATES: (*Offering POOH a scaly hand*) You're okay, bear.

POOH: So are you! Call me Pooh.

PIGLET: Don't be so nice to them. They'll eat us for sure.

POOH: Silly, piglet. Chill out. (*POOH giggles. The OTHERS laugh, except for PIGLET.*)

PIGLET: You really are a bear of very little brain.

GATES: Hey! Don't be like that with my friend or you gonna answer to me.

POOH: I like the City!

FELICIA: Where are you from?

POOH: The forest. We have trees and rivers and bridges over the river and sticks to play with and flowers and all sorts of things.

FELICIA: Ooh...sounds boring. No dance bands? No scraps outside expensive restaurants? I could never live in such a place.

MUGS: Sticks, huh? I love sticks. And rivers to run by and wet your paws in...Jees! Sounds like Heaven.

FELICIA: You're just being contrary. (*RITA ROACH enters in a spectacular new outfit.*)

ROLANDO: Wow, Sis. You look dressed to kill.

RICARDO: Not such a great thing for a roach! (*HE laughs at his own joke.*) Only teasing, Rita. You look delicious.

RITA: You think so, Ricardo? I chose this particular blue because of the color of your fur in the moonlight.

GATES: Rita's got it bad and that ain't good! (*THEY all laugh except for PIGLET.*)

PIGLET: Pooh, get a hold of yourself please.

RITA: I brought you your favorite meal. Leftover Chinese. (*SHE holds it out to him, HE grabs for it, SHE pulls it away.*) Not so fast. First a smoochie. (*SHE puckers her lips, POOH kisses her.*) Ooh, Ricardo. You scamp! (*SHE screams when SHE realizes it was POOH kissing her instead.*) Aaaghh! A bear! You've humiliated me for the last time, Ricardo! I mean business. (*RITA stomps off in a huff. The OTHERS laugh.*)

RICARDO: You're really growing on me, Poohchie.

POOH: Oh, thank you. You are great, uhm, homies, too. (*GATES teaches POOH the secret city animal handshake.*)

GATES: Cool. This guy is definitely one of us. Put out your paw. (*POOH does so. GATES manipulates it into the secret handshake.*) Memorize that. It could save your hide.

POOH: I will, Mr. Gates.

PIGLET: Shame on you, Pooh.

GATES: What is this pig's problem?

POOH: He's my friend. And—and, if you mess with him, well, I'll have something to say about it, won't I? I mean, don't be like that with my friend or you gonna answer to me.

GATES: Okay, man. I respect that. When's the party gonna be?

RICARDO: Tonight. (*Lights cross to the Heffalump trap. The Forest animals are looking for clues.*)

CHRISTOPHER ROBIN: Poohnappers always leave a clue.

EEYORE: Don't you think we thought of that?

RABBIT: I dare say we didn't, Eeyore. Don't you remember? We just ran to get help.

EEYORE: Oh. Well, I thought of it, but didn't say anything to you.

RABBIT: Oh . . . In any case, it's quite a good idea.

CHRISTOPHER ROBIN: (*Pointing at a piece of paper on the ground*) LOOK!!

OWL: Most definitely a clueus maximus.

KANGA: It's got writing on it too.

RABBIT: What does it say?

CHRISTOPHER ROBIN: An address . . . and a name. Miss Tina Robinson. That's who stole them!

RABBIT: Let's go!

OWL: But how do we get there?

EEYORE: Alright. I knew you'd have to rely on the donkey. Get on—but gently please.

TIGGER: I run next to you. Tigger fast.

KANGA: Me too. *(Checking her pouch.)* Roo will just sleep through this whole thing. It's so nice when they're still this age.

EEYORE: Yes. The mixed blessing of youth.

OWL: Have you studied philosasophy, Eeyore? Sometimes you're so profundo.

EEYORE: Sometimes?! Why doesn't anyone understand me?? What's a donkey to do?? *(CHRISTOPHER ROBIN gets on EEYORE's back as the lights cross to the city.)* Ouch! Careful.

SCENE FIVE

In the City. All the City animals, except for RITA, are in TINA ROBINSON's bedroom. POOH and PIGLET are hidden from view, behind the other animals. TINA has her leg in a cast.

RICARDO: Happy birthday, Miss Tina.

ROLANDO: Yeah.

GATES: Happy whatever.

FELICIA: Yeah, what they said.

MUGS: Double for me.

ROLANDO: And we got a special surprise for you!

RICARDO: Hey!

ROLANDO: I mean, Ricardo has a surprise for you.

RICARDO: We found him, Miss Tina. The perfect animal. Everything that's good. Everything you want to help your leg heal. *(Pushing POOH forward towards her.)* Here he is.

TINA: Thank you guys. He's cute, but he's not what I wanted.

RICARDO: Sure he is. You said you wanted to spend your birthday with the bestest animal ever. The cutest, the furriest. Somebody you could keep for your friend forever.

ROLANDO: That's him alright. Too cute if you ask me—but nobody asked, I know.

TINA: It's a beautiful thought, but . . . Ricardo? I was talking about you.

RICARDO: You were? Well . . . I'm handsome, not cute.

TINA: That's a figure of speech. Remember? We talked about those.

RICARDO: Yeah. You really mean that, Tina? You could be happy just with me by your side?

TINA: Of course. Why don't you listen? For a smart rat you sure act like a mouse sometimes. Come here. (*RICARDO goes to her and hugs her. The OTHERS make kissy-face noises.*)

RICARDO: Hey, you guys, cut that out!

FELICIA: (*beginning to cry*) I love happy endings.

PIGLET: (*Beginning to cry also*) I dare say even I am moved. Come Pooh. It's time to go home. (*RITA ROACH bursts through the door, holding a can of rat poison and roach eliminator. The OTHERS gasp.*)

RITA: You're going somewhere alright, bear. Out to the docks—with me.

POOH: I love new places.

PIGLET: Oh, dear. We were almost safe.

POOH: What's the ducks?

GATES: A place nobody comes back from.

MUGS: Even I don't dare go there.

FELICIA: And if he don't go there, nobody better!!

POOH: That doesn't sound like fun. I was thinking—though I don't think very well mind you, that we were going to visit some water birds. I like the water.

RITA: (*Taking hold of POOH and backing out the door*) And don't any of youse try to follow me. (*SHE exits and the OTHERS leap into action. Another group bursts through the door—The Forestdwellers.*)

CHRISTOPHER ROBIN: Unhand our man, Pooh, or—or—

EEYORE: Else.

CHRISTOPHER ROBIN: Thank you, Eeyore. Or else!

PIGLET: Thank goodness, you've come my friends. Pooh has been poohnapped–again.

KANGA: What are we waiting for?! Let's go after them.

MUGS the PUG: Where do you think you're going? It's a big city. You'll never find them.

TINA: Unless we go with you.

GATES: Yeah . . . that might work, y'all.

OWL: Why should we trust you? You were the ones took our indelible bear in the first place.

RABBIT: Yes. That's true. *(Pointing at ROLANDO)* That's one of the poohnappers right there.

PIGLET: Why just "poohnapper?" They took me too you know. Don't pigs count anymore?

KANGA: Of course they do, Piglet. We're very happy to find you safe and sound. *(TIGGER bounces on PIGLET, knocking him down.)*

EEYORE: What a welcome.

FELICIA: I never seen animals like you. You're all—clean and everything. Don't you eat garbage?

RABBIT: Where we come from there's fresh plants and sweet honey. No garbage.

FELICIA: Well, youse don't know what you've been missing. We should stop by Lindy's on the way. Nothing better to introduce youse to the good life than a nice old piece of cheesecake—

MUGS: Felicia, please. We have serious business to take care of.

FELICIA: Sheesh! I was only trying to be hospitable—something maybe you don't know about. Sheesh, I get picked on no matter what I say!

EEYORE: Really? So do I. We have a lot in common, Miss, uhm—

FELICIA: Feline. But my friends call me, Felicia. Can I take your hoof? I mean, for the walk to the docks?

EEYORE: Why of course, Felicia. Felicia . . . what a beautiful name! Sounds like the earth after a summer rain—soft and smoothe and—

GATES: This mushy stuff is getting on my last nerve!

MUGS: Mine too . . .

CHRISTOPHER ROBIN: Mine too. We have to find Pooh!

TINA: Yeah. We're wasting time here. There's a hundred different places they could be. *(TINA gets up and gets on her crutches.)*

RICARDO: Do you think you should do that? Get up like that? Why don't you stay home and we'll—

TINA: No way am I gonna miss another adventure. Anyway, this cast comes off tomorrow.

RICARDO: That's great.

CHRISTOPHER ROBIN: Yes. Good for you, Miss Tina Robinson!

RICARDO: Who are you anyway?

CHRISTOPHER ROBIN: I'm Christopher Robin, friend to Pooh and Piglet. And I hope your friend too.

RICARDO: I don't know about that buddy.

TINA: He's okay, Ricardo...has a bad haircut, but still okay. Let's go! (*Lights cross to the docks.*)

SCENE SIX

At the Docks. RITA stands behind POOH, about to push him into the water.

RITA: I don't really want to do this to you, bear. I got no argument with you, you understand? No hard feelings? I just want that darn rat to listen to me. To see me—like really see me like I am. I'm a beautiful roach. He knows it, but he won't even think about me. It's always Tina this and Tina that, and I wonder what Tina is doing today. There's only so much a girl can take. I—I— (*RITA faints. POOH runs to her.*)

POOH: Oh, dear! Miss Rita! Miss Rita! Poor thing. Probably hasn't had a thing to eat today. (*Taking out a jar of honey*) I'm glad I brought this—not that I think ahead very often, but today has been a very unusual day. (*POOH puts a handful to RITA's lips. Slowly, SHE revives.*) It's working. Hooray!

RITA: (*Eating noisily*) Yum! What is that stuff? I never had nothing like it.

POOH: Honey. My emergency jar. I always like to carry a little something, in case it gets to be around eleven—snack time.

RITA: I hate to be the one to break it to you, bear, but it is *not* eleven o'clock.

POOH: Silly! Any snack time is eleven. Aren't we eating?

RITA: Yeah.

POOH: Don't you like it?

RITA: Yeah.

POOH: Then it is most definitely elevenses.

RITA: Huh? You know you really confuse me. Here I was all ready to push you in the drink, and you offer me your honey. You haven't been in the city very long, have you?

POOH: My first time. But I love, love, love, love, love it. *(Pause)* But I do miss my friends.

RITA: You're a really nice guy, bear. I don't meet many nice guys. Frankly, I don't understand men. But I think it's because I never tried just being nice to them. Never occurred to me. Not till now.

POOH: What's nice?

RITA: Gentle, caring. I don't know. When you live behind a stove, and people are scared of you, just because of how you look, you don't let yourself be nice to them. It's them or me, I always think . . . always used to think anyway. *(Pause; THEY are both lost in thought.)*

POOH: I just know who my friends are. And I can't think of a better way to spend the day than just being with them. This has been so much fun, but I think I want to go home now. *(All the OTHERS enter like a charging army.)*

OWL: Ah hah!!

POOH: Ah hah what?

RABBIT: We've come to save you from the fierce roach.

POOH: She's not fierce. She's just Rita.

OTHERS: Oh . . .

RICARDO: We thought you were gonna do something crazy.

RITA: I did. I made a friend.

TINA: Well, it's about time. You were getting hard to be around. I still have a birthday cake to eat. Who wants to help me?

RABBIT: I do! I do!

GATES: Wouldn't mind a little ole piece.

EEYORE: I want a big piece. I've been working all day.

FELICIA: You have such muscular back legs, Eyeee. *(SHE touches one of his back legs.)* You shiverize me!

POOH: Yea! Hooray for cake!

MUGS: I wouldn't mind a piece myself.

ROLANDO: I'm glad you didn't hurt the little guy, Rita. Maybe you're okay after all, even if you are my sister.

KANGA: I'd love some cake. I am eating for two you know. I'll save a little piece for Roo. He loves cake.

PIGLET: I don't care for any myself. This has been a most anxious day. I don't understand why we can't just go home. (*TIGGER bounces him.*)

TIGGER: Tigger miss Piglet. Piglet he friend.

PIGLET: There's no way I can win today.

RICARDO: You're the best, Tina.

POOH: Christopher Robin is the best too.

OWL: They can't both be best. That's completely illogicus mentus. I mean, impossible.

TINA: Maybe we should hook up, you and me Chris. I mean, like an exchange program. Two weeks there. One week here.

CHRISTOPHER ROBIN: That would be most delightful. But, Miss Tina?

TINA: Yeah?

CHRISTOPHER ROBIN: Will you cut my hair goodly? Bad haircuts are for bad people, I think.

TINA: Oh, sure, Chris. I'll take of you. Don't worry. We'll hip you up.

EEYORE: I'm staying. Miss Felicia needs a donkey like me around in the city.

FELICIA: Oh, Eeyee. You're too much.

EEYORE: I'm sorry. I'll try to be less.

FELICIA: No . . . I mean. Never mind. Could definitely use a donkey around here. (*Sticks her tongue out at MUGS*) See? This is how you treat a lady.

MUGS: I'm glad he's staying too. Wanna go out tamorrow, Rita. Since we are are both, how you say, unattached?

RITA: Sure. I always liked your face.

MUGS: (*Blushing*) Oh, Jeez . . . You romanticalize me! (*RITA and MUGS hold paws shyly.*)

GATES: You're going home now, huh? After the cake?

POOH: Don't worry, Gates. We only live a wish away. Look! A star! (*ALL look up and see the first star. GATES and POOH sing/recite together.*)

GATES & POOH: A star can twinkle fiercely, but will never mean you harm. A star can bring you great new friends with chillin' wit and charm. You never have to miss them if you look up in the sky—for there you'll see a distant star that never says good—bye . . . *(Lights slowly fade)*

End of Play

Just Another Decoration Day

by

Etta L. Worthington

Production Notes

Characters

Mother–a fourty year old housewife, graying, stern

Daughter–a thirteen year old girl, slim, rather timid with her mother

Grammy–a seventy year old woman, gray hair braided and in a bun, she has a stern expression on her face but she is gentle in behavior

Nellie–early seventies, rather small and hunched over, but pleasant and smiling

Margaret—a thirteen year old girl, taller and larger than Daughter

Young Grammy—fourteen year old with long hair and glasses

Young Nellie—fourteen year old, long hair

George—late seventies, rather tired and pale, weak, speaks with effort

191

Setting: the stage is mostly bare with square and rectangular wood boxes that represent gravestones, a bed, a closet, an outhouse, a tree, etc. As the play opens, the three women are working in the kitchen cleaning and organizing things. One rectangular box is centerstage, another is downstage and to the right. This one is vertical and has a uniform hanging in it. One square box is next to the larger one and the other is downstage and to the left. As the play opens, Daughter is downstage and Mother and Grammy are upstage to the right and left respectively.

Clock strikes five dongs. (*This should be done vocally by one of the actors, probably George. Lights come up.*)

• • • • • • • • • • • • • • • • • • •

MOTHER: We'll leave at six.

DAUGHTER: (*To audience.*) I hear her and know that we won't leave a minute past six, and probably a few minutes before. I, for one, would rather sleep in a little longer. In fact, I'd rather not go at all. But I wasn't asked. I tried to talk to her about it. (*Lights come up stage left on Margaret holding the phone.*)

MARGARET: So, are you going to come?

DAUGHTER: (*Talking into an imaginary telephone.*) She won't let me go.

MARGARET: How come?

DAUGHTER: Because we always go to Coudersport. (*pause*) I can't ask her.

MARGARET: You can!

DAUGHTER: (*To mother.*) Margaret and I want to go to the parade in Olean.

MOTHER: There's one in Coudersport. You can invite Margaret along if you like. The way you two talk on the phone all the time, I'd think by now you'd be all talked out. But you could talk the whole way there and back.

DAUGHTER: She can't come. She has a picnic at her aunt's house in the afternoon.

MOTHER: Well, I'm sure the two of you'll catch up as soon as you get home. (*lights fade on Margaret*)

DAUGHTER: (*She grimaces. To audience*) It's obvious I'm going, even though I haven't really been asked. I've always gone, of course, so I will go again this year. Just Grammy and Mother and me. Never my father.

MOTHER, DAUGHTER: He always has work to do fixing something around the house, so he can't go.

DAUGHTER: I wish I could help him. He's going to start painting the house, but I know he'll just shoo me away if I ask to help. He'll send me inside to see if Mother . . .

MOTHER: Needs any housework done. (*To daughter who starts washing dishes, and starts saying "wash, wash" as Mother talks to her. This sound effect continues for as long as Mother talks.*) Did you see the flowers I picked out? I got white petunias and geraniums. I'll put some of both on each of the graves. Don't you think that'll look nice, with the red and white together? (*Daughter doesn't say anything and Mother glares at her.*) Well you didn't like the pink petunias last year, so I got white ones.

DAUGHTER: (*To Mother, smiling at her sweetly.*) They'll look wonderful, Mother. (*To audience.*) I tell her that because I know she will keep poking at me with her comments, her questions, until I answer. Until I answer yes. She always needs someone to agree with her. So I do and she leaves me alone to finish the dishes.

Mother: (*Daughter continues her "wash, wash" routine while Mother speaks.*) Make sure you clean the pan good. You miss the bottoms sometimes.

DAUGHTER: (*Changes to "scrub, scrub, scrub, scrub." To audience.*) She must have the copper bottoms to her pots polished and shined after every use. Last place we lived, she used to hang them all on the wall and she'd bring one down to shine again if it seemed in the slightest bit tarnished. I don't know why they have to be polished now, because all of them get stacked and loaded on shelves in the cupboard next to the stove. So I sprinkle the copper cleaner on the pot bottom and scour away with extra vengeance and I don't realize how hard I'm doing it until I hear Grammy say, (*She makes scrubbing sounds again.*)

GRAMMY: (*To Daughter.*) Goodness. You're bout to scour the bottom off that pan, young lady.

DAUGHTER: (*Looking at Grammy sadly.*) I always have to go. But I don't want to. I don't have a choice. I just go. One year I asked Grammy why I had to go.

GRAMMY: Well, sometimes we have to do things we don't necessarily want to do. Did I ever tell you about the time I had to get up early every morning before I went to school for a month and sweep out your Aunt

Nellie's father's store? (*She comes over to daughter and the two of them sit down.*)

DAUGHTER: No.

GRAMMY: I was just about your age I guess. It was winter and everybody would go down to the river when it froze over and have ice skating parties. (*Lights start to fade on Grammy and Daughter as lights come up on Young Grammy and Young Nellie*) We'd make big bonfires on the side of the river to get warm, and we'd skate for hours. When the river first froze that year, I dug out my skates. Try as I might, there was no way I could fit my feet in them. I wasn't going to be able to skate any more.

YOUNG GRAMMY: I can't fit my feet in these.

YOUNG NELLIE: Take a layer of socks off.

YOUNG GRAMMY: I only have one pair of socks on. I still can't get my heel in this.

YOUNG NELLIE: Doesn't your sister have old ones you can wear?

YOUNG GRAMMY: These are my sister's old skates.

YOUNG NELLIE: Here. Try these.

YOUNG GRAMMY: They fit. But they're yours.

YOUNG NELLIE: They're a little tight on me. I'll just tell my dad that I've outgrown mine and need a new pair. And you can have mine.

YOUNG GRAMMY: But won't he ask to see?

YOUNG NELLIE: No, he's too busy. He'll just get me a new pair. (*lights fade on that scene and come up on Grammy and Daughter*)

DAUGHTER: Why couldn't you buy new ones?

GRAMMY: There wasn't any money. With eleven children in the family, we were lucky just to have new shoes.

DAUGHTER: Did her father find out?

GRAMMY: Not until my father started wondering where I got skates. He thought I'd stolen them from somewhere and threatened to give me a good licking if I didn't tell him the truth. So I had to 'fess up and he went and talked to Nellie's father.

DAUGHTER: So that's how come you had to sweep the store.

GRAMMY: Our fathers decided we had to pay for the skates by working in Nellie's father's store. We swept it out every day for a month. I didn't want to get up those cold mornings, but something good come of it.

Nellie and I got to skate together all winter.

DAUGHTER: Do you want to go?

GRAMMY: Yes.

DAUGHTER: It's different for you. I didn't know any of them.

GRAMMY: You knew him.

DAUGHTER: (*She nods her head, then gets up.*) No, I didn't. I mean, I don't remember.

GRAMMY: You don't remember him at all?

DAUGHTER: No. I was only three when he was born. (*She looks expectantly at Grammy as if she will tell her more. Grammy says nothing and walks stage right to where Mother is. Daughter walks there slowly.*) As expected, it's 5:54 on the dot when we pull out of our driveway with the trunk full of

MOTHER: (*taking inventory, while Grammy points to each object*) petunias, geraniums, ice chest, sandwiches, Kool-aid, jelly. (*Each character says slam as they take their positions in the car. Mother says "slam" quickly and with determination. Grammy says it a little more tentatively. They look at Daughter who is very slowly making her way to the car. Daughter gets in and says "slam" with hesitation and frustration.*)

MOTHER, DAUGHTER: Your Grammy packed the lunch.

GRAMMY: It's the least I can do,

MOTHER, DAUGHTER: she says, and then makes more food than the three of us can possibly eat, even for a whole day.

DAUGHTER: There's a metal tin of tollhouse cookies (*she puts her hand on tin as she talks*) which I helped her make yesterday morning and I'm sitting in the backseat of the Rambler with a pillow and the cookies nearby, so this trip won't be all bad. We have a regular itinerary. I have taken this trip so many times I know it by heart. The only thing that ever changes is how long you stay at any one place.

MOTHER: We'll head out to Coudersport first. We should get there by nine and be through at the cemetery in time for the parade. After that we'll drive out to Nellie's.

DAUGHTER: (*To audience.*) I'm not sure why she tells us this, because this is what we always do.

GRAMMY: I wonder how George is doing? (*She sighs.*)

DAUGHTER: George is Nellie's husband.

GRAMMY: *(To daughter.)* He's had a couple of bouts with cancer.

MOTHER: *(Shaking her head and looking worried.)* I don't think he has long,

DAUGHTER: *(To audience.)* Mother says that in her waiting for death kind of voice.

MOTHER: He's getting weaker and the treatment didn't work before. It might be better if they just left him in peace.

DAUGHTER: *(To audience.)* That's what I don't like about our annual trip. Our Decoration Day routine. We've been doing it as long as I can remember.

MOTHER, DAUGHTER, GRAMMY: We always go and put flowers on the graves of our dead family members

DAUGHTER: and talk about those nearly ready to be laid in the cemetery. For everyone else it's Memorial Day,

GRAMMY: but in our house it's Decoration Day

DAUGHTER: and geraniums and the smell of dirt and spending time cleaning up around graves and small stone markers.

MOTHER: Nellie asked about you when she wrote last time.

DAUGHTER: *(To audience)* Nellie is my aunt, but not really. I think maybe we're related somehow, but I'm not sure. I always call her Aunt Nellie. I like going to her house. She makes the best molasses cookies. They're big and chewy and my mouth starts to water just thinking about them so I decide to grab a chocolate chip cookie for now.

MOTHER: She's been sick too. She said she's not been doing the baking she's used to doing. George doesn't eat much no matter what she fixes him.

DAUGHTER: *(To audience)* I am suddenly sad. No molasses cookies. Two hours of sitting quietly while they visit. No glass of milk to drown my sorrows . . . or . . . my cookies in. (After saying this, she reaches in the tin of cookies and takes out a couple of them to eat.)

MOTHER: You won't want anything come lunch time.

DAUGHTER: *(To audience.)* She has heard me prying open the lid to the cookie tin. She's heard me even though she and Grammy were talking and not paying any attention to me. *(To Mother.)* Grammy makes such good chocolate chip cookies.

MOTHER: Only one. We have a long ways to go and I don't want you just filling your stomach with cookies.

DAUGHTER: *(She nods meekly and guiltily covers the second cookie with her skirt, hoping Mother hasn't noticed.)* Do you want one Grammy? *(She hands one to Grammy.)*

GRAMMY: Don't mind if I do.

DAUGHTER: *(To audience.)* Grammy takes one out and offers one to Mother who professes to be

MOTHER: not the slightest bit hungry.

DAUGHTER: I wish Margaret were here so I wouldn't have to listen to the two of them talk in the front seat all the time. If Margaret were here this trip wouldn't be so boringly long. Mother finally pulls into a roadside park because Grammy needs to use the toilet. *(They get out of car. Grammy goes behind the box stage right and slightly upstage.)*

MOTHER: *(To daughter.)* Don't you need to go?

DAUGHTER: No.

MOTHER: You should go when you have the chance. You don't know when we'll be at a toilet again.

DAUGHTER: *(To Mother.)* I don't have to go.

MOTHER: *(With indignation.)* Well I don't want to hear you begging to stop somewhere along the way. That's all I have to say.

DAUGHTER: *(To audience.)* I know that means war, so I go. If I don't go now, she'll make sure we don't stop until my bladder is bursting. *(She heads in the direction of the outhouse.)* I hate the outhouses in these roadside parks. They're kept clean, usually, but they still stink and I have to breathe through my mouth so I don't smell anything. I always look in it even though I hate to because when I was little

MOTHER, GRAMMY: she went to her Aunt Martha's house

GRAMMY: and there was a snake in the outhouse when she had to go

MOTHER: and she ran out of the outhouse, screaming at the top of her lungs.

DAUGHTER: *(Peaking out from behind the outhouse.)* Yeah, and I ended up peeing in my pants.

MOTHER: We looked in the outhouse. It was only a piece of hose that looked like a snake. *(She laughs and gives daughter a little hug as Daughter comes back towards car.)*

DAUGHTER: *(To audience)* I hear that one every year. The trip drags on and when we get to Coudersport it's the same as it was last year. The fire hall is having a ham and leek dinner April 23rd, 24th and 25th. (*As she says that their eyes all follow the sign as if they are just passing it on the road.*) No. That's an old sign that nobody remembered to take down. (*To Mother*) How come people like wild leeks so much?

MOTHER: It's a spring tonic. Problem is, you stink to high heaven when you eat leeks. But grandpa used to swear by them. He said it cleaned your blood out.

GRAMMY: He'd eat so many leeks my mother would make him sleep out in the shed.

DAUGHTER: I never ate any.

MOTHER: And you're not likely to get any in my house. The smell of them nauseates me.

DAUGHTER: (*To audience.*) When we finally arrive at our destination, Mother is all business.

MOTHER: (*Taking basket with full of plants from the car.*) We'll do Grandpa first. They just don't keep the cemetery up like they used to. They always used to have it nicely trimmed next to the monuments. I don't think they do more than just mow now. And not that often. (*GRAMMY nods in agreement when she says this. DAUGHTER lays down on a box representing a gravestone, closes her eyes and folds her hands.*)

GRAMMY: Do you remember when your brother used to mow the lawn at the Daggett Hollow Church? Why it used to take him more than half a day just to do the trimming around the stones, and that was a small cemetery. I don't know. Just doesn't seem right they don't keep it up. (*She goes off shaking her head and muttering.*)

MOTHER: (*Noticing DAUGHTER.*) Grab the clippers out of the trunk. Now. And go and trim around the marker while I get out the flowers.

DAUGHTER: (*To audience.*) Daddy's oiled them up good so they work easy. Thwing thwang. (*She mimes using clippers as she says the words.*) Thwing, thwang. It's a small stone. Only about two feet high and three feet wide.

GRAMMY: Robert K. Towser. Born October 10, 1889. Died May 3, 1952.

DAUGHTER: (*To audience.*) There's a blank on the other side. Meant for Grammy when she dies. I guess then they'll carve in her name and her dates. But I don't like thinking about that. She's lived with us as long as I have. Thwing, thwang. Thwing, thwang. I am doing it very neatly. Daddy would approve of how I'm holding the clippers. If you don't do it right you'll give yourself blisters, he always warns me. Thwing, thwang. What if she does die? She could. She is very old, after all. I think she's seventy or seventy one. I never can remember. And she has to take heart pills every day.

MOTHER: *(To DAUGHTER).* Here. Give me a hand with these geraniums.

DAUGHTER: *(Drops the clippers and grabs the basket of geraniums MOTHER'S handed her. She steps back not realizing how close she is to the next gravestone and loses her balance. She pushes the geraniums out in front of her and falls on her bottom. The plants crash to her chest, the dirt in the pots get all over her and in her mouth.)*

GRAMMY: *(Both MOTHER and GRAMMY rush to DAUGHTER, but GRAMMY gets there first.)* Did you hurt yourself? Are you okay?

MOTHER: If she'd pay more attention to what she was doing instead of hopping around, she'd be fine.

DAUGHTER: *(She turns and spits and then looks at her mother.)* I had dirt in my mouth.

MOTHER: *(To DAUGHTER).* For heaven's sake, go wash your mouth out with some water. There's a pump down there. *(She points stage right.)*

DAUGHTER: *(To audience.)* I haven't the slightest idea where it is but I head down the road and figure I'll run into it sooner or later. Or maybe I'll just keep on walking until they come and get me. Ah. Here. Creak. Goosh. *(She mimes rinsing her mouth out with water from the pump.)* Dirt to dirt. Or is it earth to earth. Whatever. Creak. Goosh. *(She splashes water on her face.)* That's better. *(She washes her hands and looks around like she's trying to figure out how to dry them and considers her skirt but changes her mind and mimics her mother lecturing her.)* I don't know when you're going to learn to act like a young lady. *(She shakes her hands to dry them as she walks back.)*

MOTHER: *(To DAUGHTER.)* The plants weren't hurt, no thanks to you. Your grandmother and I repotted them. You could move a little faster. We don't have all day.

GRAMMY: *(To MOTHER, while putting her arm around DAUGHTER.)* We'll walk down to my mother's grave and get started on that one while you finish this one up.

DAUGHTER: *(To audience.)* This is a much older section of the cemetery. The stones, what ones are there, are well weathered. Some of them, in fact, are starting to crumble. I have a favorite one that I pick away at every year when no one is looking. I figure in another ten years the top third should be totally gone. Willover. That's what her mother's name was.

GRAMMY: Mary Alice Willover. 1866 to 1934. She died of consumption.

DAUGHTER: The second grave doesn't take that long. Grammy and Mother still worry over the condition of the cemetery.

GRAMMY: *(To MOTHER.)* A shame there's not more sun over here.

MOTHER: I don't know how the flowers will do with this much shade. They really should do a better job of trimming the trees back. They're just too overgrown. I just don't know.

DAUGHTER: *(To audience.)* I think she is wondering about Grammy. Whether she should be buried in this cemetery which is so far from home and so poorly kept up.

GRAMMY: *(To MOTHER.)* I'll bet Nellie can tell us who's doing the mowing here. Maybe she can get them to trim this tree back a little.

DAUGHTER: Then comes the worst part. I hate this part of our trip. Mother is always sighing and rubbing tears away from her cheeks. His grave is in the newest section of the cemetery.

MOTHER: *(To DAUGHTER.)* The plants.

DAUGHTER: Shouldn't I do the trimming first?

MOTHER: Well of course.

DAUGHTER: There's three plants. We only put two on the other graves.

MOTHER: *(Turns to DAUGHTER and glares and then says with hands firmly planted on her hips.)* What's the matter? Don't you want your little brother to have three plants on his grave? Think that's too much for him?

DAUGHTER: Don't blame me! *(She runs to the grave she likes to pick at and sits down and sobs.)* It's not my fault.

GRAMMY: *(She looks at MOTHER and then at DAUGHTER and then she starts to hum "Sometimes I Feel Like a Motherless Child.")*

DAUGHTER: *(At some point she joins in and starts humming too. She smiles.)*

GRAMMY: *(Coming to sit with her.)* Nellie and I were inseparable. Either I was at her house or she was at my house. We only lived three blocks apart. That was in South Corning.

DAUGHTER: Did you want to be with her and not with your family some times?

GRAMMY: *(smiling)* Yes. And some times I got in trouble.

DAUGHTER: In trouble?

GRAMMY: Yes. When I was fifteen Nellie was sick all summer and the doctor told her mother that she had to have her hair bobbed because long hair wasn't good for her health.

DAUGHTER: Bobbed?

GRAMMY: Cut. We called it a bob when I was young. So she was the only girl in school that year with bobbed hair. Everyone else wore theirs long, in braids, or with ribbons and curls. So, one Saturday afternoon, I walked over to Mrs. Carns and got my hair bobbed so I could be like Nellie. When I got home my mother had conniptions. And then my father—

DAUGHTER: What did he do?

GRAMMY: He said I couldn't go back to school until my hair grew long again. My mother talked him out of that, but he was mad as a wet hen until she finally told him about Nellie having to get her hair bobbed. So you see, it all worked out. Well, it looks like your Mother's finished over there. Reckon we should help her pack up the car.

DAUGHTER: Nellie's is where we go after we've stopped at the cemetery. She doesn't really live in Coudersport, even though we always talk about going to Nellie's and Coudersport in the same breath. She and George live in North Eulalia which is ten miles down the road, near a farm that Grammy lived on when Mother was growing up. Grammy tells me

DAUGHTER, MOTHER: stories, sometimes after we get through playing Chinese checkers or dominoes, about

DAUGHTER, MOTHER, GRAMMY: taffy pulls, or making maple syrup, or going swimming in the dammed up creek and swinging from a rope out over the water and jumping. (*GEORGE and NELLIE enter. GEORGE sits on long rectangular box center stage where he will soon lie down on his bed. NELLIE is downstage right.*)

DAUGHTER: When we reach their house in North Eulalia—odd name for a town—I don't know what it means.

MOTHER: (*To DAUGHTER.*) Take the jelly.

DAUGHTER: When we reach their house, Nellie greets us at the door wearing an apron over her house dress and wiping her floury hands. (*NELLIE hugs GRAMMY.*)

MOTHER: You take it in to George. (*DAUGHTER shakes her head no.*)

NELLIE: (*To visitors.*) Oh I'm sorry. I'm just about to take the last batch of cookies out of the oven. I wanted to have some fresh ones for you when you got here. And I was going to change my dress.

MOTHER: You look wonderful. (*She goes over to NELLIE who gives her a hug and kiss.*)

NELLIE: Oh.

GRAMMY: And how is George doing?

NELLIE: He had a couple of bad days last week, but he's better now. He's waiting in the den for you. (*MOTHER is still motioning to DAUGHTER to take the jar but DAUGHTER still refuses.*)

MOTHER: We brought a jar of elderberry jelly for you and GEORGE.

NELLIE: (*She takes jar from DAUGHTER.*) Oh that's his favorite. Go ahead on in. (*GRAMMY and Mother do but DAUGHTER hangs back.*) Hi honey. My, how much you've grown since last year. (*She gives DAUGHTER a hug.*)

DAUGHTER: (*Stands there looking a little bored and like she doesn't know what to say*) Aunt Nellie, you made the cookies without me!

NELLIE: Sorry honey. Did you want to help me?

DAUGHTER: I like making cookies with you.

NELLIE: The last batch is in the oven. You can help me eat them. (*She looks tenderly at DAUGHTER.*) You know your mother is a very lucky woman, having a daughter like you.

DAUGHTER: Huh.

NELLIE: She loves you very much you know. (*DAUGHTER rolls her eyes and grimaces.*) Oh, I know, sometimes it doesn't seem like it. I remember back when, you know, when your brother died. She was so terrified of losing you she wouldn't let you out of her sight. Once when you came here she wouldn't even let George take you out on the swing in the rose garden, she was so afraid you'd get hurt.

DAUGHTER: Really?

NELLIE: (*Nods yes.*) I kind of understood her. She relaxed after a while. So, would you like to help me get our snack ready?

DAUGHTER: Can I go up and use your bathroom first?

NELLIE: Oh sure, honey.

DAUGHTER: (*To audience.*) I'm saved. There are fresh molasses cookies. This trip won't be a total loss. I do know where that bathroom is. Right after George's closet. I've never understood why they built a bathroom off a closet, but it must have made sense to someone back then. There are old suits and a wool topcoat hanging in George's closet. And a uniform. That's why I go up there. It belonged to Daniel, their

DAUGHTER, NELLIE, GEORGE: son who died in the war. He was in the Navy and was killed in a bombing raid.

DAUGHTER: *(To audience.)* The uniform has hung there as long as I can remember— it's blue wool, edged with gold trim, and rows of medals on the chest. *(As she says this the light comes up on MOTHER who is stroking the uniform and fingering the medals)* I touch the bright colored medals and try to memorize them so I can go home and look them up in Encyclopedia Britannica and figure out what each one is for. *(She comes upon her MOTHER in the closet with her face buried in the uniform. MOTHER jumps back, startled, and DAUGHTER looks just as startled.)*

MOTHER: *(Composes herself and says softly.)* Don't dilly dally up here. You need to spend some time with Nellie and George. They look forward to seeing you. *(She leaves.)*

DAUGHTER: *(Looks confused, quizzical, and goes over and touches the uniform and then pulls a stools out, climbs up and reaches the sailor hat.)* There. *(She models the hat, hums "Anchors Away" and looks in the mirror and strikes several different poses.)*

NELLIE: *(In the background)* Yoo hoo. Cookies are done.

DAUGHTER: Oh, better get downstairs. *(She puts the hat back on the shelf and then fingers the medals again.)* I wish I could take one or two of these. *(She takes a medal off and holds it in her hand, weighing whether she should keep it. She decides not to.)*

NELLIE: What happened up there? Did you fall in?

DAUGHTER: Goodbye Daniel. Molasses cookies, here I come. *(She returns to kitchen)*

NELLIE: *(To DAUGHTER.)* Last batch, hot out of the oven. Here. You make up a plate of cookies for us to eat while we visit. I'll put the water on for tea. *(NELLIE grabs a cooler cookie, breaks it in two and offers half to DAUGHTER.)* We have to make sure they taste okay.

MOTHER: *(Coming into the kitchen)* Why don't you go in there and give your Uncle George a cookie and talk to him. You don't know if you'll get to see him again.

DAUGHTER: *(She shakes her head, looking defeated. She notices some daisies in a vase on the table and goes over and breaks one off which she puts in her hair. She goes to the den and finds GEORGE with his eyes closed and she stands timidly at the edge of the room. She sits and looks at him.)* Uncle

George. Are you awake?

GEORGE: (*His eyelids flutter open*) Just resting my eyes. (*He motions her to bedside.*)

DAUGHTER: Can I ask a question?

GEORGE: What would you like to know?

DAUGHTER: How old would Daniel have been, you know, if he was still alive?

GEORGE: Oh God, I don't know. You'll need to ask your Aunt Nellie that one. Can't remember years any more. (*He thinks for a minute.*) Daniel was—well, he and your mother were friends. I think they were just about the same age.

DAUGHTER: She's old. I think she's forty. Well, I guess I shouldn't say that she's old, I mean—

GEORGE: (*Laughs a little.*) That's okay. I thought everybody was old when I was your age. My parents for sure. Now I'm old.

DAUGHTER: Do you mind being old?

GEORGE: No. Don't have to do much any more. People wait on me hand and foot. That's not so bad. (*He closes his eyes for a while and DAUGHTER watches him. He starts talking again without opening his eyes.*) Being sick . . . It drives me crazy. I'm driving your Aunt Nellie crazy too. Sometimes I get up and walk to the living room. Then I have to rest all afternoon because it tires me out. Old's okay, but sick . . .

DAUGHTER: (*Doesn't say anything for a while.*) Uncle George.

GEORGE: What?

DAUGHTER: What was Daniel like?

GEORGE: (*Struggles to open his eyes again.*) He was strong. Good looking. He had wavy brown hair and big dark brown eyes. You've seen pictures of him, haven't you? We have some of him and your mother together.

DAUGHTER: But what was he really like? Why did he go to war?

GEORGE: It was the honorable thing to do, defending your country. (*Sighs.*) I would have gone if they would have taken me. But I was too old by that time. When the war broke out, he was working with me at the dairy.

DAUGHTER: Didn't you take me there once?

GEORGE: Yes. That was after I'd retired. You were just a little bit of a thing. But you and your dad came on a tour of the dairy.

DAUGHTER: And we made butter.

GEORGE: What a memory you have! I'd totally forgotten about that but you're right. We brought home some cream.

DAUGHTER: And put it in jars and shook it up until it became butter. Except I couldn't shake mine very long.

GEORGE: So I finished it off for you.

DAUGHTER: And then we had some on bread. But I didn't really like it.

GEORGE: Hadn't been salted yet. You liked it better after we mixed some salt with it. *(He closes his eyes again and sighs.)* Haven't made butter in years.

DAUGHTER: I go look at his uniform sometimes when I'm here.

GEORGE: *(Smiles.)* Hmm.

DAUGHTER: I look at the medals sometimes too. He had lots of them. I always wonder what they're for. What about the one with the star on it?

GEORGE: I don't remember them all. You'll have to ask Nellie. She's got it written down some place, what he got them for. I only remember the ones that came after he was gone. *(He closes his eyes like he is thinking but seems to half doze, but once and a while comes out with the name of a metal.)* The Department of the Navy sent them to us. . . Air Medal. . . Purple Heart. . . *(Trailing off)* Distinguished Flying Cross. *(Finally he sleeps. DAUGHTER ever so slowly tiptoes to his bedside and reaches up and pulls the daisy out of her hair and puts it on his hands on his chest and then she whispers.)* Bye. *(She starts to tiptoe out of the room.)*

GEORGE: Wait.

DAUGHTER: *(Looks startled then as if she is dreading what he might ask.)* What?

GEORGE: *(DAUGHTER goes back to his side and he takes off a dog tag he has around his neck.)* Here. This was his.

DAUGHTER: *(She takes it hesitantly and then slowly leaves the room. In the kitchen area she encounters MOTHER who is waiting for her. MOTHER looks at what she has in her hand, puzzled.)* He gave it to me. *(She looks at it and then puts the chain around her neck. Light fades.)*

End of Play

The Case of the Kidnapped Nephew
by
Sue Alexander

Characters

Court Clerk
Judge Alexander Fairman
Timothy Crane
Ms. Garfield, attorney for the accused
Mr. Bradbury, prosecuting attorney
Pamela Madison
Edith Allwell
Jonathan Slote
Brian Farley

Production Notes

The play requires a minimum of props and furniture and can be staged in a classroom, a club meeting room, or at home. Young people will enjoy using their imaginations in developing the characters and deciding on costumes and makeup.

The scene is a courtroom. There are three tables and ten chairs. A gavel is on the judge's table. Pamela Madison walks with the aid of a cane (or stick) and carries a purse containing a letter in an envelope and a folded piece of yellow paper. Brian is wearing one green sock and one red sock. Each attorney has a folder of papers.

The Judge's chambers are to the audience's left, the doorway is to the audience's right. The Court Clerk and the Judge enter and exit from the Judge's chambers. All others enter and exit on the doorway side.

General note: The attorneys stand while they are questioning witnesses.

As the play begins, everyone except the Court Clerk and the Judge enters. Garfield and Timothy are talking to each other. The witnesses are talking among themselves. They sit down Garfield and Timothy are at the audience's left, and Bradbury is at the audience's right.

● ● ● ● ● ● ● ● ● ● ● ● ● ● ● ● ● ●

TIMOTHY: This whole thing is crazy! I can't believe it's happening. I'm on trial for something I didn't do!

GARFIELD: You know you didn't do it, Tim, and I know it. But the only way we're going to be able to prove it is to discover who did!

CLERK: *(The CLERK enters and stands, facing the audience, in front of the JUDGE'S table.)* Hear ye, hear ye, court is now in session. Judge Alexander Fairman presiding. All rise. *(Everyone stands up. The JUDGE comes in and sits down. Then everyone except the CLERK sits down.)*

CLERK: The People versus Timothy Crane! *(The clerk sits down.)*

JUDGE: Timothy Crane, you are charged with kidnapping and extortion. How do you plead?

TIMOTHY: *(He stands up.)* Not guilty, Your Honor. *(He sits down.)*

JUDGE: The clerk will enter the plea in the record. Ms. Garfield, as counsel for the defense, are you ready to proceed?

GARFIELD: *(She stands.)* Yes, Your Honor.

JUDGE: Mr. Bradbury, as prosecutor for the People, are you ready to proceed?

BRADBURY: *(He stands up.)* Yes, Your Honor.

JUDGE: Very well. Begin then, please, Mr. Bradbury. *(MS. GARFIELD sits down.)*

BRADBURY: *(He walks back and forth while he is talking.)* Your Honor, the People will prove that Timothy Crane did, on the 22nd of May this year, kidnap Brian Farley and extort money for his release from Mr. Farley's aunt, Mrs. Pamela Madison. To begin testimony, I call my first witness, Pamela Madison . . . *(PAMELA rises with difficulty and walks haltingly, leaning on her cane, to the witness chair and stands in front of it.)*

CLERK: *(The CLERK stands.)* Do you swear to tell the truth, the whole truth, and nothing but the truth?

PAMELA: I do. *(She sits down. So does the CLERK.)*

BRADBURY: Mrs. Madison, you are a writer, is that correct? And Timothy Crane is your secretary?:

PAMELA: Yes, that's correct. Tim is my secretary and research assistant. As you can see, I'm not able to get around easily—I have chronic arthritis. So Tim goes here and there on errands for me.

BRADBURY: I see. Now, Mrs. Madison, will you please tell us in your own words what occurred on the 22nd of May.

PAMELA: Well, Tim had gone out and I don't like to be alone in the house, so my friend Edith Allwell had come to stay with me. I was waiting for my nephew Brian to arrive from England. Earlier that day I'd received a telegram from him telling me not to meet him at the airport, that he would take a cab. Then, shortly before noon, the doorbell rang, and a messenger hand-delivered a letter. As soon as he put the envelope in my hand, he left—even before I had time to open it. The letter stated that Brian had been kidnapped!

BRADBURY: Do you have that letter?

PAMELA: Yes. *(She opens her purse and pulls out the envelope.)* Here it is.

BRADBURY: Read it aloud, please.

PAMELA: *(She takes the letter out of the envelope and reads.)* "If you want to see your nephew Brian alive, put ten thousand dollars in a suitcase and wait for further instructions. Do not call the police."

BRADBURY: Your Honor, I would lilke to have the letter entered as the People's exhibit A.

JUDGE: It is so ordered.

BRADBURY: *(He takes the letter from PAMELA and hands it to the clerk.)* Go on, Mrs. Madison, what happened next?

PAMELA: For a while, I didn't know what to do. I was terribly frightened. And I was afraid to call the police for fear that something would happen to Brian. Then I remembered that I had enough money. I own several racehorses and the day before I'd sold one to Admiral Denay. He'd paid me in cash. I got the money from my safe, and my friend Edith got one of my suitcases from the closet. I put the money inside and waited for further instructions. About an hour later the doorbell rang again. But this time there wasn't any messenger. There was just an envelope on the doorstep. It contained the instructions.

BRADBURY: What were you instructed to do?

PAMELA: To take the suitcase of money and put it in back of the newsstand at the corner. The letter said that if I did as I was told within ten minutes, Brian would be freed.

BRADBURY: And did you follow the instructions?

PAMELA: Yes, of course! Edith took the suitcase there for me since I'm unable to carry anything heavy while I'm walking.

BRADBURY: And was Brian freed?

PAMELA: Yes. He arrived at my home about an hour later.

BRADBURY: Mrs. Madison, where was your secretary, Timothy Crane, at this time?

PAMELA: I don't know. He had come to me quite early that morning and asked if he might have the day off. He seemed quite nervous about something. I told him he could, and he left immediately.

BRADBURY: I see. Now, Mrs. Madison, who besides yourself knew that your nephew Brian was due to arrive that day?

PAMELA: Only Tim and, of course, my friend Edith.

BRADBURY: Tell me, Mrs. Madison, did Timothy Crane know what your nephew looked like?

PAMELA: I would think so. When Brian wrote and said he was coming, he enclosed his picture so I'd recognize him. The picture had been on the mantel over the fireplace since I got it about two weeks before.

BRADBURY: Thank you. (*He turns toward GARFIELD.*) Your witness. (*He sits down.*)

GARFIELD: (*She walks toward PAMELA while she is talking.*) Mrs. Madison, could you describe the messenger who brought the ransom note?

PAMELA: Not really. I couldn't see his face at all. He was bundled up in a rain slicker and hat—you know, the kind that covers most of your face. And I really wasn't paying much attention to him. (*She stops and thinks for a moment.*) I did notice that he had on one red sock and one green sock. I remember thinking how peculiar that was.

GARFIELD: So the messenger could have been anybody at all?

PAMELA: Yes.

GARFIELD: You say that Timothy Crane was the only one besides your friend Ms. Allwell who knew that Brian was arriving from England. But a great many people—almost everyone—knew about the money you had, isn't that true?

PAMELA: Yes, I suppose so. It had been in the papers that morning. Admiral Denay is a bit eccentric in that he always pays cash for the racehorses he buys, and newspaper reporters like that kind of story.

GARFIELD: Thank you, that's all. *(She goes back to her seat and sits down.)*

BRADBURY: *(He rises.)* One question on redirect, Your Honor.

JUDGE: Proceed, Mr. Bradbury.

BRADBURY: Mrs. Madison, could you say definitely that the messenger was *not* Timothy Crane? Think before you answer.

PAMELA: *(She thinks for a second.)* No, I couldn't say that.

JUDGE: You may step down, Mrs. Madison. *(PAMELA gets up and goes back to her original seat.)*

BRADBURY: My next witness is Ms. Edith Allwell. *(EDITH gets up and walks to the witness chair and stands in front of it.)*

CLERK: *(The CLERK stands.)* Do you swear to tell the truth, the whole truth, and nothing but the truth?

EDITH: I do. *(She sits down. So does the CLERK.)*

BRADBURY: Ms. Allwell, are you acquainted with Timothy Crane?

EDITH: Yes, of course, He's been Mrs. Madison's secretary for a number of years. And I am a regular visitor at her home.

BRADBURY: Did you ever have occasion to see him elsewhere?

EDITH: Yes, as a matter of fact. Like Mrs. Madison, I own some racehorses. I go to the racetrack quite often. And I've seen Tim there— bumped into him, you might say.

BRADBURY: And did he win or lose?

GARFIELD: *(She rises.)* Objection! That's immaterial, Your Honor!

BRADBURY: *(He turns toward the JUDGE.)* Your Honor, I intend to show that it is not. In fact, it may be the *reason* for this crime.

JUDGE: Very well. Objection overruled. You may answer the question, Ms. Allwell.

EDITH: I've no idea whether Tim won or lost.

BRADBURY: Hmmm. All right. Now let's go back to the day of the kidnapping. What time had you arrived at Mrs. Madison's home?

EDITH: Oh, I'd say around 10 a.m., or so. She'd called me shortly after nine, and I got there as quickly as I could. I stayed with her until sometime after Brian arrived—about an hour or so.

BRADBURY: Were you there when Timothy Crane returned from wherever he'd been?

EDITH: Yes, I was.

BRADBURY: And when was that?

EDITH: About half an hour after Brian came in. We were listening to Brian tell about what had happened to him when Tim came in.

BRADBURY: And how did he seem to you?

EDITH: He seemed to be agitated, nervous. But we were so taken up with Brian that I didn't pay too much attention to Tim.

BRADBURY: Thank you. Your witness, Ms. Garfield. (He goes to his seat.)

GARFIELD: Ms. Allwell, you say Timothy Crane seemed agitated. Yet, you admit you weren't paying too much attention to his mood.

EDITH: That's true.

GARFIELD: Weren't you agitated at that point, given the events of the day?

EDITH: Indeed I was! My heart was still jumping. I can't remember ever being so frightened or upset!

GARFIELD: Why, then, wouldn't Timothy Crane be agitated? After all, he had been in Mrs. Madison's employ for a long time. Certainly you would credit him with caring about her.

BRADBURY: (He rises.) Objection! That's calling for an opinion!

JUDGE: Objection sustained. The witness will not answer the question.

GARFIELD: No further questions. (She returns to her seat.)

JUDGE: You may step down, Ms. Allwell. Mr. Bradbury, call your next witness. (EDITH goes back to her seat.)

BRADBURY: (He rises.) I call Jonathan Slote. (JONATHAN gets up and walks to the witness chair.)

CLERK: (The CLERK stands.) Do you swear to tell the truth, the whole truth, and nothing but the truth?

JONATHAN: I do. (He sits down. So does the CLERK.)

BRADBURY: Mr. Slote, what is your occupation?

JONATHAN: I'm—I work for a literary agency. Mrs. Madison's agent is my employer.

BRADBURY: And do you know Mrs. Madison's secretary, Timothy Crane?

JONATHAN: Oh, yes. We come from the same town in Illinois. I've known him all my life. In fact, it was he who recommended me to my employer.

BRADBURY: And do you have occasion to see him often?

JONATHAN: Yes, sir. We have the same day off and generally spend it together.

BRADBURY: And what do you and Mr. Crane do on your days off?

JONATHAN: Usually, we go to the races. We both like to bet on the horses.

BRADBURY: Mr. Slote, do you know if Mr. Crane won or lost at the races?

JONATHAN: Well, lately he'd been losing.

BRADBURY: I see. Mr. Slote, do you know how much money he had lost?

JONATHAN: Not exactly. It has to be quite a lot, though. Because he's borrowed money from me—he owes me over a thousand dollars.

BRADBURY: And has he expressed an intention to repay you?

JONATHAN: Oh, yes. He told me that he'd have it for me very soon.

BRADBURY: When did he tell you that?

JONATHAN: Two days before Brian Farley was kidnapped.

BRADBURY: Thank you. Your witness. *(He returns to his seat.)*

GARFIELD: *(She rises.)* I have only one question for Mr. Slote. Tell me, Mr. Slote, since you have known the defendant so long, do you think him capable of committing this crime?

BRADBURY: *(He rises.)* Objection, Your Honor! Opinion!

JUDGE: Hmmm. I think I'll overrule your objection, Mr. Bradbury. The witness may answer.

GARFIELD: Mr. Slote?

JONATHAN: No, I don't *think* so.

GARFIELD: Thank you. No further questions. *(She sits down.)*

JUDGE: You may step down, Mr. Slote. Before you call your next witness, Mr. Bradbury, we will take a recess.

CLERK: *(The CLERK stands up.)* All rise!

(Everyone stands as the JUDGE goes out the chambers side, followed by the CLERK. Then everyone but GARFIELD and TIMOTHY go out the doorway side. GARFIELD and TIMOTHY sit down.)

TIMOTHY: It doesn't look good for me, does it?

GARFIELD: No, Tim, I'm afraid it doesn't. *(She thinks for a second.)* The nephew will probably be the next witness. What's he like?

TIMOTHY: He seems nice enough. A bit down on his luck at the moment, I'd guess from his conversation. But he's got a good sense of humor. Takes after his father, according to Mrs. Madison. She says he has all the family traits.

GARFIELD: What do you mean, all?

TIMOTHY: Oh, just the odd things that occur in some families. You know, allergies and that sort of thing. Mrs. Madison says that all the men in her family are color-blind, hate squash, and are allergic to strawberries.

GARFIELD: Hmmmm. Color-blind. *(She thinks for a moment.)* I wonder . . *(Everyone except the JUDGE and the CLERK returns to the courtroom. They don't all come at once—they straggle in. When everyone is in his or her seat the clerk comes in and faces them all.)*

CLERK: All rise! *(Everyone stands up. The JUDGE comes in and takes his seat.)*

CLERK: Be seated.

(Everyone, including the CLERK, sits down.)

JUDGE: Mr. Bradbury, call your witness.

BRADBURY: *(He rises.)* Mr. Brian Farley. *(BRIAN comes to the witness chair and stands in front of it.)*

CLERK: *(The CLERK stands.)* Do you swear to tell the truth, the whole truth, and nothing but the truth?

BRIAN: I do. *(He sits down. So does the CLERK.)*

BRADBURY: Mr. Farley, please tell the court what happened to you on May 22nd.

BRIAN: Yes, sir. Just before my plane landed, the airflight attendant told me that I'd got a message not to go to my aunt's house. I was to meet her at a different address. I took a cab there. No sooner had I rung the bell, when the door opened and somebody grabbed me. I never did see the man's face. Before I knew what was happening, I was bound, gagged, and blindfolded. Then I heard the man go out. He came back some time later, pushed me out the door, and into a car. We drove for quite some time. Then he stopped the car, untied my hands, and pushed me out. He drove away before I could get the blindfold off. When I finally managed to remove it, I found that I was back at the airport. I hailed a cab and went to my aunt's house.

BRADBURY: Thank you, Mr. Farley. Your witness, Ms. Garfield. (*He sits down.*)

GARFIELD: (*She is talking to herself in a loud whisper.*) Something isn't . . . but what is it? (*She rises.*) I would like to reserve my cross examination until later, Your Honor. (*She sits down.*)

JUDGE: Very well. Call another witness, Mr. Bradbury. (*BRIAN returns to his seat.*)

BRADBURY: (*He rises.*) The prosecution has no other witnesses, Your Honor. (*He sits down.*)

JUDGE: Then we will hear from the defense. Ms. Garfield.

GARFIELD: (*She rises.*) The defense calls Timothy Crane. (*TIMOTHY goes to the witness chair and stands in front of it.*)

CLERK: (*The CLERK stands.*) Do you swear to tell the truth, the whole truth, and nothing but the truth?

TIMOTHY: I do. (*He sits down. So does the CLERK.*)

GARFIELD: Mr. Crane, please tell the court what you did on the day in question.

TIMOTHY: I left the house a little after nine in the morning and went to the racetrack. I was to meet a guy I know. He'd promised to give me a good solid tip on the sixth race. And I needed that tip. I'd lost a lot of money, including most of what I'd borrowed from my friend, Jon Slote. I figured that with a good tip, I could make back what I'd lost—and maybe more. But the guy never showed up. I hunted all over for him. Then the races started. I bet—and lost. I felt sick so I went home, back to Mrs. Madison's.

GARFIELD: Did you see anyone you knew at the racetrack?

TIMOTHY: No. If it had been my regular day off, I probably would have—the same people seem to be there all the time. But this was a different day. Besides, I was busy looking for the guy I was supposed to meet. I didn't pay any attention to who was there.

GARFIELD: Were you aware that it was the day that Mrs. Madison's nephew was to arrive?

TIMOTHY: Yes. His telegram had come just before I left the house.

GARFIELD: *(She walks back and forth for a moment, thinking. Then she stops.)* Mr. Crane, did you read the telegram?

TIMOTHY: Yes. I open all the mail. As soon as I read it, I gave it to Mrs. Madison.

GARFIELD: Do you happen to know what she did with it?

TIMOTHY: Hmmm. I think she put it in her purse.

GARFIELD: *(She turns toward the JUDGE.)* Your Honor, if Mrs. Madison still has the telegram in her purse, perhaps we might see it?

JUDGE: *(He nods, then turns and looks at PAMELA.)* Mrs. Madison, do you have that telegram?

PAMELA: I'll see, Your Honor. *(She opens her purse and searches through it. After a second or two she pulls out a folded piece of yellow paper.)* Yes. Here it is.

JUDGE: Give it to the clerk, please. *(The CLERK takes the telegram and brings it to Ms. Garfield.)*

GARFIELD: Thank you. *(She takes it from the CLERK and reads aloud.)* It says: "Arriving 1:30 p.m. Do not meet me. Will take a cab." And it's signed Brian. *(She hands it to TIMOTHY.)* Is this the telegram you saw? *(He looks at it.)* Yes, it is. *(He hands it back to GARFIELD.)*

GARFIELD: Thank you, Mr. Crane. I have no further questions. Your witness, Mr. Bradbury. *(She returns to her seat and puts the telegram on the table in front of her.)*

BRADBURY: Your testimony was very interesting, Mr. Crane. But do you really expect us to believe that you saw no one you knew at the racetrack? After all, it is a place you go often.

TIMOTHY: Yes, but I didn't see anyone I knew that day.

BRADBURY: Of course, you didn't. Because you weren't there! You never went to the racetrack. Instead, you were holding Brian Farley prisoner! You knew your employer had a great deal of cash on hand and that she would gladly exchange it for the safe return of her nephew.

TIMOTHY: No! That's not true! I didn't do it! I didn't!

BRADBURY: I submit that you did, Mr. Crane. No further questions. *(He returns to his seat.)*

JUDGE: You may step down, Mr. Crane. Ms. Garfield, call your next witness. *(CRANE returns to his seat.)*

GARFIELD: *(She rises.)* I have no other witnesses, Your Honor. But at this time I'd like to have Brian Farley recalled to the stand for cross-examination.

JUDGE: Very well. Brian Farley, take the stand. *(BRIAN goes to the witness chair and sits down.)*

JUDGE: Remember, Mr. Farley, you are still under oath.

BRIAN: Yes, Your Honor.

GARFIELD: Mr. Farley, before you left England, you sent a telegram to your aunt not to meet your plane. Why was that?

BRIAN: I wanted to save her a trip to the airport.

GARFIELD: That was very considerate of you. By the way, what time did your plane arrive?

BRIAN: One-thirty in the afternoon.

GARFIELD: And it was a direct, non-stop flight from England?

BRIAN: Yes.

GARFIELD: *(She walks over to the table and picks up the telegram.)* Can you tell me then, Mr. Farley, how your aunt received this *telegram* from you and not a cablegram? Telegrams are *land* wires, not overseas wires.

BRIAN: Why—uhhh . . .

GARFIELD: Mr. Farley, how long have you been out of work?

BRIAN: About six months. But I don't see what that has to do with anything.

GARFIELD: Let's let the court decide that. Tell me, if you've not worked in six months, where did you get the money for the trip?

BRIAN: I—I—borrowed it. I'm to pay it back within a month.

GARFIELD: I see, Mr. Farley, what would you say if I contended that you were never kidnapped at all? That you, in fact, landed in the United States in the morning, saw the newspaper report of your aunt's sale of a racehorse to Admiral Denay, guessed that she had a lot of cash on hand—and cooked up this scheme to rob her?

BRIAN: That's ridiculous!

GARFIELD: Is it? Tell me, Mr. Farley, what color socks are you wearing?

BRIAN: What . . .? *(He pulls up both legs of his pants so that his socks show and looks down at them.)* They're green. But I don't see . . .

GARFIELD: No, *you* don't. But perhaps the court will. You are not wearing two green socks, Mr. Farley. Only one is green. The other is red. You can't tell the difference because you are color-blind.

BRIAN: So what?

GARFIELD: Isn't it strange that the messenger who brought the ransom note also wore one red sock and one green one? Perhaps he, too, is color-blind. Or perhaps, Mr. Farley, you were the messenger!

BRIAN: I—I—oh, what's the use! Yes, I did it. Just the way you said. I thought no one would find out! *(He covers his face with his hands.)* I'll give the money back!

JUDGE: *(He pounds the gavel.)* Mr. Bradbury, I think a motion to dismiss the case against Mr. Crane is in order.

BRADBURY: *(He rises.)* I so move, Your Honor.

JUDGE: Motion granted. Case dismissed! *(He pounds the gavel once.)* The clerk will escort Mr. Farley to the bailiff where he will be advised of his rights and then removed to the jail. *(The clerk goes over to the witness stand and takes Brian's arm and escorts him out the doorway side.)*

JUDGE: Court is adjourned. *(He gets up and goes out. Everyone, except TIMOTHY and GARFIELD, rises and heads for the doorway, talking among themselves.)*

TIMOTHY: *(He turns to GARFIELD.)* I don't know how to thank you . . .*(On her way to the door, Pamela has stopped next to TIMOTHY'S chair. She puts her hand on his shoulder and faces GARFIELD.)*

PAMELA: Let me add my thanks, too. Though it hurts to know that my own nephew tried to rob me, it makes me feel better to know that my trust in Tim all these years hasn't been misplaced.

GARFIELD: No thanks are necessary. Tim's telling me that Brian is color-blind was what gave me the answer. The path to truth, in this case, was marked in red and green. *(GARFIELD and TIMOTHY rise. TIMOTHY takes PAMELA'S arm and all three go out together.)*

End of Play

A Scene from
Rockway Cafe II
A play with rock music
by
Max Bush

Characters

ROXANNE . . . 14 Years old
DELLA . . . Roxanne's Mother

TV Characters
ERIC . . . Rock and Roll Singer
RACHEL . . . Eric's Girlfriend
JOHN . . . Rachel's Father
DIGGS . . . Stage-Manager
TONYA . . . Back-up Singer
CHARLEEN . . . Back-up Singer
JASMINE . . . Back-up Singer
BRANDY . . . Dancer
CASSIE . . . Dancer

Production Notes

TIME: Present

PLACE: A Suburb

SETTINGS: The family recreation room

219

MUSIC NOTE: If a live band is used, there can be interplay between band and actors throughout. Five musicians are suggested—two guitars, drums, keyboard and bass. If a music tape is used with no live accompaniment, when the characters sing only part of a song, it is sung acappella. For music, contact the playwrite.

AT RISE: Rec room and TV area; the two worlds are clearly delineated; there is strong contrast between the two. Right, the rec room, has a couch, floor lamp, shelves and an end table with a jar of candy and a phone. Rec room is fairly small and simple; left, Rockway Cafe is spacious and brilliant. The Cafe's walls contain high cathedral windows with colorful curtains. Bolts of material hang from the ceiling. A series of platforms lines the walls that will be used by the band, singers and dancers.

The TV actors [Rachel, Eric, John, Candy, Diggs] stand scattered around the stage, unlit, unmoving, their heads down.

For the pre-show, the band—up left and on platforms—plays "Was It The Night." When they are not playing, they are unlit but do not lower their heads and freeze as the TV actors do when the TV is off.

Roxanne enters rec room, the band finishes playing. She walks up to her practice mike stand and mike and breaks into singing "Fantasy Man". The song has potentially a lot of energy but Roxanne sings it self-consciously and joylessly, going through the motions of choreography she's created for herself.

● ● ● ● ● ● ● ● ● ● ● ● ● ● ● ● ● ●

ROX: (Sings accapella.)
HE'S MY FANTASY MAN,
AND GIRL HE'S ALWAYS THERE.
HE'S MY FANTASY MAN,
(DELLA enters.)
WHEN I NEED SOMEONE TO CARE.
HE'S MY FANTASY, FANTASY, FANTASY, FANTASY MAN.
HE'S MY FANTASY, FANTASY, FANTASY, FANTASY MAN.

DELLA: Well, that's a little better, Roxanne, isn't it?

ROX: Hey, it's a lot better, mom.

DELLA: But it's still not what you want, is it?

ROX: I couldn't do better if I was Whitney Houston. It's a rank song.

DELLA: Who chose it for you?

ROX: I did.

DELLA: Why did you choose a rank song?

ROX: Because I love myself, Ma!

DELLA: I've heard you sing better, honey.

ROX: I never sang it any better. I can't sing it any better. I will never sing it any better.

DELLA: Like when you're listening to headphones or watching "Rockway Cafe." You sing loud, you jump around, you have fun. Try again.

ROX: Don't you have court in the morning? (*DELLA indicates yes.*) Shouldn't you be figuring out your cross exams?

DELLA: I've already done them.

ROX: I hate Mr. Berry!

DELLA: Roxanne—

ROX: You don't know what kind of teacher he is.

DELLA: He's letting you choose your own rank music.

ROX: You know what Mr. Berry's first name is? It's Dingle. What does that tell you about his teaching methods?

DELLA: (*Covering a smile.*) Roxanne, don't be rude. He doesn't deserve that from you. Now, go ahead, sing. Only let yourself go. Have fun.

ROX: (*Suddenly sitting on floor. DELLA lets this run its course.*) Why does everyone have to sing? Why not just the best people in the class? I sing like a trollqueen . . . giving birth.
(*Sings like a trollqueen.*)
HE'S MY FANTASY MAN
MORE THAN A FRIEND TO ME—
(*DELLA throws a couch pillow, hits ROXANNE.*) I wish I had someone to sing with. Everybody was already stuck together by the time Berry finished his sentence: "You can sing by yourselves or with others." Zip, superglued in groups. "Ha-ha, Roxanne." I'm the only one singing by her stupid self.

DELLA: (*Seeing she's finished.*) Come on. I'll help you.

ROX: Don't you have to go to the jail tonight to talk to that drug dealer?

DELLA: Drunk driver.

ROX: Or that cat burglar?

DELLA: Dog catcher.

ROX: Don't you have to research something or update your folders or make some notes or look up some other cases?

DELLA: Always.

ROX: Ma, you got to pick out your clothes!

DELLA: I will.

ROX: You're perfect, aren't you?

DELLA: And I'd love to hear you sing.

ROX: I want to watch "Rockway Cafe".

DELLA: So that's it.

ROX: I'll practice afterwards.

DELLA: Roxanne, you said you'd practice tonight because last night you had to watch "The Bradford Show" and "Our Times" or you would die of television withdrawal.

ROX: But I've been looking forward to this episode for five months; ever since it was first on.

DELLA: It's a rerun?

ROX: You heard me talk about it. They sing the whole intro tonight. And Eric sings "I'm Ready For Love" to Rachel. (*ROXANNE sings to DELLA part of the song with more enthusiasm than her recital song.*)
I'M READY FOR LOVE
THE LOVE THAT SAYS THERE IS ONLY YOU.
YES, I'M READY FOR LOVE
(*She kisses DELLA.*)
I GIVE YOU EVERYTHING YOU KNOW IT'S TRUE.

DELLA: I'm worried about you and that TV.

ROX: We're just going steady.

DELLA: I mean it, Roxanne.

ROX: I'm worried, too. I'm worried about Eric. He's blowing it with Rachel. I keep telling him what he needs to do but he won't listen to me.

DELLA: Don't you have this on tape?

ROX: I did but I accidently taped over it. Mom, I'll clean the porch or I'll do the laundry for a month or—

DELLA: Roxanne—

ROX: I'll call gramma and talk to her about her operations.

DELLA: You want to live to see your next birthday? (*ROXANNE sulks.*) Don't pull that face.

ROX: What face?

DELLA: That thing you do with your eyes. It's just like your father.

ROX: You mean this? (*She does it again.*)

DELLA: Stop it. You only do that to irritate me.

ROX: I'm sorry. I am his daughter. I look like him.

DELLA: Roxanne, you chose to be in this class. You chose that rank song. You knew you'd have to sing in this recital.

ROX: Dad lets me watch as much TV as I want at his house. He even watches Rockway with me sometimes.

DELLA: You sing the song through once—to me—we'll talk about it, then sing it again and you can watch TV All right?

ROX: All right.

DELLA: All right.

ROX: After "Rockway Cafe".

DELLA: Before "Rockway Cafe". Before any more TV.

ROX: It's almost time for it to start.

DELLA: Then tape it and watch it after you're done.

ROX: I will, but—I'll practice all night. I'll sing it to you three times! Mom! I'll-have-fun!

DELLA: Roxanne!

ROX: I haven't won one argument since you became a lawyer.

DELLA: That's enough! You practice, now—

ROX: I know.

DELLA: With or without me helping you.

ROX: Without, please.

DELLA: Don't you think it would help you—

ROX: Without, please.

DELLA: All right. Call me when you're ready to sing to me.

ROX: All right.

DELLA: You can do this, Roxanne; the only thing stopping you is yourself. *(DELLA exits.)*

ROX: "The only thing stopping you is yourself." God, Mom, what do you know? I'm on my deathbed! It's my last wish! *(She flops on couch.)* Rockway Cafe. . .Rockway Cafe. . .*(She falls off the couch, dies. The phone rings. She sits up, checks her watch, picks up remote, turns on the TV [Note: The remote has a clicker on it that the TV actors can hear.])* Just starting. *(Lights up on TV, the TV actors begin to animate, ROXANNE hears mother coming, turns TV off, jumps up to mike and sings. The TV lights fade out, the actors put their heads back down.)* HE'S MY FANTASY MAN, MORE THAN A FRIEND TO ME—

DELLA: *(Entering.)* The phone's for you.

ROX: Who is it?

DELLA: Rob.

ROX: Tell him I'm practicing.

DELLA: Why won't you talk to him? I think he's charming.

ROX: Mom, I think I'd better accept the responsibility for things like practicing, don't you? *(Sings.)* HE'S MY FANTASY MAN HE'S WHAT A FRIEND SHOULD BE. . . *(DELLA exits shaking her head. ROX quickly turns on TV. Spot up on JOHN in the Rockway Cafe; the other characters remain frozen in the dark [RACHEL, ERIC, TONYA, JOHN, DIGGS] This is the introduction of the weekly TV show. The bass pulses underneath the lines.)*

JOHN: It's finally Friday; *(Rhythm guitar strikes a chord, the bass continues to pulse.)* finally nine o-clock. Leave the world behind. The door is open. Come in to where fantasy lives and rocks. None of that other stuff matters. Come find yourself in "Rockway Cafe."

(Guitar player hits a chord, lets it hang over the scene as the lights come up and the TV actors animate. DIGGS begins placing the four mikes for ERIC'S upcoming song, "Rockway Cafe." DIGGS is the stage-manager/technical wizard wearing jeans and a heavily stocked tool belt. CANDY, a dancer, is doing some extra stretches to warm for song. Both JOHN and ERIC converge on RACHEL.)

ERIC: Rachel . . .

RACHEL: Are you ready?

ERIC: Yea, I'm ready.

RACHEL: Well, I'm not. And we go on in five minutes. *(She begins to move, JOHN cuts her off.)*

JOHN: Eric is right. Listen to him.

RACHEL: What is it you think I haven't heard?

ERIC: I can help you, Rachel. Let me talk to the recording company.

RACHEL: If you do I won't go to the audition.

ERIC: John, am I trying to do something wrong?

JOHN: No. Rachel, I don't know where this stubborn streak comes from. Certainly not me.

ERIC: What are you afraid of?

ROX: She told you!

RACHEL: I told you. I told you both.

ROX & RACHEL: I want my talent to get me in the door.

RACHEL: I want my music to get this recording contract,

ROX & RACHEL: not you.

ROX: Leave her alone.

ERIC: I'm not singing for you; I'm just asking someone to listen to you.

CANDY: God, stop arguing. It's too early. I'll throw up. *(She moves toward DIGGS, JOHN and ERIC follow.)*

RACHEL: Diggs, are the mike's hot?

DIGGS: I'm working on it.

RACHEL: We're at three minutes.

DIGGS: It'll be ready, Miss Rachel, and we'll be doing good.

ERIC: Rachel—*(RACHEL sees the back-up singers, JASMINE, TONYA and CHARLEEN enter, moves to them. ERIC and JOHN let her go, for now.)*

RACHEL: *(To CHARLEEN.)* You don't want this. *(Takes off CHARLEEN'S headband, pockets it.)*

CHAR: *(To JASMINE.)* I told you she wouldn't like it.

JASMINE: Is this all right? *(Her costume.)*

RACHEL: Yes, that's what I meant. *(To TONYA.)* Like the new hair, Tonya.

But it needs a little help.

TONYA: Of course.

RACHEL: What does that mean?

TONYA: There's always something wrong, isn't there, Rachel?

ROX: As long as you're on the program, Tonya. (*BRANDY, a featured dancer in Rockway Cafe, enters, moves to DIGGS, who has begun to work on a cable.*)

RACHEL: Let me fix it.

TONYA: (*Sweetly*) How about I fix your face?

RACHEL: What?

TONYA: Your rouge is uneven. (*RACHEL fixes TONYA'S hair.*)

BRANDY: Diggs, is my collar all right? How do I look?

DIGGS: You look fine, Brandy.

BRANDY: You didn't even see. (*One of the other dancers, CASSIE, enters, dressed in a tight, revealing outfit.*)

DIGGS: Ask Rachel how you look. I have to get this plug ready or nobody will hear anything, tonight.

CASSIE: Hello, Mr. Diggs. (*DIGGS stops working for a moment, watches her.*)

DIGGS: (*Impressed.*) Cassie.

BRANDY: Is that what you like? (*She moves to her place.*)

JOHN: (*He and ERIC once more converge on RACHEL.*) You don't understand how the industry operates.

ROX: You don't understand your daughter!

JOHN: I've worked in the studios and I know how they think.

ERIC: I came from the streets of nowhere and I needed lots of help.

ROX: Eric, try not to talk.

ERIC: My music was always hot, but no one would hear it—until your father told them to listen. Suddenly, they had ears and contracts. But I still feel pride in my music; it's still mine.

RACHEL& ROX: That's your story.

DIGGS: Back-ground test, please.

JASMINE: Hello, hello—

DIGGS: Next.

CHAR: Are we going to be ready, Diggs?

DIGGS: Next.

TONYA: Does anybody mind if I move my mike?

DIGGS, RACHEL, JOHN, ROXANNE: Yes!

TONYA: (*Satisfied.*) The world is still the same—all is well.

DIGGS: Everything's set.

RACHEL: Where are the rest of the dancers?

DIGGS: Places everybody. We're at one minute. (*DIGGS hustles off.*)

JOHN: Just let me tell them you're my daughter.

ROX: I don't think so.

RACHEL: I waited years until my music was good enough until I was good enough to get this audition. My music got me in the door and now it's up to me to win a contract. It's time, Father. (*Lights dim, spot up on JOHN'S mike.*)

ROX: Just sing, Eric. That's all you need to do.

RACHEL: (*Pushing JOHN up platform.*) Father, go! JOHN (*JOHN steps into spot, speaks into mike, directly to audience.*) Welcome. Welcome to Rockway Cafe! (*BAND PLAYS INTRO TO ROCKWAY CAFE.*) We know why you're here and we'll bring him right on. (*DIGGS hurries in other dancers, then takes his position near the band. RACHEL fixes ERIC'S hair.*) But first I'd like to personally thank this young man for not forgetting those who knew and loved him before he became a legend. Many have come through here, but none so hot, none with so much class. Hey! Returning to The Cafe where it started for him! Here, with the Rockway Dancers, The Man! The Rockman of Rockway! Eric Cortland! (*JOHN exits.*)

ERIC: It's great to be home!

ERIC & ROX: "Rockway Cafe!"

ERIC: (*Sings.*)

DON'T YOU WORRY 'BOUT TOMORROW

DON'T YOU FRET ABOUT ABOUT TODAY. (*Lights flash, the dancers dance, the spot picks out featured singers and dancers. It's flashing, colorful, exuberant rock and roll.*)

'CAUSE THERE'S A PLACE, YOU CAN ROCK TONIGHT

AND ROLL YOUR CARES AWAY.

ERIC & BACK-UP: YOU CAN GO THERE JUST THE WAY YOU ARE.

JOIN YOUR FRIENDS WHO KNOW YOU ARE A STAR.

COME ON TO THE ROCKWAY!

BABY, IT'S YOUR CAFE!

COME ON TO THE ROCKWAY!

BABY IT'S OUR CAFE!

ERIC: COME AND MEET ME FOR THE SHOW TONIGHT

LEAVE YOUR MONDAY WORLD FAR BELOW.

LET YOUR SOUL GO SAILIN' WHEN THE BAND STARTS WAILIN'

IT'S FRIDAY NIGHT, LET'S GO!

ERIC & BACK-UP: JOIN THE BEAT THAT ROCKS THE U.S.A.

CELEBRATE; GET DOWN; COME OUT; COME PLAY.

(COME ON, COME ON, COME ON)

COME ON TO THE ROCKWAY!

GET DOWN AT THE CAFE!

JOIN US AT THE ROCKWAY!

DANCIN' AT THE CAFE!

ROCK—WAY—CA—FE *(five times)*

TAKE ME TO THE ROCKWAY!

TAKE ME TO OUR CAFE!

COME ON TO THE ROCKWAY!

BABY, IT'S OUR CAFE!

ERIC: Thank-you! Thank-you! Rockway Cafe! *(ERIC bows, everyone follows* him, bows. Dancers exit, lights fade. TONYA, JASMINE, CHARLEEN, DIGGS, ERIC and RACHEL slowly put their heads down, become inert.)

ROX: Commercial. I hate—NO COMMERCIALS! Why don't they put them all at the beginning or the end. *(She hits mute button, stands fidgeting for a time.)* "You could sing while you're waiting." Oh, I didn't think of that. "Sure, let yourself go, jump around, have fun." Thank-you. I'd rather eat my dad's socks. *(She looks at TV, then turns away in disgust. She sings absentmindedly.)*

GIRLS YOU KNOW THE STORY

YOU KNOW ALL THE RULES

BUT THERE'S NOTHING 'BOUT—I was singing! *(She freezes. She begins to say something inaudibly, repeatedly, without moving her jaw. She says it three times; finally we're able to understand:)* Oil can. Oil can. *(She loosens a couple joints, then slumps. She glances at TV, sees the commercials are still running. She moves up to mike, resolutely sings.)*

HE'S MY FANTASY MAN

MORE THAN A FRIEND TO—

(She stops, having made a mistake.) HE'S MY FANTASY *(She goes off key.)* HE'S MY *(Another mistake.)* I need help. *(She takes a fistful of candy out of the jar on the end table, stuffs it in her mouth with the wrappers still on. She moves back to mike, sings with her mouth full.)* HE'S MY FANTASY MAN *(Pieces fall out of her mouth to the floor.)*

AND GIRL, HE'S ALWAYS THERE.

HE'S MY FANTASY MAN

WHEN I NEED SOMEONE TO CARE. "Well, that's a little better, Roxanne, isn't it." Yup. I never sang it better. I'm the star of the recital. *(She takes the last piece of candy from her mouth, offers it to her Mother.)* Would you like a piece of candy, Mom? *(She sees the program is resuming, picks candy up, stuffs it back in candy dish.)* That took forever. *(Scene opens in the Rockway Cafe, late at night. DIGGS stands near band, the back-up singers stand at their mikes, exhausted. RACHEL paces.)*

CHAR: Rachel

RACHEL: Later.

RIC: What are you

RACHEL: Don't talk to me for a minute.

TONYA: Diggs?

RACHEL: *(Sings.)* TELL ME BABY

DIGGS: How long will this take, Miss Rachel? The band is fried.

RACHEL: Until I have the song.

ERIC: Why don't you come out to the beach house, I'll turn on the jacuzzi

RACHEL: Not now.

ROX: I can make it. 555-4585! Say your name is Rob!

ERIC: After this?

RACHEL: I'm sure it will be too late.

ROX: I bet it won't be too late for you, Eric.

ERIC: It won't be too late for me.

ROX: I knew it. You're so predictable.

RACHEL: Charleen

CHAR: We're just doing what you wanted.

RACHEL: Try coming in a little stronger on the verses.

JASMINE: We could do that.

RACHEL: Thank you, Jasmine.

JOHN: *(JOHN walks on.)* Rachel!

RACHEL: I'm right here, I wasn't hiding from you.

ROX: What time is it, John?

JOHN: It's two o'clock in the morning.

ROX: How's the band?

JOHN: The band is exhausted.

ROX: I like fried, better.

RACHEL: They're getting paid.

DIGGS: How much longer—

RACHEL & ROX: Until we get it right.

TONYA: Great.

RACHEL: All night if I have to. The audition is next week. I want to be ready.

JOHN: *(Help.)* Eric.

RACHEL: (*Looking to the band.*) Try the first line of the chorus; just the guitar. (*Sings; the rhythm guitar tries to follow her.*)

TELL ME NOW, BABY, IS THIS ALL A DREAM.

ERIC: No. (*Nods to band, sings; guitar tries to follow.*) TELL ME BABY, NOW

RACHEL: Let me get it.

ERIC: But I hear it.

RACHEL & ROX: I'll get it.

RACHEL: (*Sings, guitar follows.*) TELL ME BABY, NOW, IS THIS ALL—

ERIC: That's your mistake.

RACHEL: Eric!

ERIC: I'm just showing you

RACHEL: I'll find my mistake. I'm writing this song. It's my song.

ERIC: (*Sings; guitar follows him.*) TELL ME BABY, NOW, IS THIS ALL A DREAM. Clean and simple, just how you like it. Now you have it, you can sing it and we can all get out of here.

JASMINE: That'll work, Rachel.

CHAR: Yeah.

TONYA: Thank-you.

CHAR: That's the way I hear it.

ROX: Kill him!

JOHN: (*Infuriated, RACHEL pushes ERIC.*) Rachel! (*RACHEL tries to slap him, he catches her arm. She swings the other, he grabs that wrist, too. They wrestle, she trying to get free of him and hit him, he protecting himself.*)

ERIC: What's wrong with you?

ROX: She told you to let her do it!

RACHEL: Let me go! Let me go!

ROX: Hit him!

JOHN: He was trying to help you!

ERIC: Rachel! Rachel!

ROX: Kick him! Kick him!

RACHEL: Eric! Let me go! (*He pushes her away, she falls, he immediately tries to help her up. She scrambles away from him.*) Let me make mistakes!

It's my song!

ERIC: I was helping you!

JOHN: He was only—

RACHEL: I make mistakes! They're my mistakes! I need to make them! Let me go! Let me go! *(She runs off.)*

JASMINE: Rachel, he wasn't trying to. . .

TONYA: Does this mean we're finished?

DIGGS: No, it doesn't. Ladies and gentleman, stay where you are. *(TONYA, JASMINE and CHARLEEN all sit. BRANDY enters, dressed much more glamourously, like the dancer that caught DIGGS' eye earlier.)*

BRANDY: Hello, Mr. Diggs.

DIGGS: Hello, Brandy. What are you still doing here?

BRANDY: Waiting for you, sweetheart.

DIGGS: What? Why are you dressed like that?

BRANDY: I should think almost anybody wearing a toolbelt could figure that out. *(DIGGS realizes she's there for him, pulls her aside.)*

DIGGS: Do you think that looks good on you?

BRANDY: Well, I don't know.

DIGGS: You want to know what I think?

BRANDY: Yes I do, Mr. Diggs.

DIGGS: I think you should go home, lady, and get some sleep. I wish I could.

ERIC: What am I doing wrong? Is it me, John? *(BRANDY exits.)*

ROX: There's nothing wrong with her!

ERIC: Maybe you can explain it to me.

ROX: Let me explain it to you. Hah! *(She kicks at the TV She then lets her hair down.)*

CHAR: Maybe the mix is sounding dry to her. Put more reverb on it.

JASMINE: And pull back the keyboards, especially on the verses.

CHAR: Yeah, she sounds like she's fighting them.

DIGGS: Hey, that's what the woman wants.

TONYA: She doesn't know what she wants.

ROX: It's my song and. . .(*ROXANNE steps toward TV. The lights flicker and flash. There is searing sound as if the fabric of the universe is torn, as ROXANNE moves into the TV and assumes RACHEL'S character. The TV characters all turn and focus on her. As RACHEL.*) I'll make it work.

ERIC: Whatever I did, I'm sorry. I was just trying to help.

JASMINE: I think that's true, don't you?

ERIC: Babe, you're just burning on nerves. Let's go to the beach house. You'll sleep forever.

ROX: (*To JOHN*) You taught me it's my music, in my style, from myself. That's what people want; that's good music.

CHAR: Honey, you nailed it—three times in a row.

JASMINE: Smooth and clean, just like you want it.

ROX: But it didn't feel right. I'm not Eric. He rehearses a song once and he's ready. It comes hard for me. I have to work at it. (*To ERIC*) Will you wait? I'd still like to sing it to you.

ERIC: Yeah. Yeah, I'll wait.

ROX: Only if you want.

ERIC: I said I'd wait.

ROX: Then maybe you should go.

ERIC: I said I'd wait.

ROX: Both of you. I can do this myself.

JOHN: We'd love to hear it again.

CHAR: Anyone who makes a mistake, dies. (*CHARLEEN and JASMINE stand, move to mikes. TONYA remains seated, pulls the mike down to her level.*)

ROX: One and two and (*Band plays, She sings, clearly and with feeling, avoiding looking at ERIC.*)

WAS IT THE NIGHT

WAS IT THE NIGHT?

WAS IT THE NIGHT?

WAS IT THE NIGHT OR THE SHINE OF YOUR HAIR

IN THE CANDLELIGHT?

WAS IT THE NIGHT?

YOU'RE SO FREE.

YOU'RE SO FREE

YOU'RE SO FREE GOOD FRIENDS IS ALL

I THOUGHT WE'D BE.

YOU'RE SO FREE.

TELL ME BABY, NOW, IS THIS ALL A DREAM?

OR, AM I TRAPPED INSIDE SOME CRUEL SCHEME?

MY MIND SAYS, BABY, NOW, DON'T YOU BE A FOOL.

MY HEART SAYS, BABY, YOU'LL LOOSE HIM IF YOU PLAY TOO COOL.
   (*She nods "yes" to back-up singers who have come in a little stronger on the verse.*)

MY HEART SAYS, BABY, YOU'LL LOOSE HIM IF YOU PLAY TOO COOL.

MY HEART SAYS, BABY, YOU'LL LOOSE HIM IF YOU PLAY TOO COOL.
   (*ERIC moves up behind her, puts his hand on her, moves away. She turns to him, sings the rest of the song to him.*)

THE MOON WAS RIGHT.

THE MOON WAS RIGHT

THE MOON WAS RIGHT AND SENT US ON A MAGIC FLIGHT.

THE MOON WAS RIGHT.

YOU CAME TO ME.

YOU CAME TO ME

YOU CAME TO ME AND YOU TAUGHT ME ALL ABOUT HARMONY.

YOU CAME TO ME.

TELL ME BABY, NOW, IS THIS ALL A DREAM?

OR, AM I TRAPPED INSIDE SOME CRUEL SCHEME?

MY MIND SAYS, BABY, NOW, DON'T YOU BE A FOOL.

MY HEART SAYS, BABY, YOU'LL LOOSE HIM IF YOU PLAY TOO COOL.

MY HEART SAYS, BABY, YOU'LL LOOSE HIM IF YOU PLAY TOO COOL.

MY HEART SAYS, BABY, YOU'LL LOOSE HIM IF YOU PLAY TOO COOL.

MY HEART SAYS, BABY, YOU'LL LOOSE HIM IF YOU PLAY TOO COOL.

WAS IT THE NIGHT?

WAS IT THE NIGHT?

That was it, everybody! Thank-you! *(Reactions from everyone.)*

TONYA: *(Aside to ERIC.)* Was it any different?

ROX: That's how it goes!

JOHN: Let's pack it up! *(He exits. JASMINE pats ROXANNE on back, then exits with TONYA, CHARLEEN and DIGGS. Band withdraws.)*

ERIC: You sing it like that and they'll book your first world tour in a week.

ROX: *(Embracing ERIC.)* Yes!

DELLA: *(Entering rec. room.)* Roxanne?

ROX: *(Aside.)* Mom. . .

ERIC: That was strong. Clean as always but more from yourself.

ROX: I felt more, like I was singing it for the first time.

DELLA: Roxanne?

ROX: Having you listen made a difference. That's how you can help me. Just listen. *(DELLA picks up remote.)*

ERIC: You sing to me any time.

ROX: Eric, you know that *(To DELLA.)* No! *(Della turns off TV Slowly, as the scene fades out, ROXANNE and ERIC put their heads down, stay still.)* Oh, no. *(From that position, ROXANNE can see but can't move.)* I can't. . . *(DELLA exits looking for ROXANNE.)*

ROX: Eric? Mother! Come back and turn on the TV! I'll miss the rest of the show. I'll miss the rest of my life! She never watches TV, I'll have to wait until Gramma comes over on Christmas to watch the Nutcracker. Maybe I. . . *(She tries to move, can't. Laughing at herself.)* Oil can! Oil can! . . . Mom? *(DELLA enters rec. room.)* Mom! *(She picks up remote.)* I don't believe it.

DELLA: Roxanne, come in here and turn this TV off yourself.

ROX: I will, just turn it back on.

DELLA: You're smarter than this.

ROX: I am! I am soooo smart! *(DELLA turns TV on. ROXANNE and ERIC animate.)*

ERIC: . . .take a walk on the beach. I have a new song I may want to sing to you. *(ROXANNE begins to exit TV into living room.)* Rachel, talk to me, don't keep pushing me away.

ROX: There are parts of my life you just don't understand.

JOHN: *(Entering, carrying sport coat over his arm.)* All packed. Let's go home.

DELLA: Roxanne?

ROX: I'm sorry, I have to go for a while.

ERIC: What?

ROX: I'll meet you at the beach house tomorrow, *(To herself.)* if I can. *(To him.)* Then you can sing your new song.

ERIC: *(The lights flicker and flash, a sound rips the air as ROXANNE steps out of TV into rec. room.)* Rachel, what are you doing? Where are you going?

(Simultaneously)

ROX: I'm right here.

DELLA: Well, Roxanne.

ROX: I'm right here. I wasn't hiding from you.

DELLA: You were too hiding from me.

ROX: All right I was.

DELLA: Turn off the television. *(Giving ROXANNE remote.)*

ROX: May we talk about this later?

ERIC: I wait all night for her, she finally sings the song and she runs away again.

JOHN: Let me talk to her.

ERIC: I don't care. I don't care. *(He exits.)*

JOHN: Rachel *(JOHN takes a couple steps toward ROXANNE, she turns off TV JOHN lowers his head.)*

DELLA: Are you ready to sing to me?

ROX: No.

DELLA: Have you been practicing?

ROX: No.

DELLA: Roxanne, what is the big deal? You agree you have to practice, you can't even answer the telephone because you're "accepting the responsibility for things like practicing", then I catch you sneaking on the TV while I'm in the kitchen making your favorite brownies because you're practicing.

ROX: I know.

DELLA: You be careful. You're going to grow up to sell real estate with a reputation like what's-his-name.

ROX: "Dad."

DELLA: Sometimes I think he gives you an allowance to do things like this. Do you want to just sing to me now?

ROX: No.

DELLA: There must be something more I don't understand. What is it, Roxanne?

ROX: Nothing.

DELLA: Then why won't you sing to me? (*Silence.*) Do you like to sing?

ROX: I love to sing.

DELLA: Why won't you sing to me then? (*Silence.*) Come on, Rox, what is it? (*Silence.*) Are you afraid you'll make a mistake? (*ROXANNE stares back at her mother.*) That's why you have to practice. I swear if you can't do something in two seconds you're sure you're going to fail. (*ROXANNE begins a slow slide down off the couch to the floor.*) It takes work. Everyone has to practice. Even Rachel. Why can't you? And it isn't just this recital. It's your school work—remember that government project? And your art class? It's seeing something through to the end. (*ROXANNE, now sitting on the floor, puts her head in her hands and her elbows on the floor. DELLA continues directly at her.*) Roxanne, you can sing. I can't imagine anybody being better than you at this recital. And you're interesting to watch, the way you move, your choreography. Do you know how many kids would give anything to have your talent? It's a shame to waste it all by not practicing. (*ROXANNE picks up cassette player and headphones and starts to leave room.*) Where are you going?

ROX: I'm sorry. I have to go for a while.

DELLA: Stay here. (*ROXANNE drops cassette player and headphones on table.*) Where is the sheet music?

ROX: Why?

DELLA: Do you even have it in here?

ROX: Here; why? *(She reaches in her pocket, takes out a wadded up piece of paper, hands it to DELLA.)*

DELLA: *(She looks at paper a moment, then opens it, looks at music, hums tune.)* You know the song really isn't that difficult.

ROX: Oh, I'm glad. It is for me.

DELLA: *(DELLA taps some of it out, sings.)*

HE'S MY FANTASY MAN.

MORE THAN A FRIEND TO ME.

ROX: I can't sing that low.

DELLA: *(Singing higher, and, once she has the beat, rather well.)*

HE'S MY FANTASY MAN

HE'S WHAT A MAN SHOULD BE.

Come on, sing with me. *(ROXANNE begins half heartedly and goes down from there until she's barely mouthing the words. DELLA notices this but pushes on with song anyway, has a little fun with it.)*

ROX & DELLA: HE'S MY FANTASY MAN,

AND GIRLS, HE'S ALWAYS THERE

HE'S MY FANTASY MAN WHEN I NEED SOMEONE TO CARE.
   (ROXANNE mocks DELLA, quits singing, sits on the couch.)

DELLA HE'S MY FANTASY, FANTASY, FANTASY, FANTASY MAN;

HE'S MY FANTASY, FANTASY, FANTASY, FANTASY MAN. *(A big finish. DELLA laughs, looks at ROXANNE for applause.)*

ROX: You sing it, then.

DELLA: I could. And I don't even know the rank song.

ROX: Then you sing it and I'll stay home.

DELLA: I was just trying to help you.

ROX: That's not helping me. You're not helping me.

DELLA: Because you won't be helped!

ROX: You want to help me? Let me watch my program! That will help me! Just let me watch my program!

DELLA: You need to practice!

ROX: I've practiced but . . .

DELLA: No more argument! God, this isn't the end of the world, it's just a recital! It's just a recital! Now stop your poor Roxanne act and get on with it! *(Silence.)*

ROX: *(Quietly.)* I have to do it myself, first. I have to sing it alone, first.

DELLA: What have you. . . ? Fine. Fine. I don't have time for this. *(DELLA exits.)*

ROX: Why do I do that? That's my mom. I'm the Original Daughter of Doom. *(ROXANNE flops face down on the couch, talks to JOHN who lifts his head, speaks back to her from inside the TV.)* Maybe you can explain it to me.

JOHN: *(Putting on his coat.)* Oh, I think you're just a little confused, like the rest of us.

ROX: I am.

JOHN: I wish you could see what I see when I look at you. You'd know you're already a success in every important way.

ROX: Yeah, I'm a success—at torturing my mother. It's this recital. Getting up in front of all those people, it scares me. Do you think I can sing?

JOHN: Do I know music?

ROX: Yes.

JOHN: *(As JOHN steps out of TV into rec. room. lights flicker and flash, the sounds tears the air.)* Will you believe me if I tell you?

[. . . As the play continues, ROX learns to except herself, her mother, and her television friends just the way they are. . . .]

End of Scene

Dark Doings at the Crossroads
or, Who Stole the Salad Dressing?
by
Arthur L. Kaser

Characters

Laurinda Kerplunk: the heroine
Augustus Kerplunk: her father
Bartholomew Wow: the hero
Jack Dalton: the villain
Theodosia Tadpole: the woman of mystery

Production Notes

All the parts are carried to the extreme, both in the acting and costumes. Laurinda is a very decided blonde, a wig being worn. Her dress is very fluffy, and her makeup clearly shows that she is trying to play a role much younger than she really is. Her father is a very quivery old man, speaking in a high-pitched voice. Bartholomew is of the sissy type dressed in clothes somewhat too large for him. His attempts at bravado are ludicrous. He rides a dilapidated bicycle. The villain is of the very heavy type, although he is a spindly type man. Theodosia is dressed in black, wearing a heavy black veil. She speaks in a sepulchral voice.

Scene: The stage is almost bare of scenery. An old table and a broken cooking range may be in evidence. Store boxes, barrels, etc., are at random about the stage and on these various pieces are plainly printed signs: "This is a tree," "This is a railroad track," "This is the old mill" "This is the crossroads," "This is the mortgaged farm," etc.

At the rise of the curtain: We discover Laurinda seated despondently on a box with her clenched hands between her knees. Augustus is seated on the box marked "Railroad Track." He, also, is very sad.

• • • • • • • • • • • • • • • • • • •

LAURINDA: (*Casts her eyes upward and squints.*) Ah, the day is done. . .

AUGUSTUS: Done what?

LAURINDA: (*Ignores him and speaks dreamily.*) The day is done! The sun has set, and having set, it sits.

AUGUSTUS: And the moon, having risen, rizzes. (*He sobs very loudly and hysterically.*)

LAURINDA: Father, sob not. All swell that ends swell. All will be well in the end.

AUGUSTUS: (*Daubs his eyes with a kerchief.*) Which end?

LAURINDA: (*Stands up and steps to her father.*) Father, dear Father, we have been cast out of the old home, but soon you will sell your salad dressing for millions . . .

AUGUSTUS: (*Pats her hand that she has lain on his shoulder.*) Ah, my daugher, all my life have I labored to perfect that salad dressing, and now that it is perfect, all except the texture and taste, I cannot sell the darn thing. (*Looks about.*) Where's Ma?

LAURINDA: Father, you forget.

AUGUSTUS: Yes, Laurinda, I remember now that I forgot. What did I forget? I don't remember.

LAURINDA: Why, Father, you know Mother is in Europe.

AUGUSTUS: Yes, yes, so she is. Ma's in Europe. She's over there selling tractors, ain't she? And when . . . when she comes back there will be no home for her. We have been ejected, kicked out . . .

LAURINDA: Father, we have been turned out only because you are old and decrepit. It was only because that villain, Jack Dalton, was stronger than you. Many's the time I've told you to eat more onions. We have until midnight tonight to pay the mortgage on this old home. Father. Oh, if only my sweetheart, the hero, Bartholomew Wow, would come to me in my hour of need.

AUGUSTUS: What about me? I'm here. I'm here, I say, shivering in the cold wintry blasts that blow.

LAURINDA: Father, you're cuckoo. This is June.

AUGUSTUS: June? Only six more months 'til Christmas? Laurinda, what are we to do? No money, no home, no dog, nobody to buy my salad dressing formula . . .(*Enter THEODOSIA, Left. She marches stiffly to Center, stops and looks steadily at AUGUSTUS.*)

THEODOSIA: Ah! (*She turns abruptly and marches off Left.*)

AUGUSTUS: That woman again!

LAURINDA: Father, who is she? That is the fourteenth time she has come here and said "Ah!"

AUGUSTUS: Gal, thar's gold in them hills . . . No, that was last night. I mean, she must be a woman of mystery. (*Stands.*) But I must go, daughter, or my name isn't Augustus Kerplunk. More salad dressing must be mixed before the villain steals the vinegar. (*He exits Left, walking very feebly.*)

LAURINDA: (*Clasping her hands in despair.*) Oh, woe is me! Woe is me! Father, dear Father, is old and decrepit, his knee joints squeak. My hero does not come to me, and Ma is in Europe! Woe is me, and what a mess I turned out to be. (*Enter JACK, Right.*)

JACK: Ah, me proud and haughty beauty, either marry me or give me the salad dressing formula!

LAURINDA: Never, Jack Dalton! Only over my dead body will you get Father's salad dressing.

JACK: Then at twelve tonight you lose the old home, including the oil stove. (*Villainous laugh.*)

LAURINDA: Jack Dalton, you shall due the ray . . . day the dew . . . rue the day that you threatened me thusly. For years Father has labored night and day to perfect his salad dressing formula. For years we have been unable to pay on the mortgage, and now . . . now when success is within his reach you foreclose on the old home. (*Pleadingly.*) Please, Mr. Dalton, only a few more days and we shall have millions . . . thousands . . . maybe hundreds!

JACK: Curses!

LAURINDA: Did you speak?

JACK: No, I sneezed. Very well, beautiful one. I'll wait one week.

LAURINDA: Oh, goody! (*She claps her hands childishly.*) I'll tell Father. (*She runs off Left.*)

JACK: *(Twists his mustache and laughs.)* Ha, ha! The little fool! Little does she know I had a purpose in mind. I have only given them more time that I may have more opportunity to steal the formula. But I do wish it was cheese instead. Curses! But I must not curse. Things are coming my way. *(Laughs.)* When the formula is in my hands I will tie the old man to yonder railroad track . . . *(Points to box.)* . . . steal the girl and be off. *(He exits Right, walking very pompously. Enter AUGUSTUS and LAURINDA, Left. He has a roll of wallpaper.)*

AUGUSTUS: It is such heartening news, daughter. Another whole week. *(Holds up the wallpaper.)* By that time I shall sell this formula for several millions of dollars and fifty cents and be able to save the old woman—I mean the old home. I hope Ma comes back then from Europe. Laurinda, the villain is a good man, isn't he? Perhaps, after all, you should marry him.

LAURINDA: Never, Father, except over your dead body.

AUGUSTUS: I hope I never live to see my dead body. . . . I always get that line wrong. Jack Dalton is rich and handsome . . .

LAURINDA: Never! Never, not even if I live till I die . . . never! I love the hero of this show, Bartholomew Wow. He is a manly men of man . . . menly min of mon . . . manly men . . . Well, anyway, he is. I shall marry no one but him.

AUGUSTUS: But my salad dressing?

LAURINDA: With or without, I shall marry him. He is the idol of my heart.

AUGUSTUS: He's been idle ever since you knew him.

LAURINDA: Father, he has no peer.

AUGUSTUS: Not even a peer of socks. *(Enter BARTHOLOMEW on a bicycle. He falls from it as he rides on from Right. He is panting in an exaggerated manner.)*

LAURINDA: My hero!

BARTHOLOMEW: Am I on time?

AUGUSTUS: No. Supper is already et.

BARTHOLOMEW: *(Daubs his eyes with a kerchief and sobs bitterly.)* Gone! Supper all gone! Oh, my goodness! Now I've got to spend my own nickel for a hamburger. *(Turns sadly to Right.)* Goo—Goodbye, my love! No eats . . . no stay! *(Goes Right.)*

LAURINDA: Bartholomew, wait. In a few days Father will sell his saddle dressing . . . I mean draddle sessing. . . . Anyway, when we get the millions I'll give you a nickel.

BARTHOLOMEW: (Brightens.) Oh, bliss! (He turns to LAURINDA with outstretched arms.) My sweetheart! A whole nickel!

AUGUSTUS: Daughter, unhand him at once! He is naught but nix. You shall marry no one but the villain, Jack Dalton. He's the baby with the dough.

BARTHOLOMEW: (Takes a comedy bravado pose.) Sir, he may have the dough, but I can loaf as much as he. I am college bred.

AUGUSTUS: And only half baked. Begone from my sight.

LAURINDA: Oh, Father, dear Father, come home with me now . . . I mean, do not hinder our betrothal.

AUGUSTUS: (Pointing to off Right and speaking to BARTHOLOMEW.) Go! Never darken my eyes again!

BARTHOLOMEW: Very well, sir, as you say, sir, I will go, sir. You have forced me to go. But I warn you, sir. I will get upon your house and cry till the roof leaks.

AUGUSTUS: You do not frighten me, young man. I have an umbrella. (Enter THEODOSIA Left. She goes to AUGUSTUS, points a finger at him and speaks in a sepulchral voice.)

THEODOSIA: Ah!

AUGUSTUS: Woman, who are you?

THEODOSIA: I am Theodosia Tadpole.

AUGUSTUS: I hope you turn into a frog and croak.

THEODOSIA: (Pokes him on the nose with her finger.) Ah! (She goes Left. Then turns and looks steadily at them.)

BARTHOLOMEW: Me go now. Ugh! (He mounts the bicycle and starts Left. THEODOSIA jerks her thumb in hitch-hiking manner.) O.K. (She tries to sit on the handlebars, they both tumble. She rises painfully and exits Left. BARTHOLOMEW shakes his head sadly, and pushes his bicycle off Left.)

AUGUSTUS: Now, dear daughter, we have until midnight to sleep, so you should retire to your bed.

LAURINDA: Yes, Father, I need my beauty sleep.

AUGUSTUS: And plenty of it. Go now. I will soon retire myself, as soon as I hide this formula in the old mill. (JACK sneaks on Right and hears AUGUSTUS speaking. He is not seen by the others.)

LAURINDA: Good night, Father dear, don't let the bugbeds bite. And be sure you hide the formula well.

AUGUSTUS: Fear not, Laurinda. The formula shall be in yonder old mill. Go now, daughter, and rest in the arms of Morpheus.

LAURINDA: I cannot never rest in nobody's arms save those of my dear, beloved Bartholomew Wow.

AUGUSTUS: Daughter, if you refuse to give him up I will disinherit you. You shall not be left one penny that I owe everybody.

LAURINDA: My heart is sad. (*She exits Left.*)

AUGUSTUS: Now to hide the salad dressing formula in the old mill yonder. Ah, the old mill! Its wheel has turned and creaked for these many a year, and now within its environs shall rest this valuable paper . . . the formula of my famous salad dressing. (*He places the wallpaper back of the box marked "The Old Mill" and exits Left. JACK comes to Center, looking furtively about the stage.*)

JACK: At last the formula is mine. Soon I will be rolling in wealth as once I rolled in the gutter. (*He approaches the box.*) Curses! The old man has locked the key and thrown the door away. But Jack Dalton has never been foiled. Where there's a will there's a lawsuit. A villain must be a brainy cuss, and no barrier must be left unturned to procure yonder valuable document. (*He twists his mustache as he stands in deep thought.*) Ah! I have it! I will enter the old mill. (*He kicks over the box and picks up the wallpaper.*) At last! (*Enter AUGUSTUS, Left, wearing a nightshirt over his other clothes. He is walking in his sleep.*)

JACK: Curses! The old buzzard is a sleep-walker.

AUGUSTUS: I walk in the garden of beautiful flowers. I smell the attar of roses.

JACK: He has found me.

AUGUSTUS: (*Stubs his toe and as he stumbles he awakens.*) Where am I? Jack Dalton, what are you doing here? My formula! You have stolen my salad dressing formula! (*Holds out his hand.*) Gimme.

JACK: Ha, ha! Do you think that once I have this formula in my possession that I give it up so easily? No, no. I will bind you securely to yonder railroad track.

AUGUSTUS: No, no!

JACK: Yes, yes. (*He takes a ball of kite string from his pocket, leaps forward and wraps a few turns of the string about AUGUSTUS' wrists.*) Now you are in my power. (*He leads him to the "Railroad" box and places him face down* *on the box.)* Now to gag him so he cannot utter an outcry. Oh, where, oh, where can I find an old gag?

AUGUSTUS: On the radio. *(Sound of a train whistle in the distance.)*

JACK: The fast mail approaches. Soon, Augustus Kerplunk, you will be naught but hamburger.

AUGUSTUS: And not an onion in sight. What a way to end it all!

JACK: Ha, ha! Now to steal your beautiful daughter and get away before the train does its work.

AUGUSTUS: *(Hardly audible.)* Help! Help!

JACK: *(Takes a big cigar from his pocket and places it in AUGUSTUS' mouth.)* My last election cigar. Now you cannot cry for help. *(Train whistle is much nearer. Enter LAURINDA, Left, running.)*

LAURINDA: Father! Father! Where are you? *(Sees AUGUSTUS.)* Father! You're on the track. The train approaches o'er yonder hill and is coming this way at sixty miles an hour. *(Screams.)* Help! Help!

JACK: Silence, you vixen! *(He grasps her and places his hand over her mouth. Enter BARTHOLOMEW on the bicycle, Left. He tumbles off, then rises painfully.)*

BARTHOLOMEW: Oh, my goodness, gracious me. Is something wrong?

LAURINDA: *(Struggles and frees her mouth.)* Bartholomew! Stop the train! The mail approaches at sixty miles an hour, and father is securely tied to the track in the path of the train.

BARTHOLOMEW: *(Takes a red bandana from his pocket, and poses as he holds it aloft.)* Stop, train! Stop at once! *(There is a sound of creaking brakes and hissing steam.)*

JACK: Curses! But I am not yet tinfoiled. I have the formula. *(He starts Right.)*

BARTHOLOMEW: *(Places his hand in his coat pocket and bulges the pocket to make it appear there is a revolver in the pocket.)* Stop, I say, Jack Dalton! Desist and halt!

JACK: Curses! *(He stops with upraised hands. Enter THEODOSIA at Left, as BARTHOLOMEW removes his hand from his pocket with a banana in it which he proceeds to eat. THEODOSIA approaches Jack and takes the wallpaper.)*

THEODOSIA: *(Pointing a finger at JACK.)* Ah!

LAURINDA: Another ah!

THEODOSIA: Ah, Jack Dalton, your time has come. Five hundred men from Scotland Yard have surrounded this old farm and you cannot escape.

JACK: Scotland Yard?

THEODOSIA: Yes, Scotland Yard, F.O.B. England. They have traced you here for stealing the House of Parliament. You cannot escape.

JACK: They shall never capture me alive. (*Looks about quickly.*) I will leap into the old mill stream. (*He dives behind the box marked "Old Mill Stream," landing heavily.*) Ouch! The old mill stream is frozen over and I've broken my neck. I am dying. Forgive me, all.

LAURINDA: He's a goner for sure.

AUGUSTUS: (*Looking up and twisting the cigar about in his mouth.*) Woman, who are you?

THEODOSIA: (*Removes the veil.*) Look!

AUGUSTUS: Ma!

LAURINDA: Mother!

THEODOSIA: Both right. My commission for selling tractors in Europe amounted to twenty-two million dollars and sixteen cents. I came back to surprise you. I find you in trouble. I came over with Scotland Yard and brought them here to capture the villain.

LAURINDA: My hero! (*Embraces BARTHOLOMEW.*) My hero!

BARTHOLOMEW: Aw, it wasn't nothin'. I only done my duty. (*Train whistle very loud and insistent.*)

THEODOSIA: Pa, get off the track the train's coming.

AUGUSTUS: Maybe I'd better. (*He stands and breaks the strings on his wrists.*)

BARTHOLOMEW: (*Bows to the audience.*) Tomorrow night we play "Ten Barrooms in a Night."

End of Play

Credits and Acknowledgments

For information and permissions, please contact the playwright, agent, or publisher directly.

1. *Cinderella, Cinderella* by Steve and Kathy Hotchner, reprinted with permission of McIntosh and Otis. **7.** *Dorothy and the Wizard of Oz,* by Steve and Kathy Hotchner, reprinted with permission of McIntosh and Otis.

2. *Hansel and Gretel,* an adaptation by William Glennon. **3.** *Dragon of the Winds* by Carson Wright. **8.** *Alice in Wonderland,* an adaptation by William Glennon, reprinted in whole or in part with permission from THE DRAMATIC PUBLISHING COMPANY P.O. Box 129, Woodstock Illinois 60098. All inquiries concerning rights, royalties and permissions should be addressed to them.

4. *An O. Henry Holiday* and **10.** *The Magic Wood* by Ric Averill © 1988 These plays are fully protected by copyright, and anyone presenting them without the consent of the author will be liable to the penalties provided by the copyright law. Professional and amateur producers are encouraged to apply for royalty quotations or scripts to RIC AVERILL 2 Winona, Lawrence, KS 666046-4848 (Phone) 913-842-6622, (Fax) 913-842-7753.

5. *A Game of Catch* by Jack Theis. The author gratefully acknowledges the assistance and encouragement of the Pegasus Players and their playwriting competition staff and Mr. Richard Westley of St. Ignatius College Prepatory School, Chicago. All inquires regarding rights should be addressed to JOHN T. THEIS 29 South LaSalle Street, Chicago, IL 60603 (Phone) 312-782-1121. Amateur and stock acting rights to this work are controlled exclusively by Jack Theis. Royalty must be paid for each performance, unless waived in writing by Jack Theis or John T. Theis.

6. *The Fall of the House of Usher,* a radio adaptation by Dorothy C. Calhoun from One Hundred Non-Royalty One-Act Plays by William Kozlenko, © 1940 by GREENBERG PUBLISHER, INC.

9. *Uncle Vanya* by Anton Chekhof adapted by Lorraine Cohen, © 1973 from Scenes for Young Actors, Edited by Loraine Cohen, by permission of AVON BOOKS, 1350 Avenue of the Americas, New York, NY 10019.

11. *Scraps* by Tagore J. McIntyre , © 1986 . from Meeting the Winter Bike Rider and other Prize–Winning Plays, Edited by Wendy Lamb. The author acknowledges his mom, dad, and sister for encourageing him and also Gerald Chapman. For permission contact, TAGOKE MCINTYRE, 1960 W Keating Ave, Building 46 #462, Masa, AZ 85202